The Beauty

of Naked

Skin 2

Jürgen Prommersberger: The Beauty of Naked Skin 2
Regenstauf , January 2016

First Edition:
CreateSpace Independent Publishing Platform

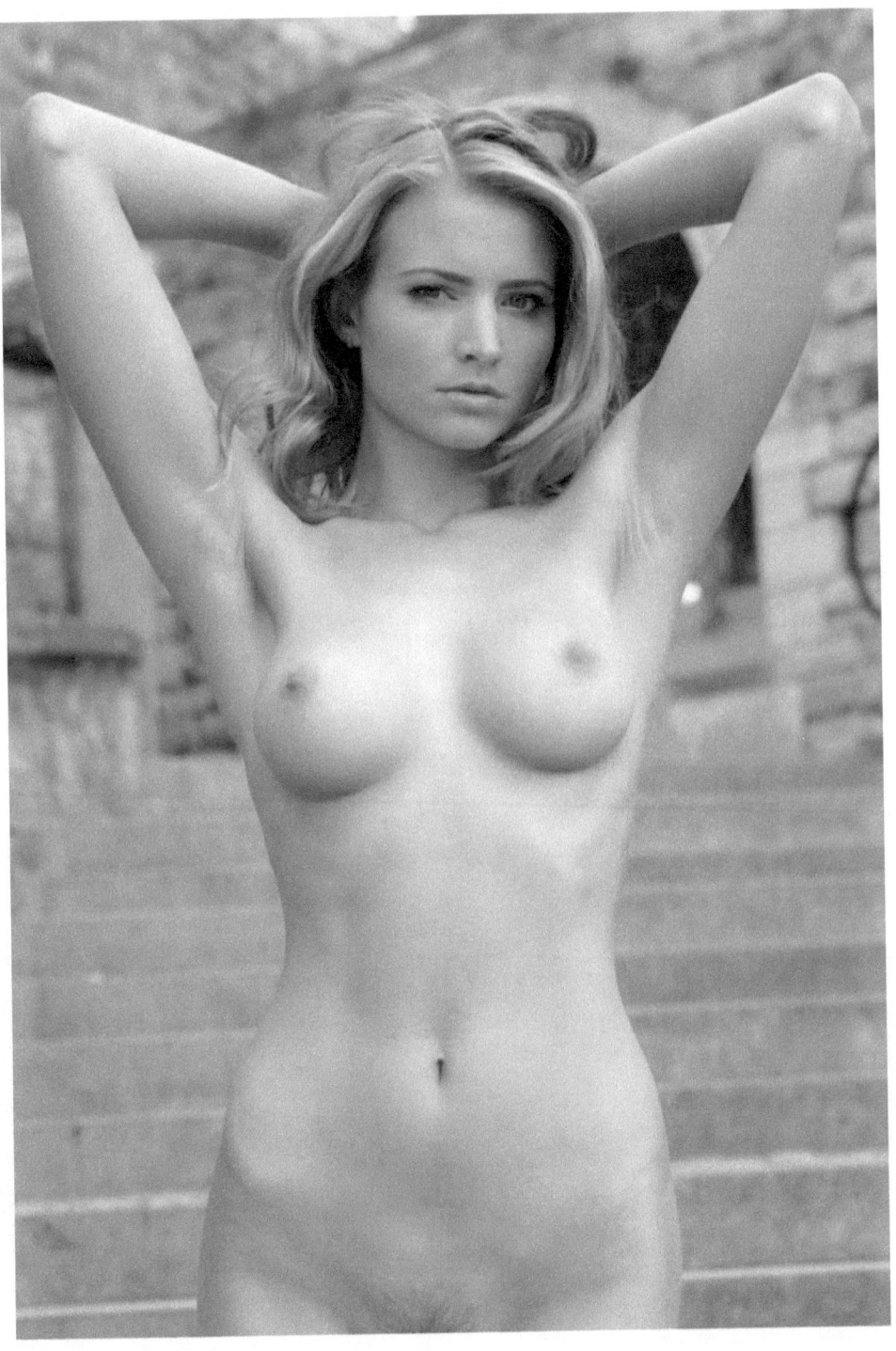

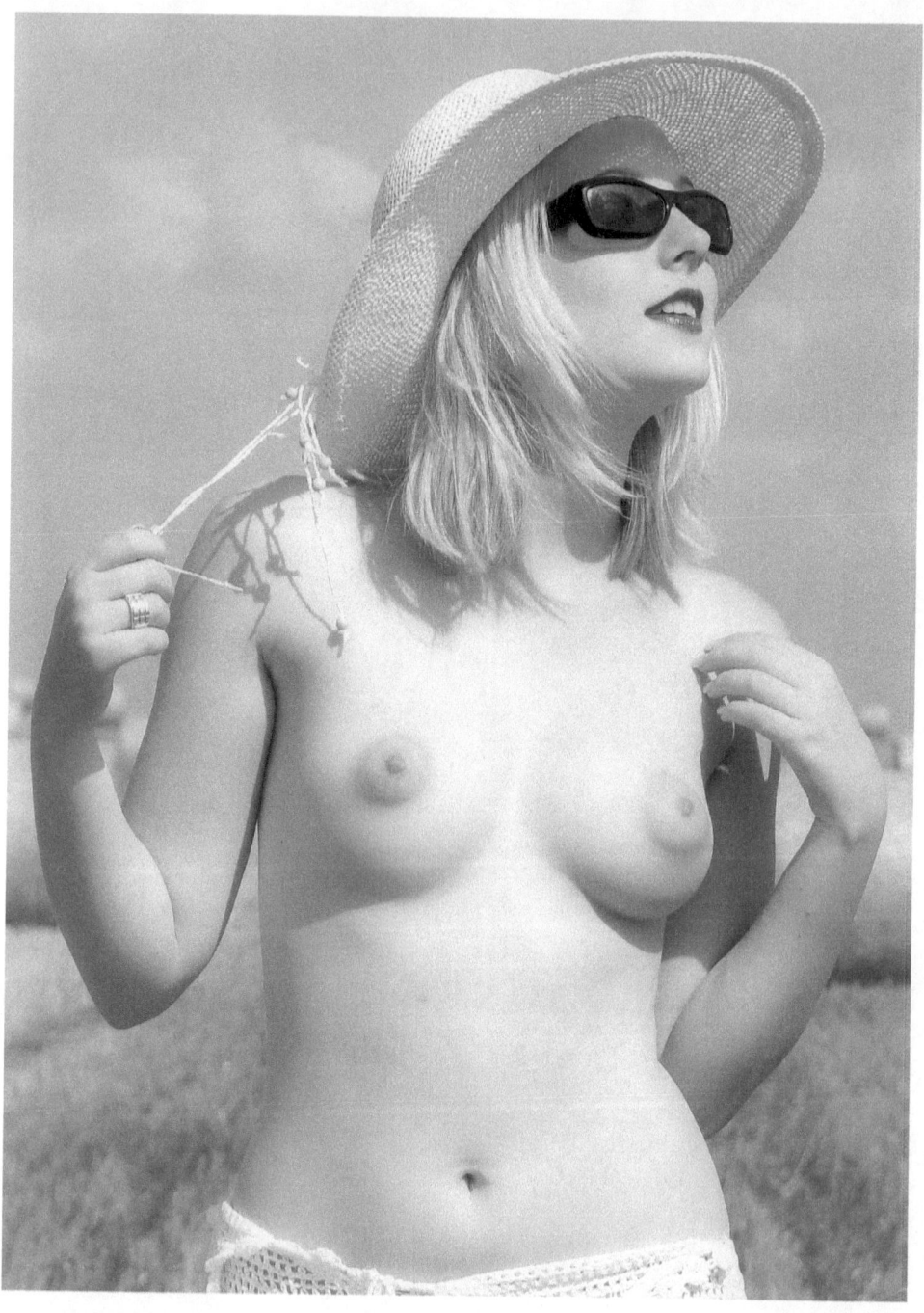

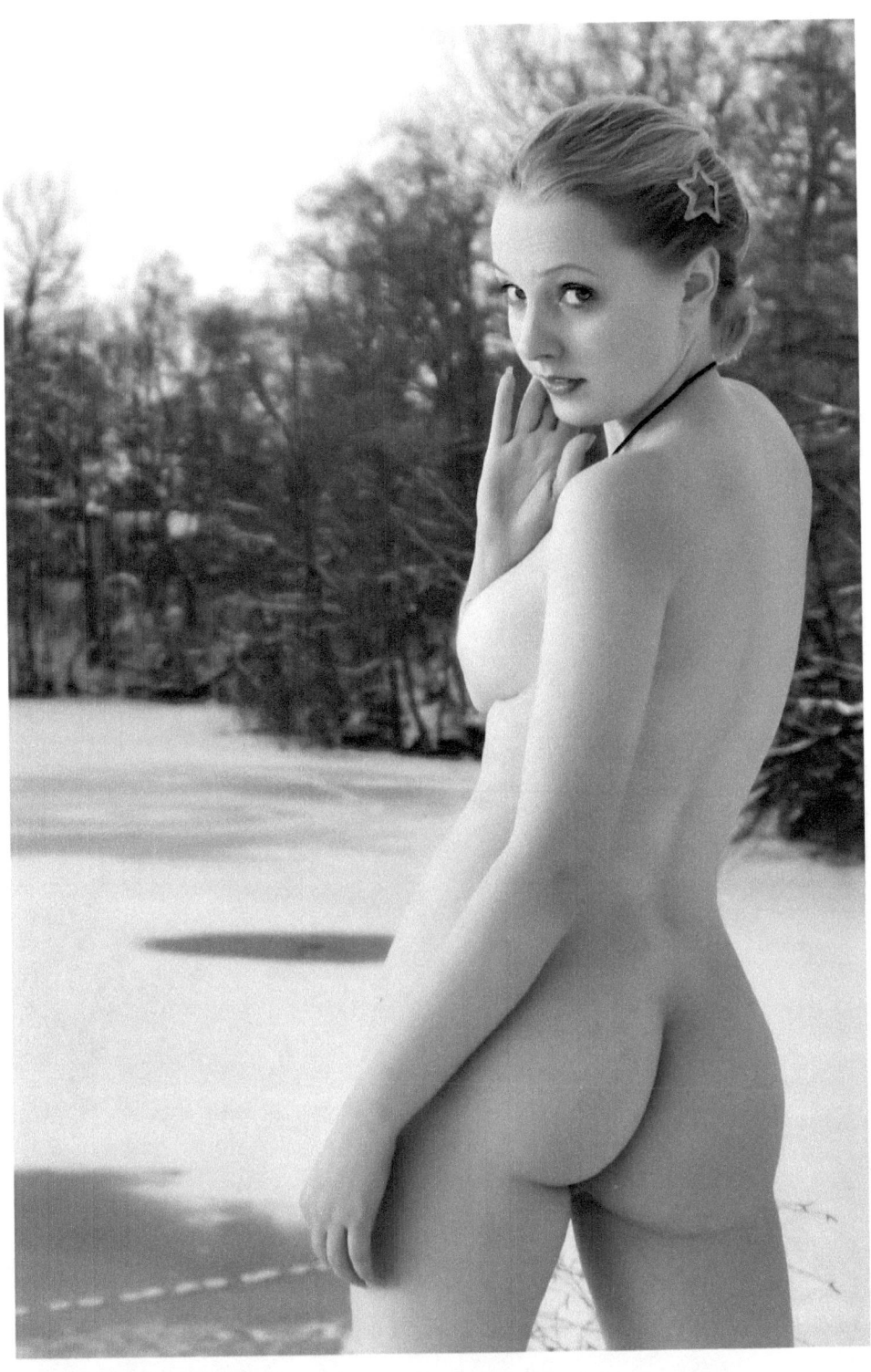

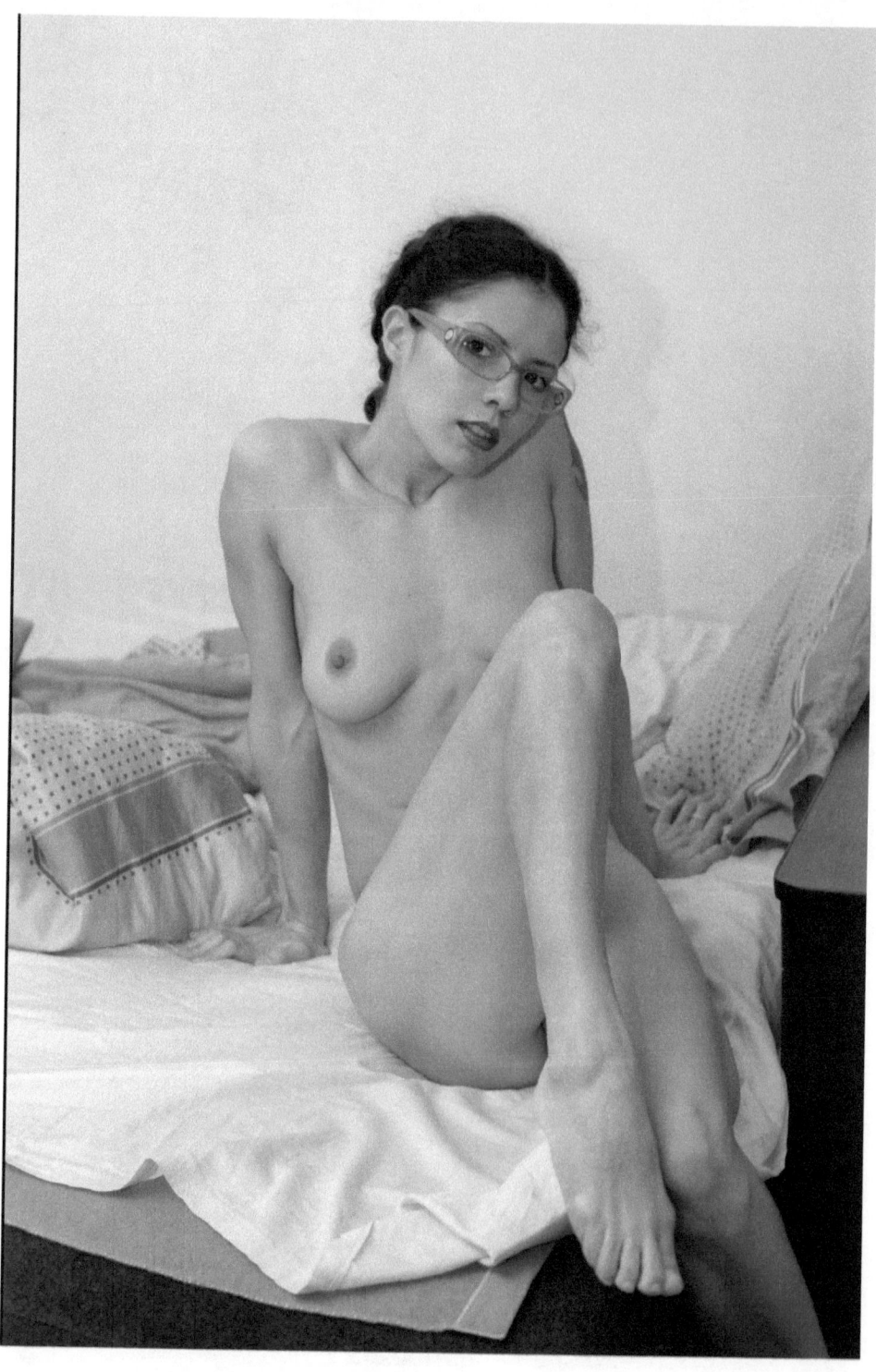

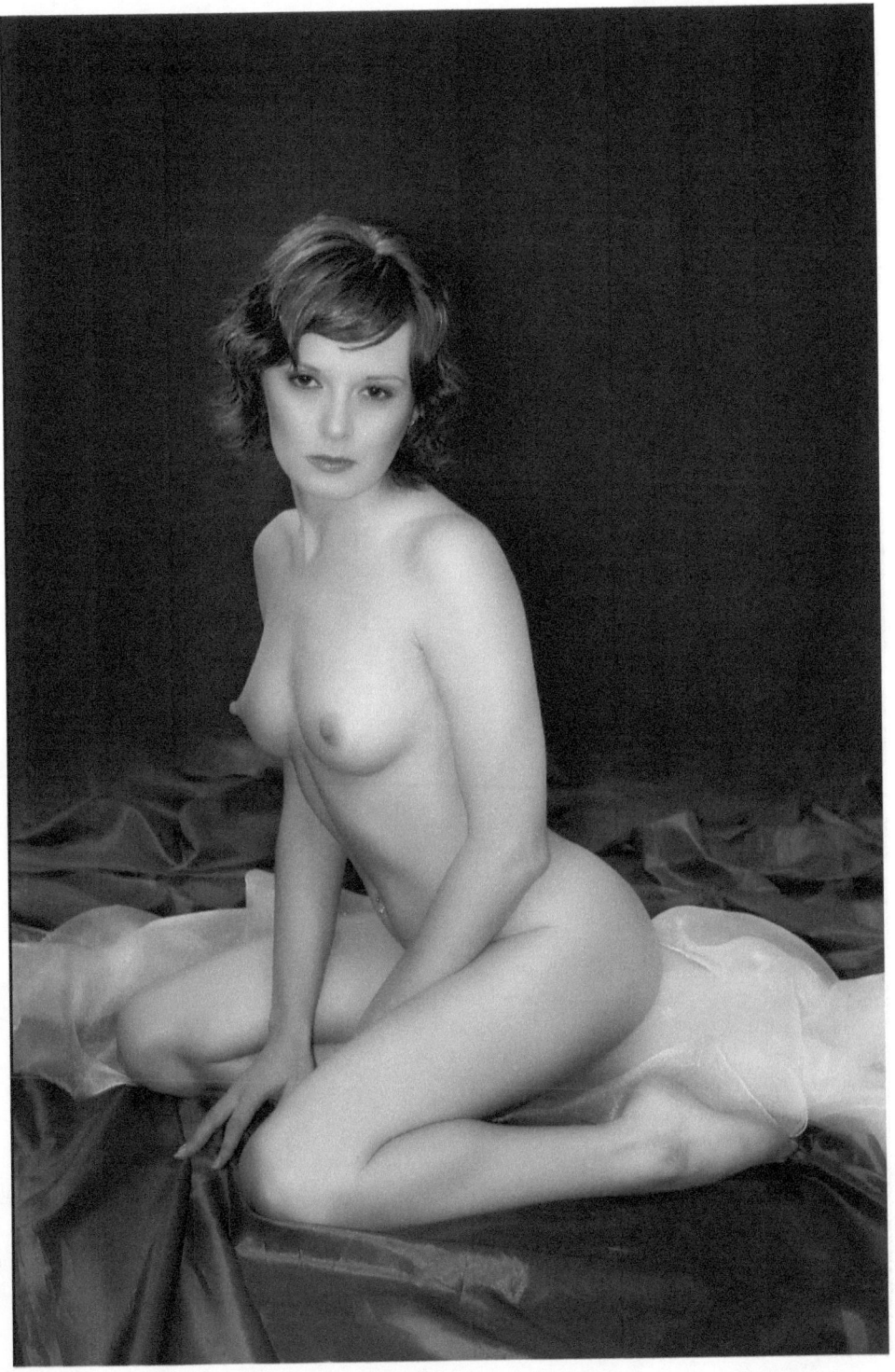

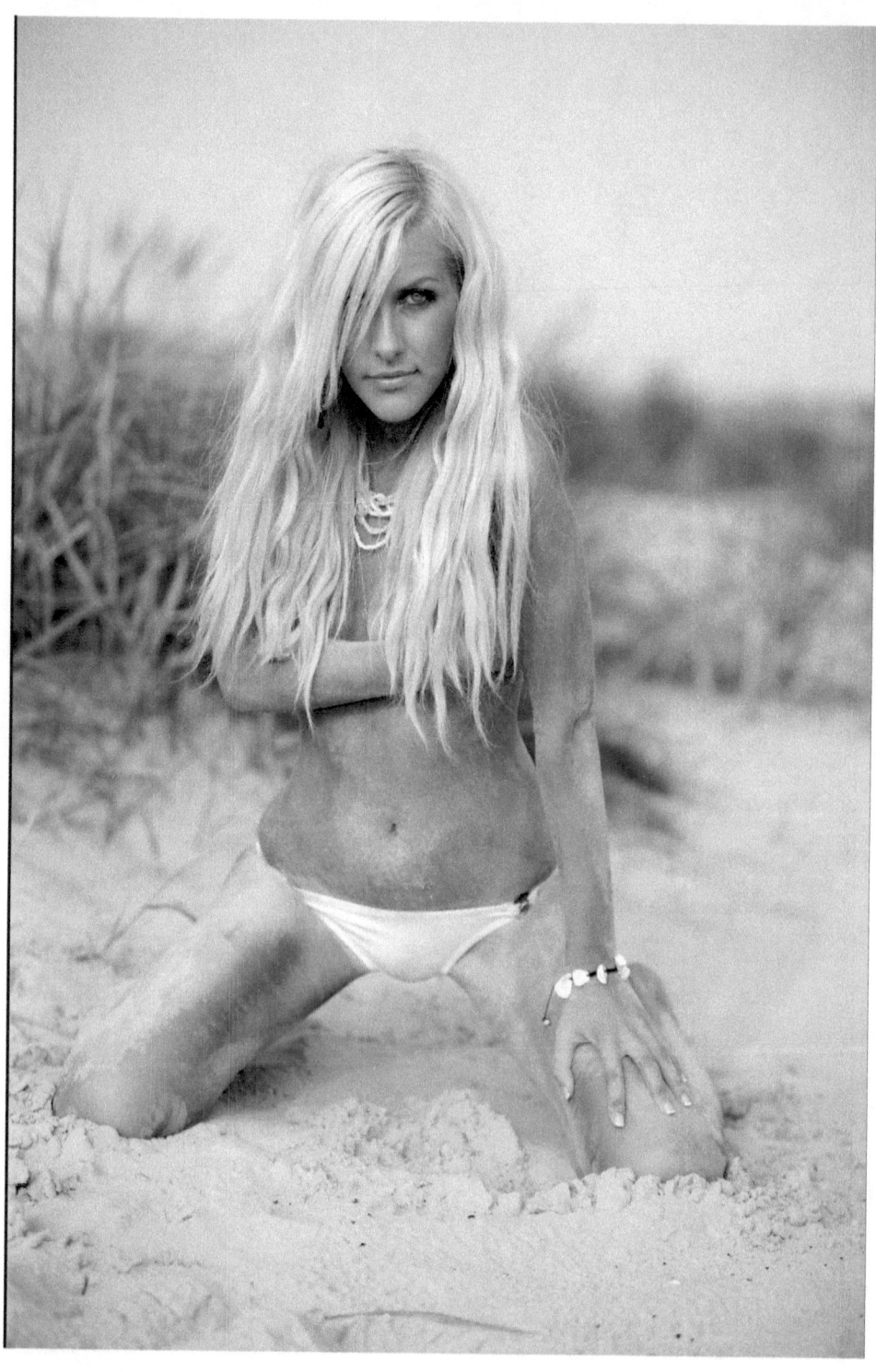

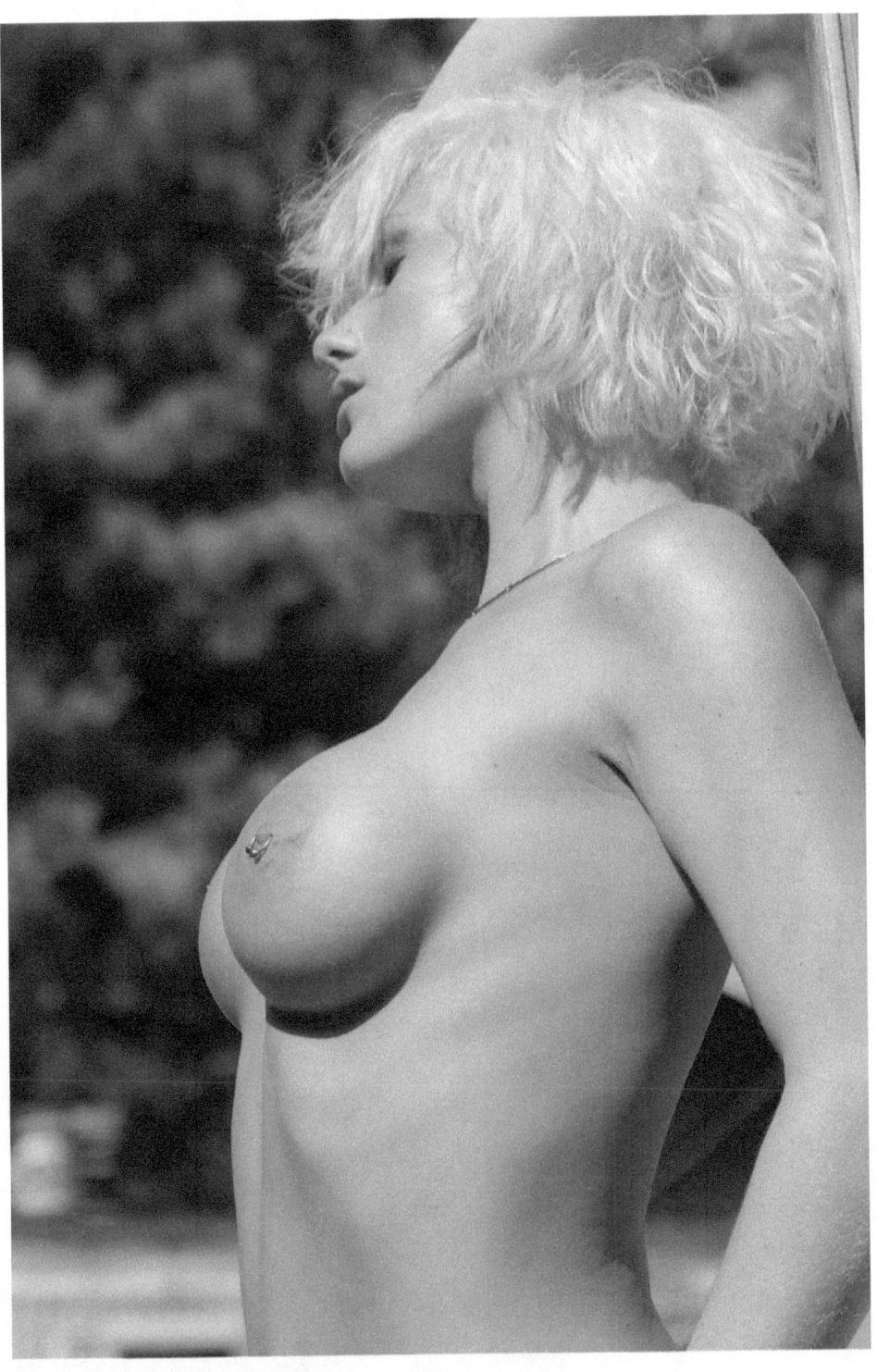

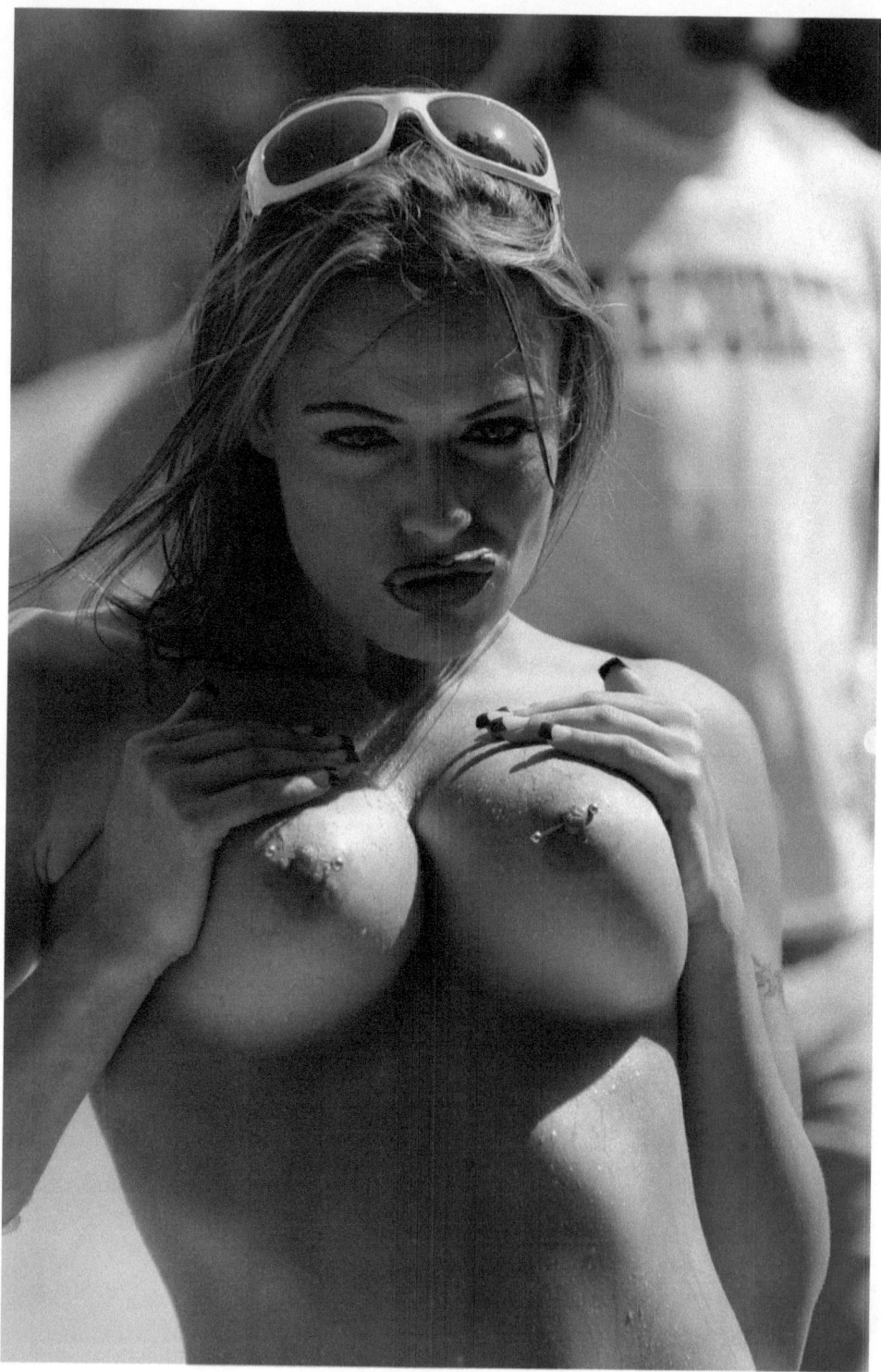

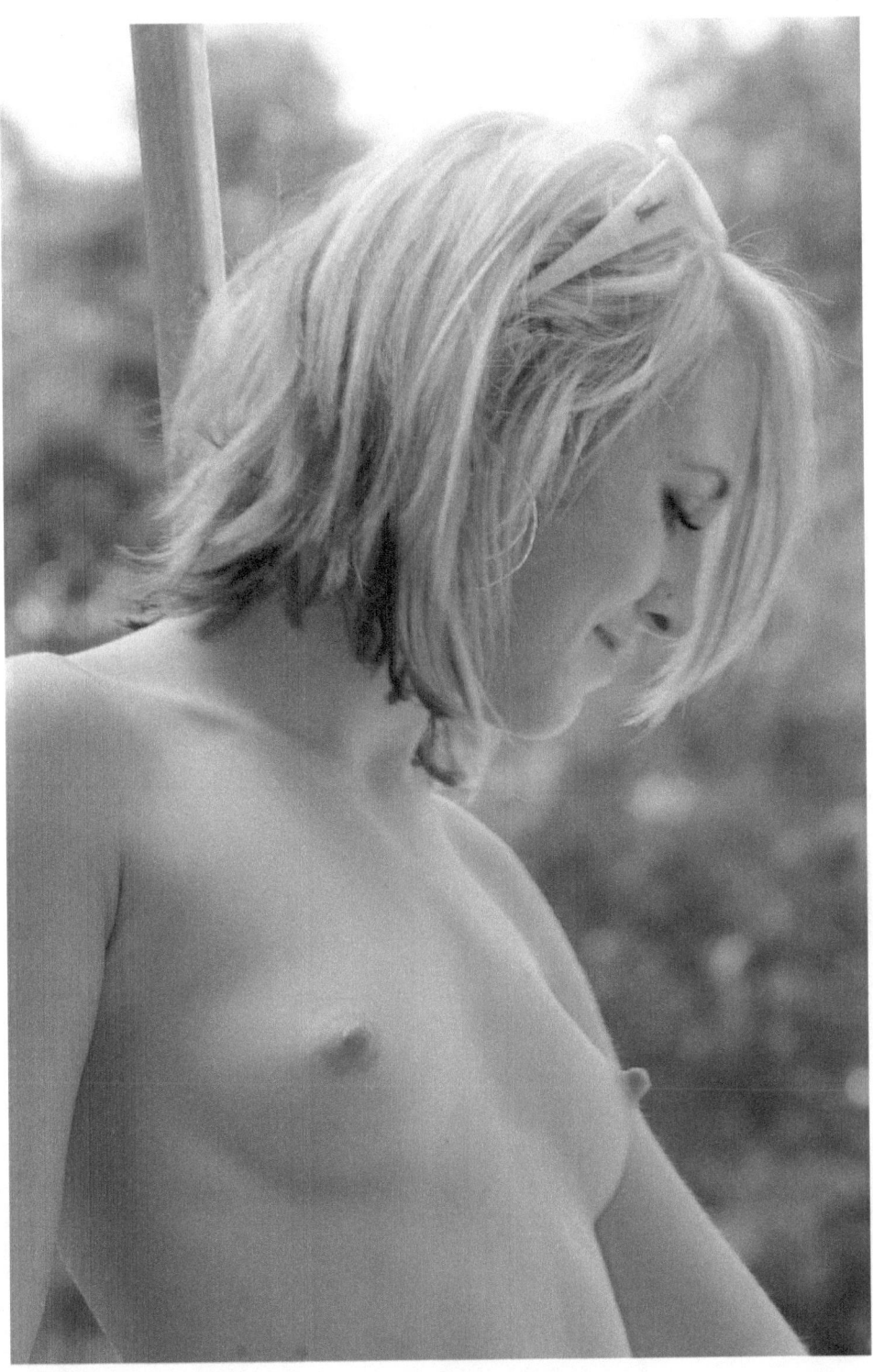

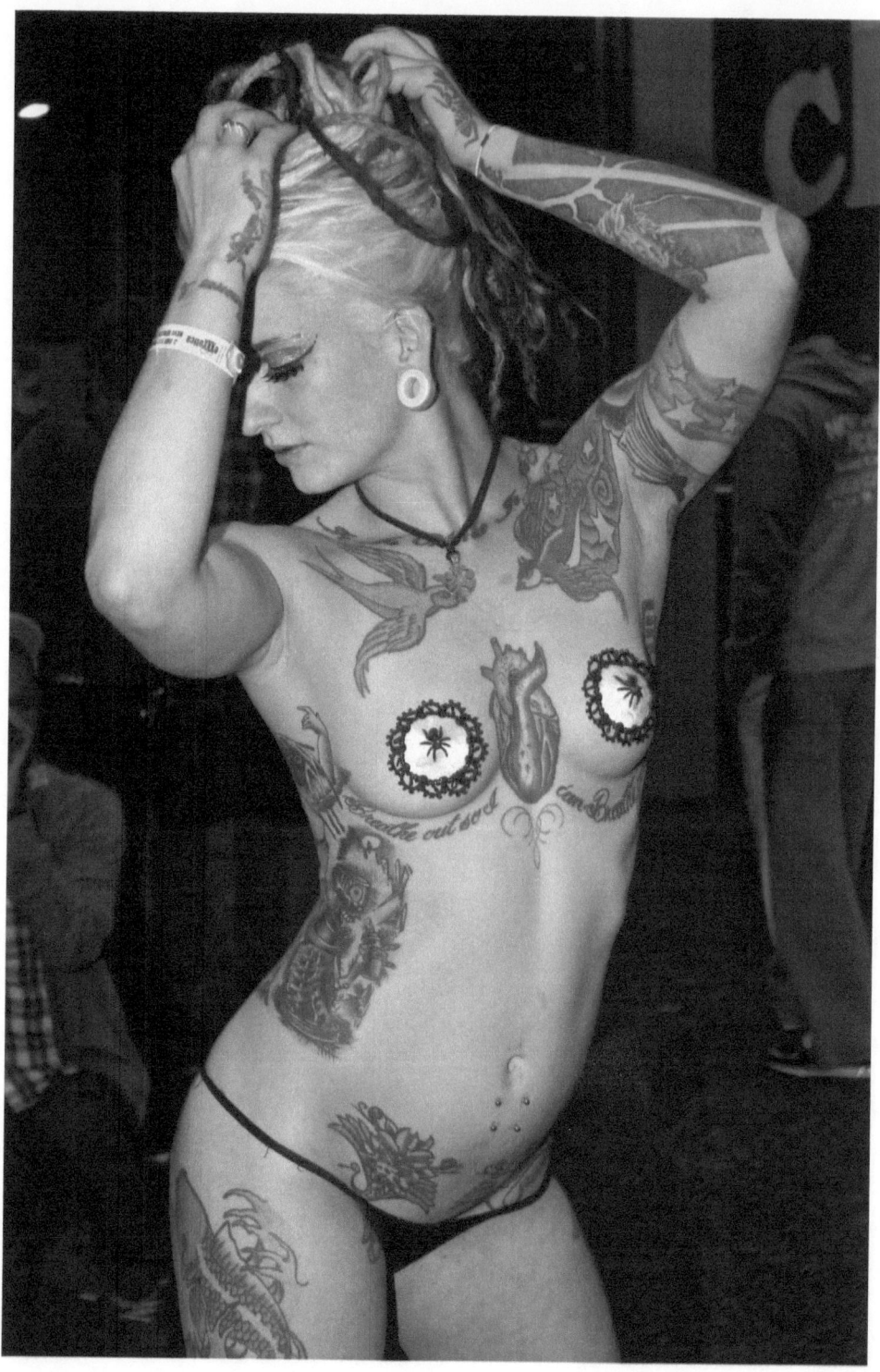

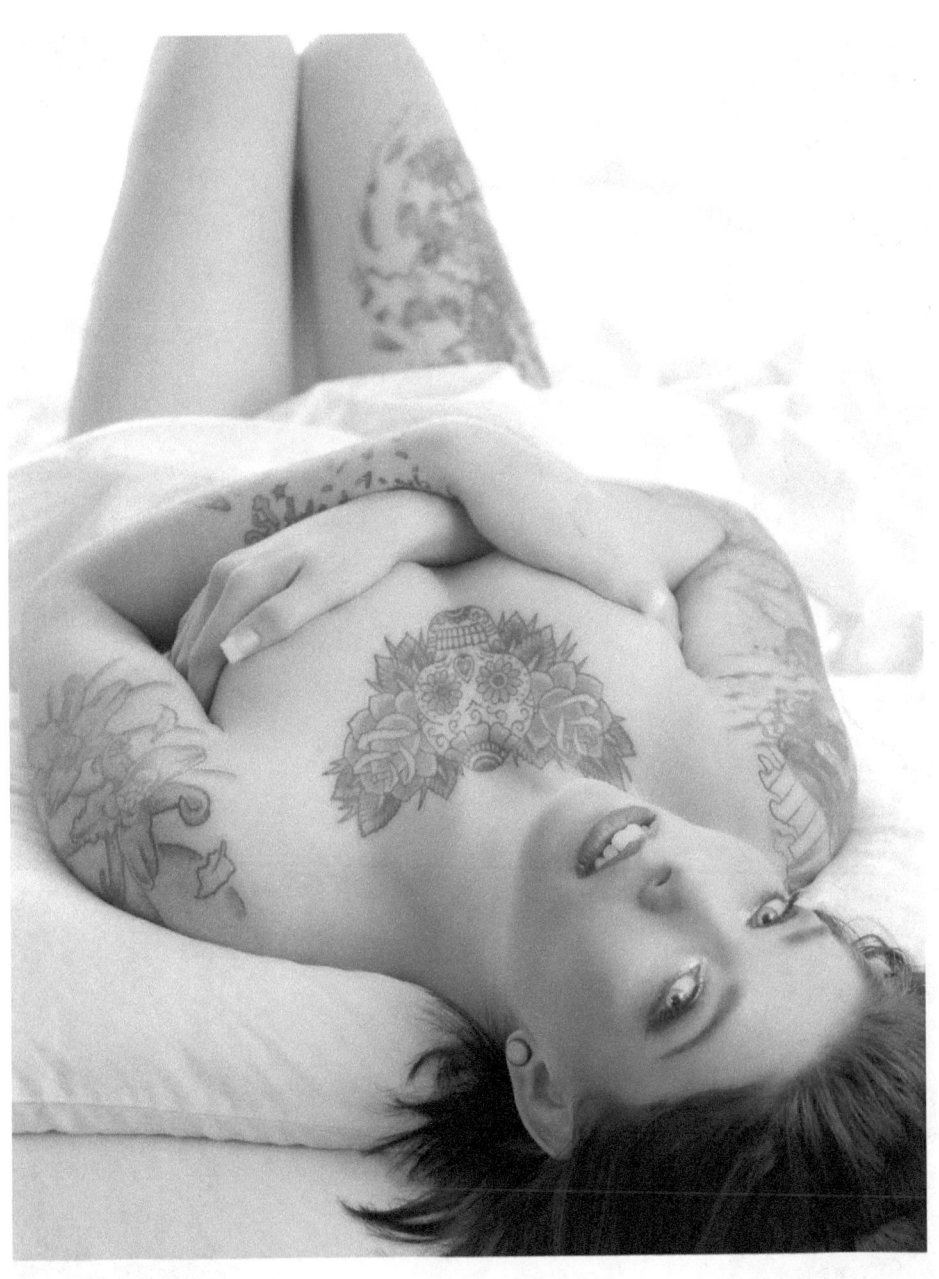

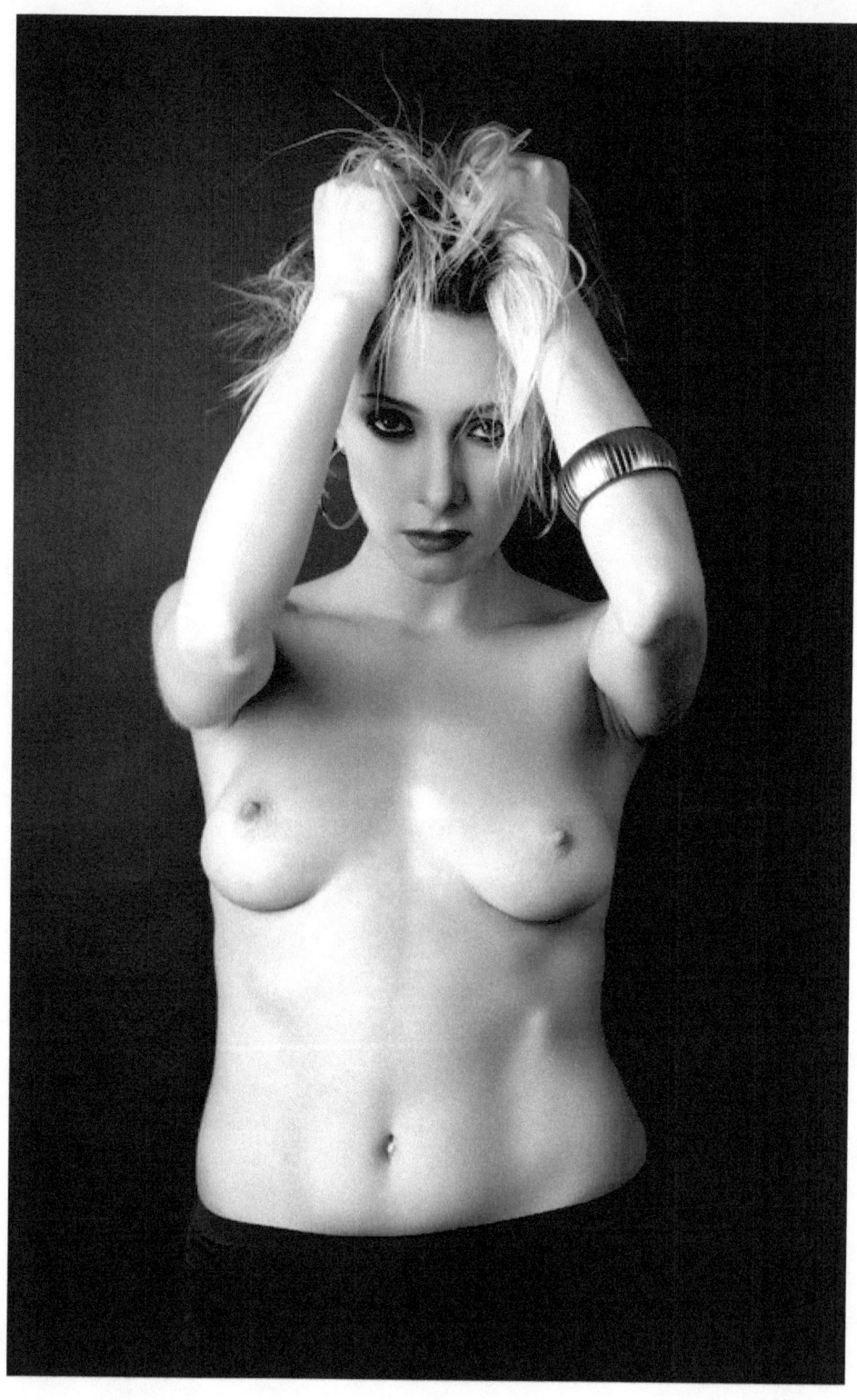

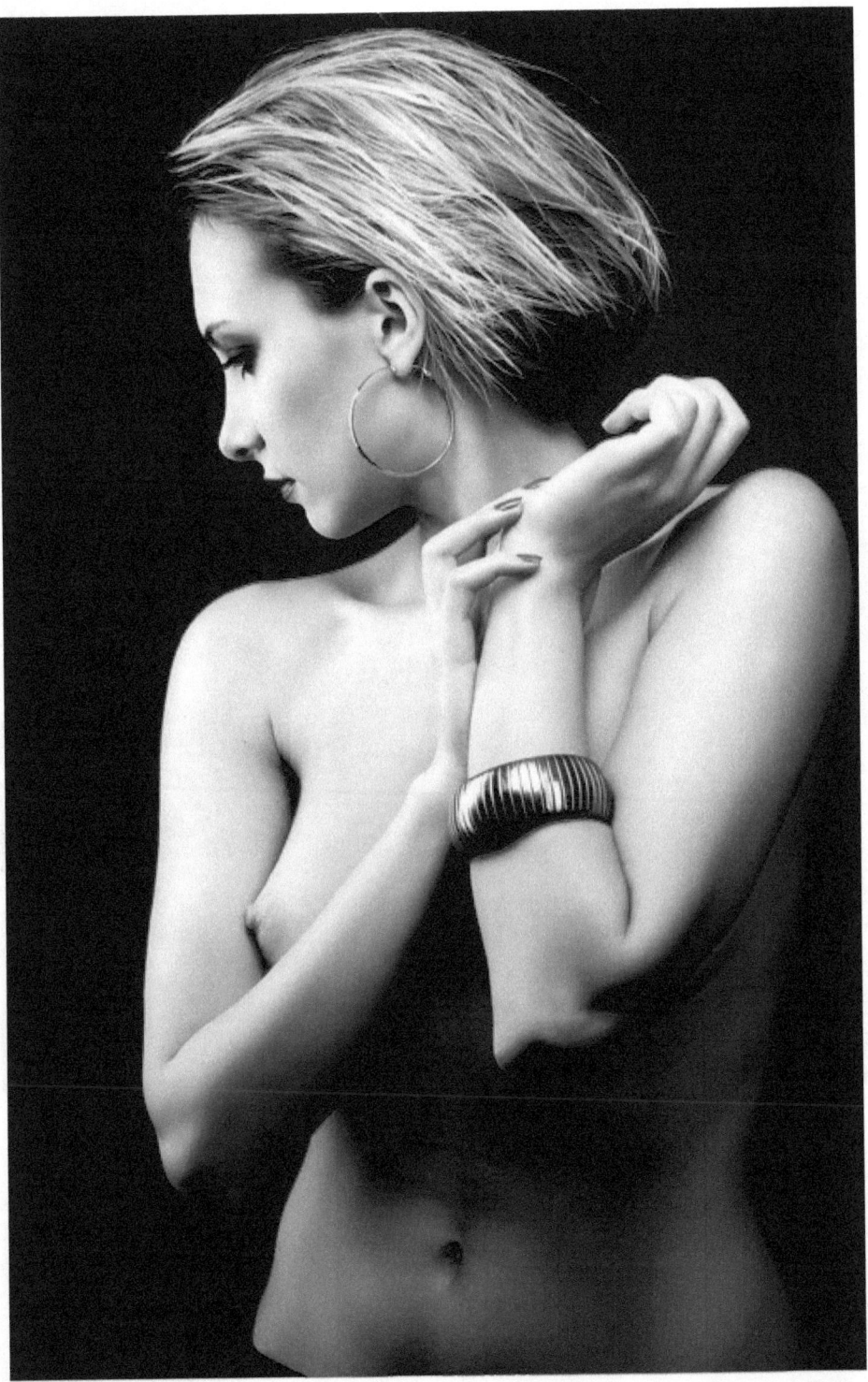

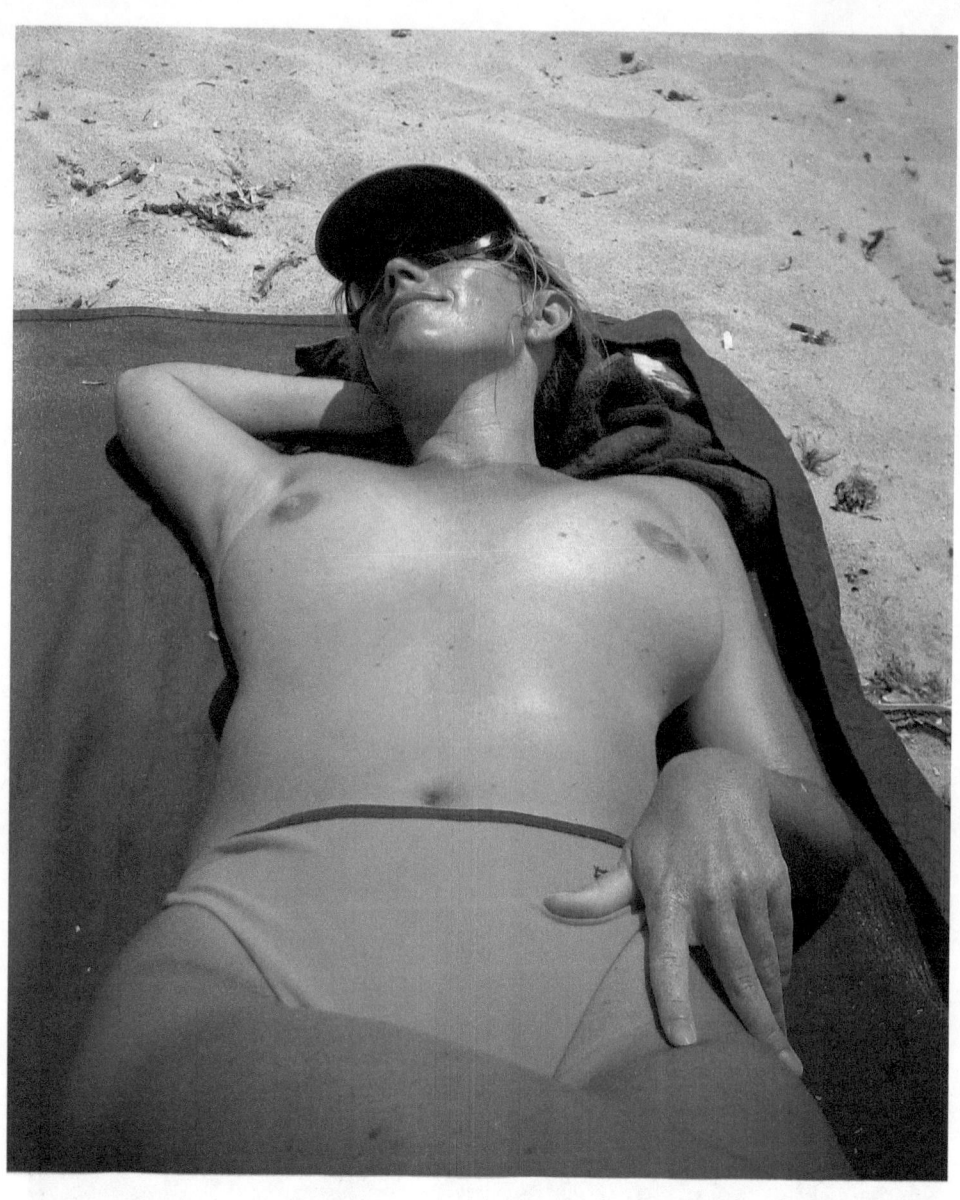

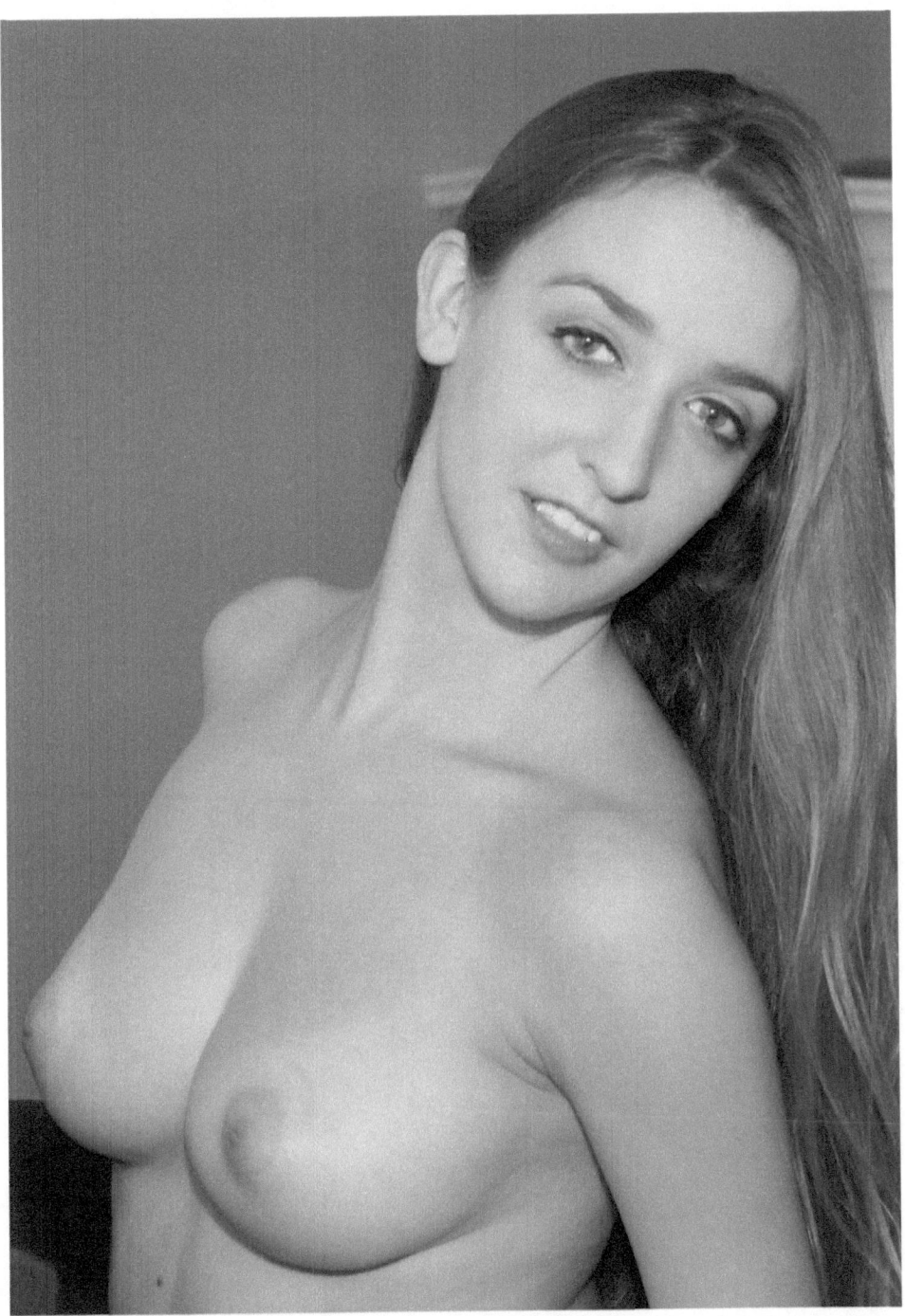

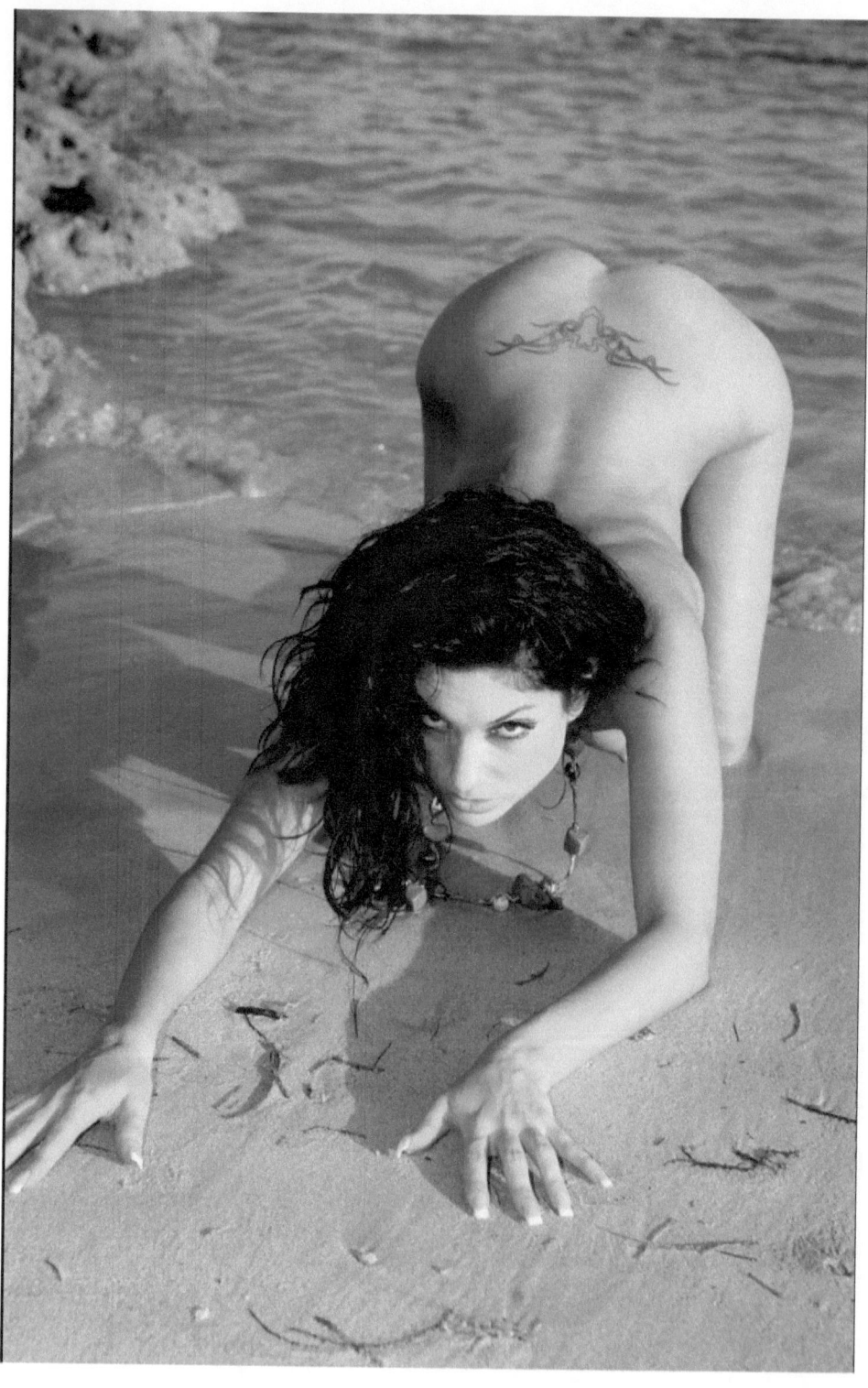

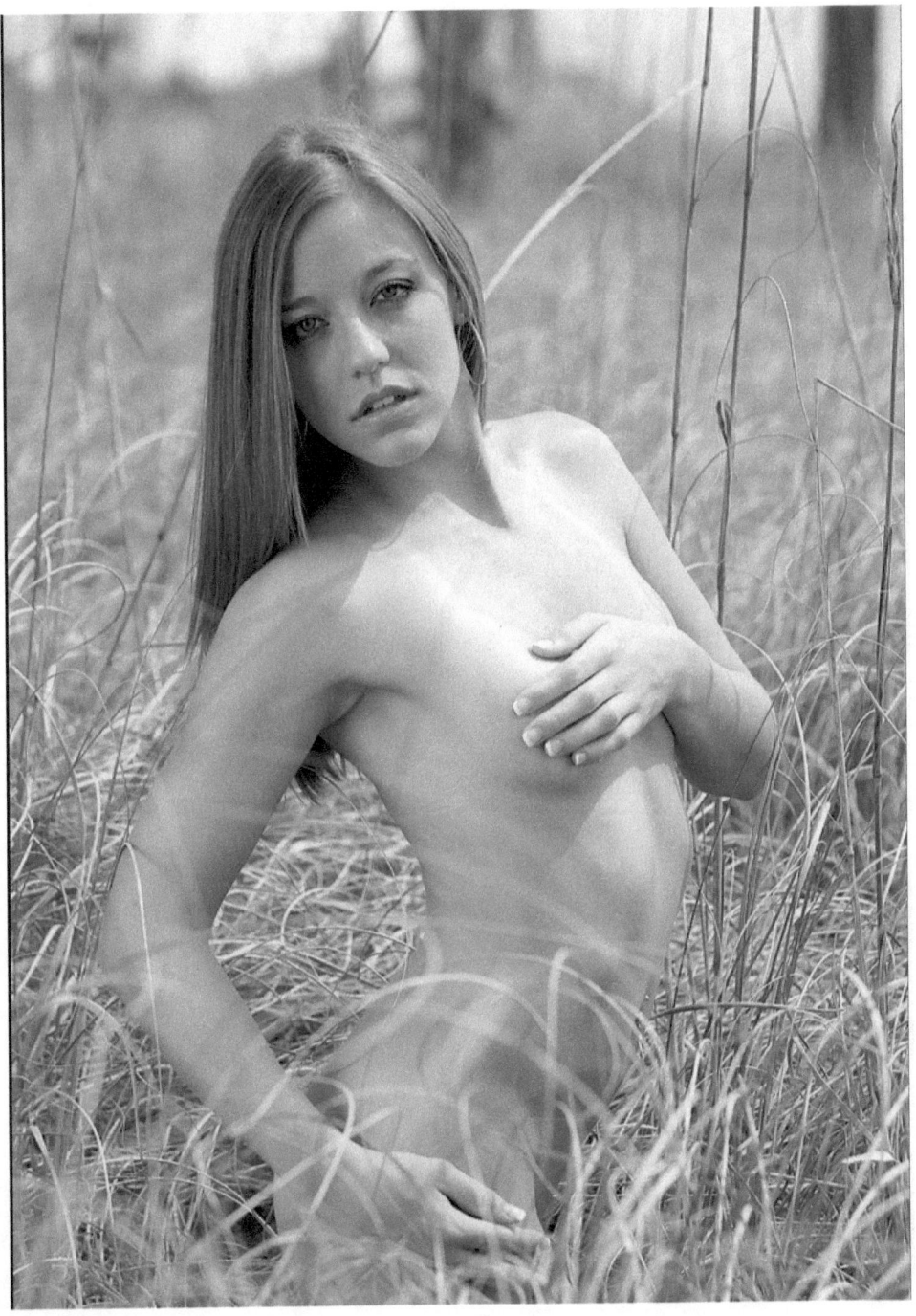

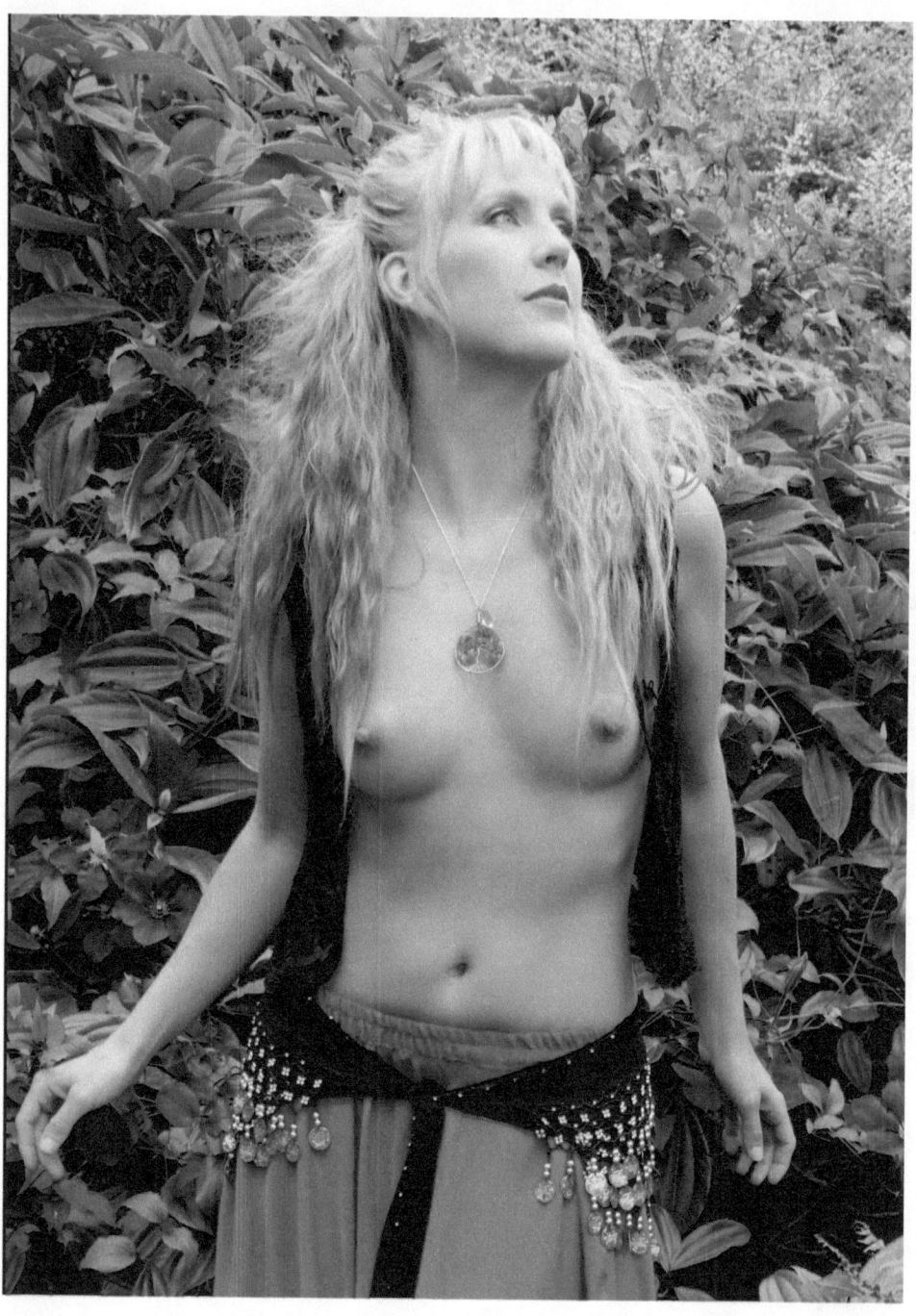

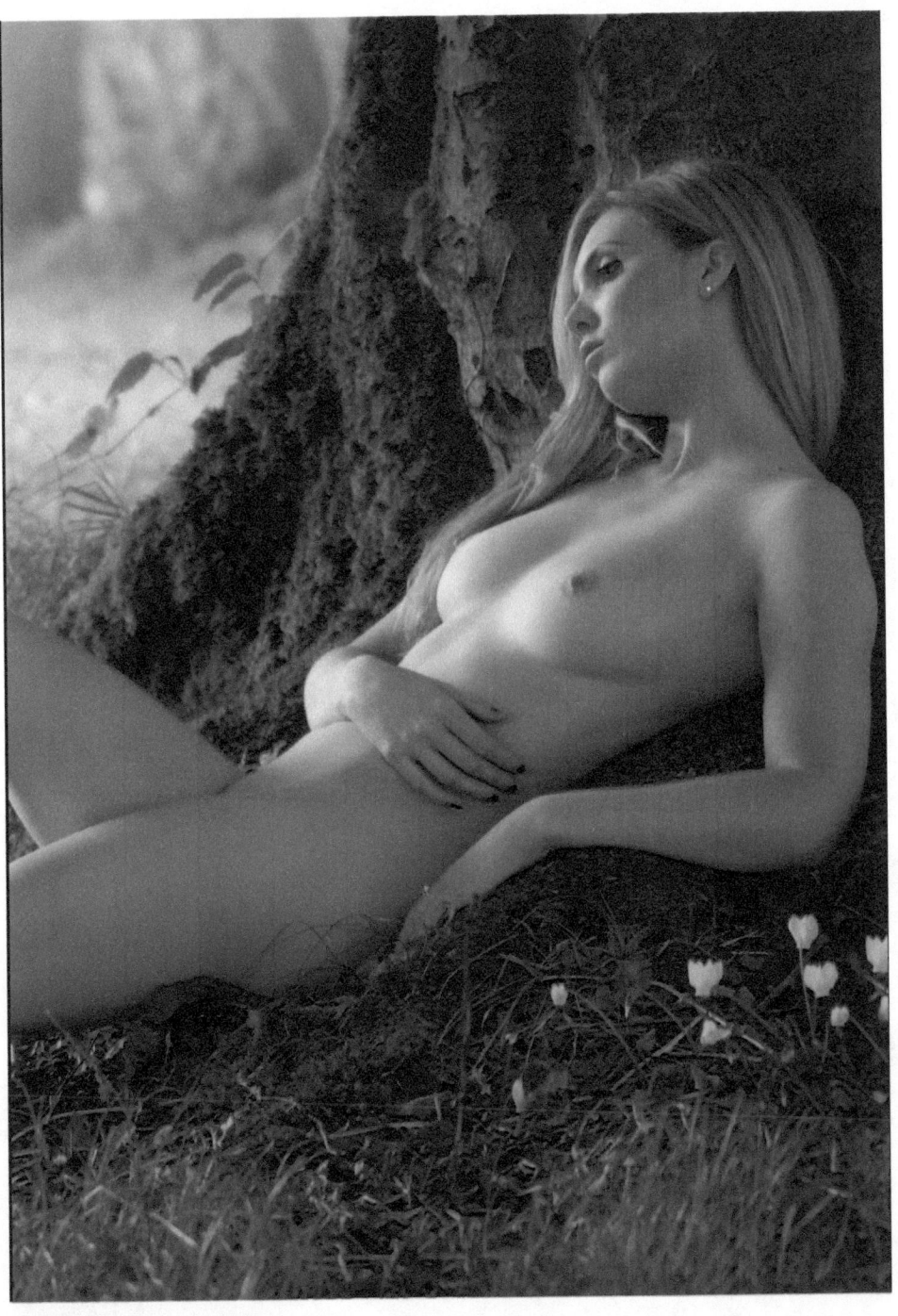

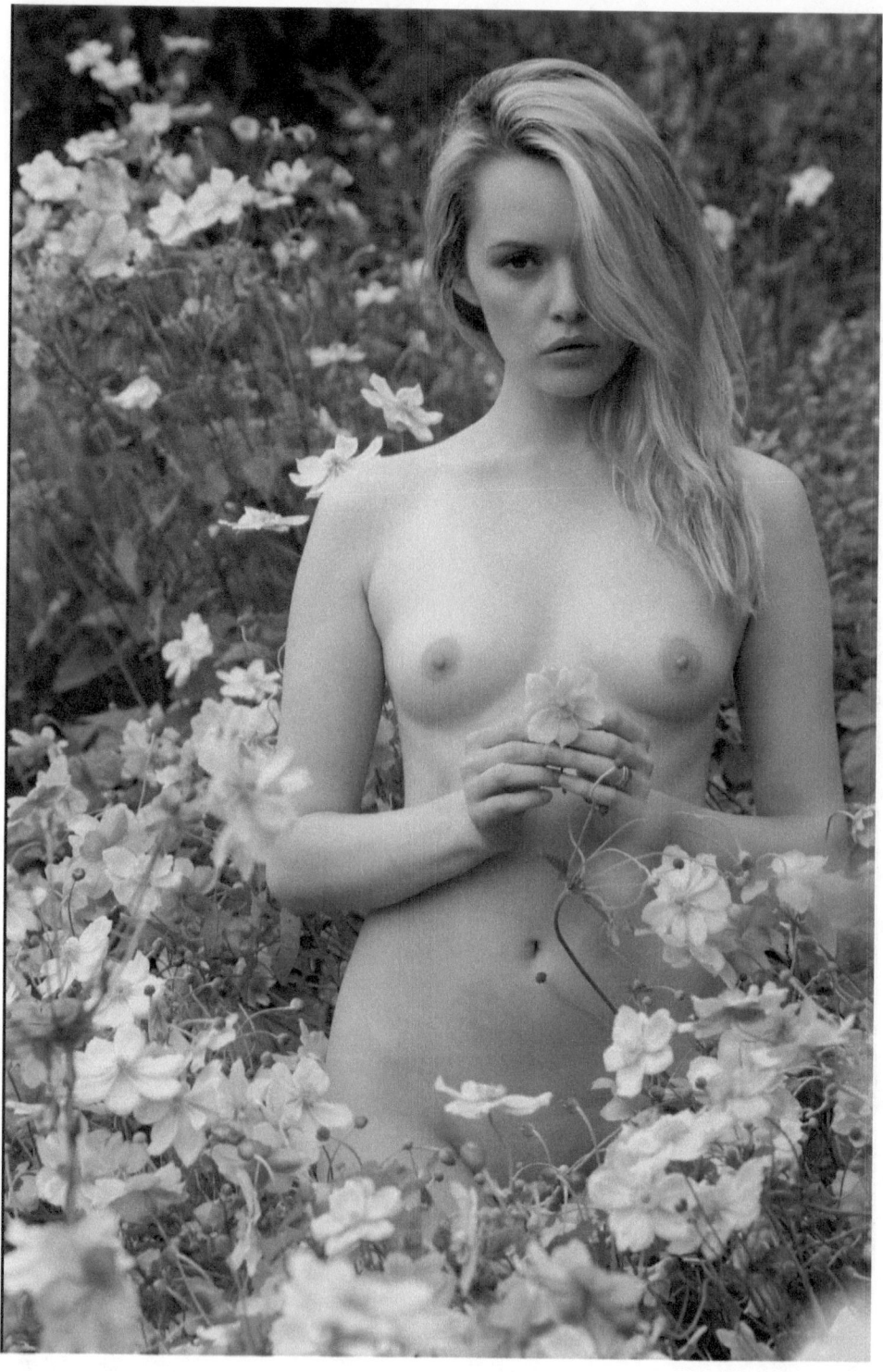

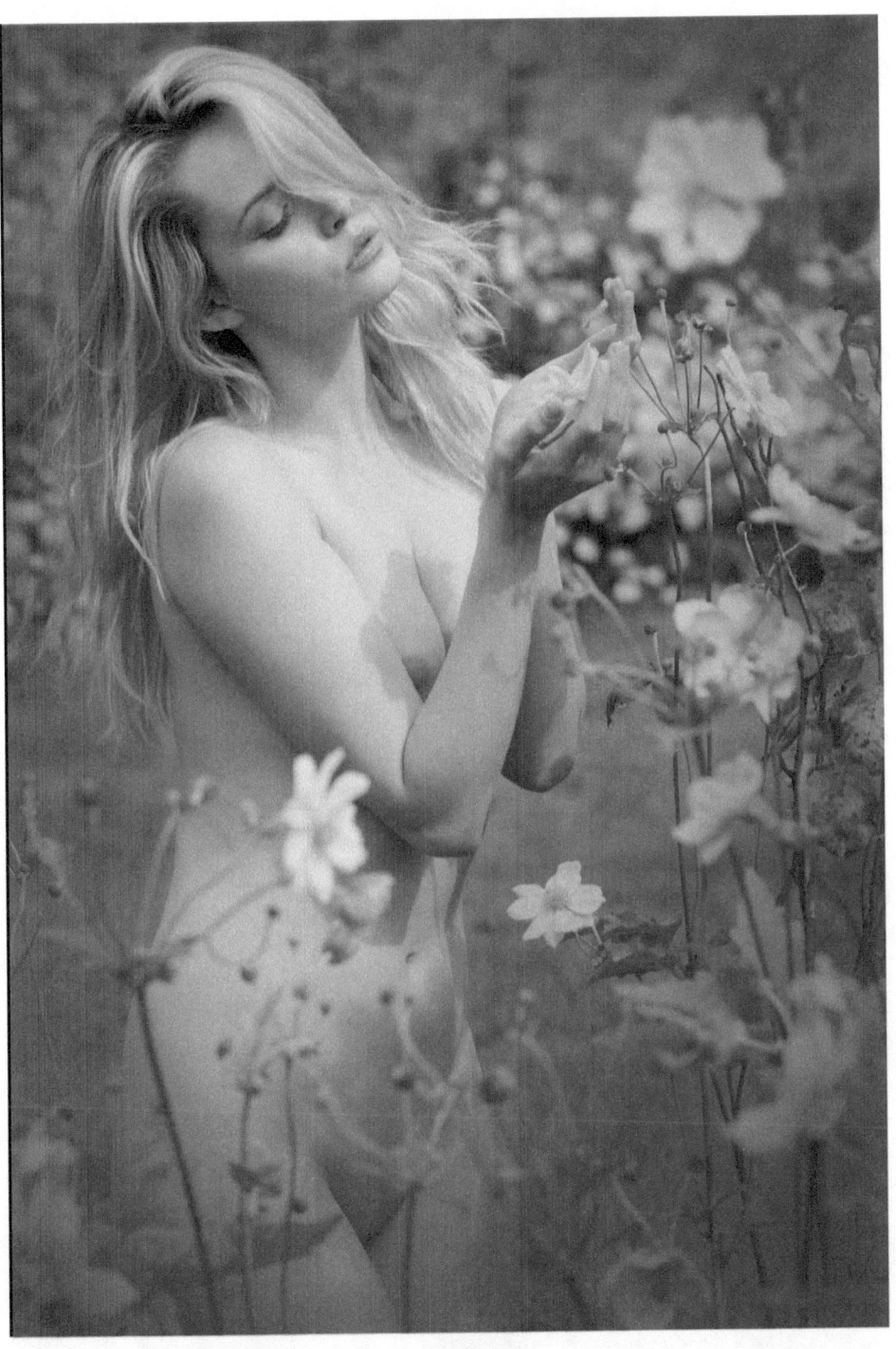

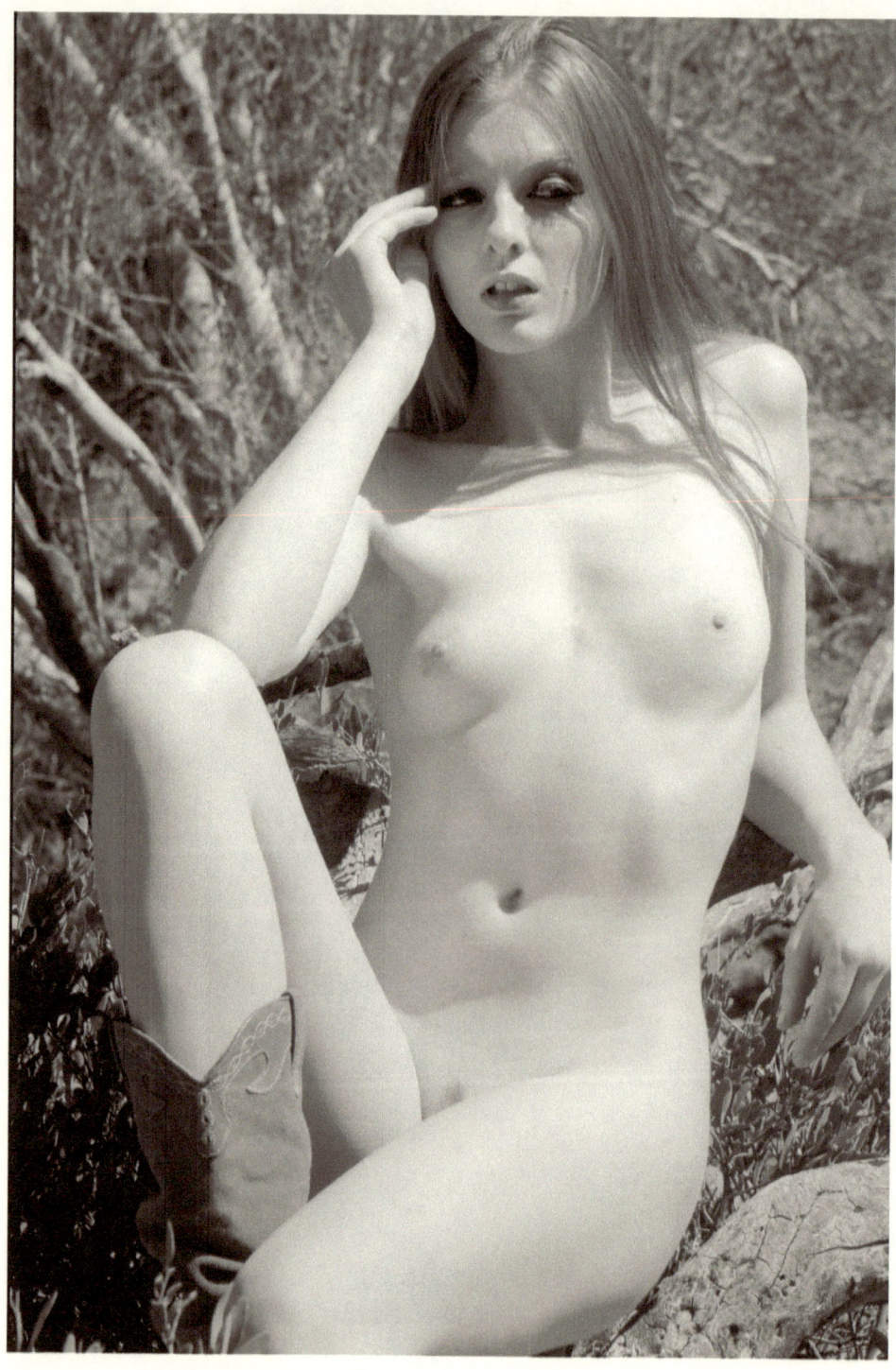

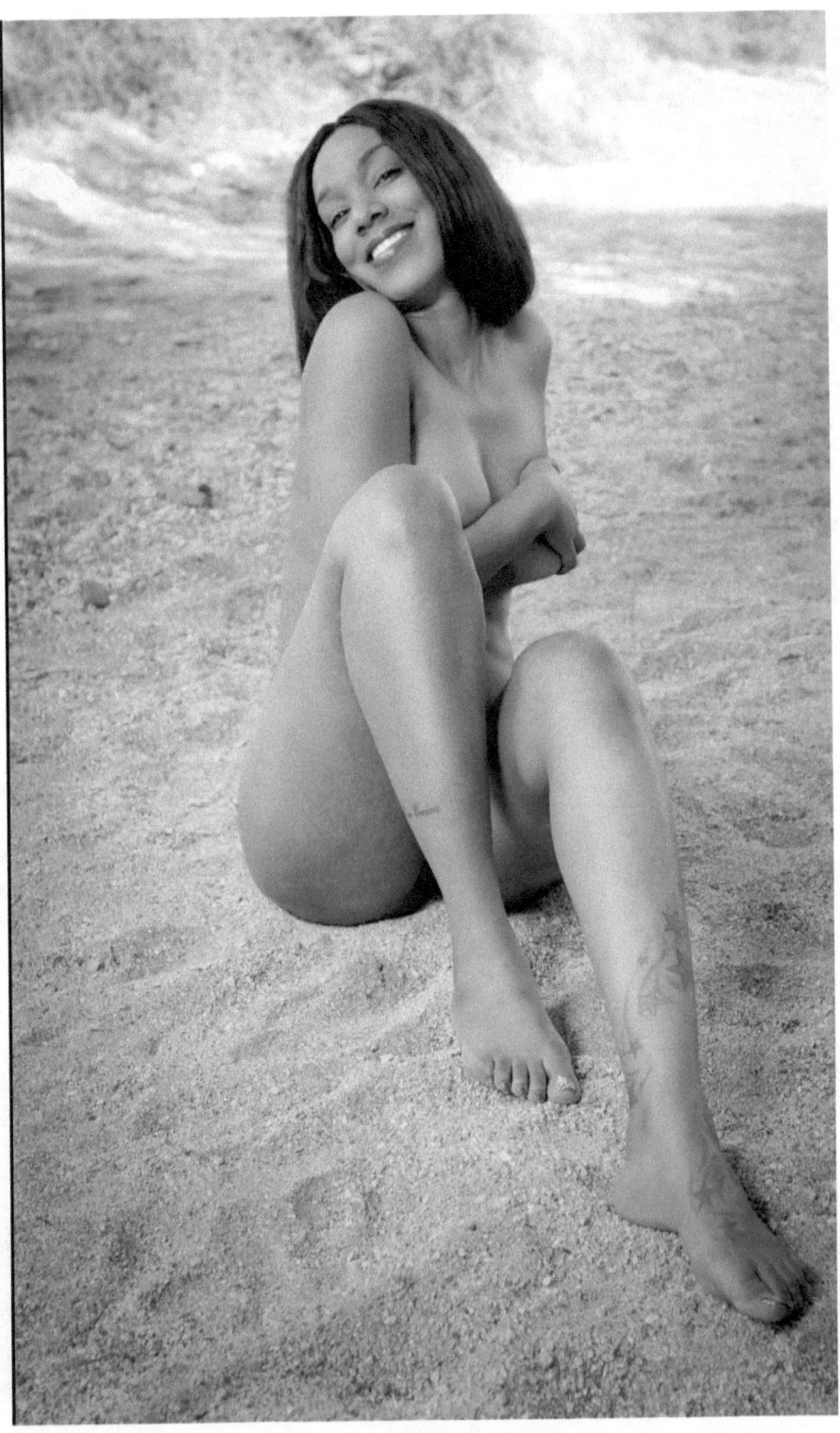

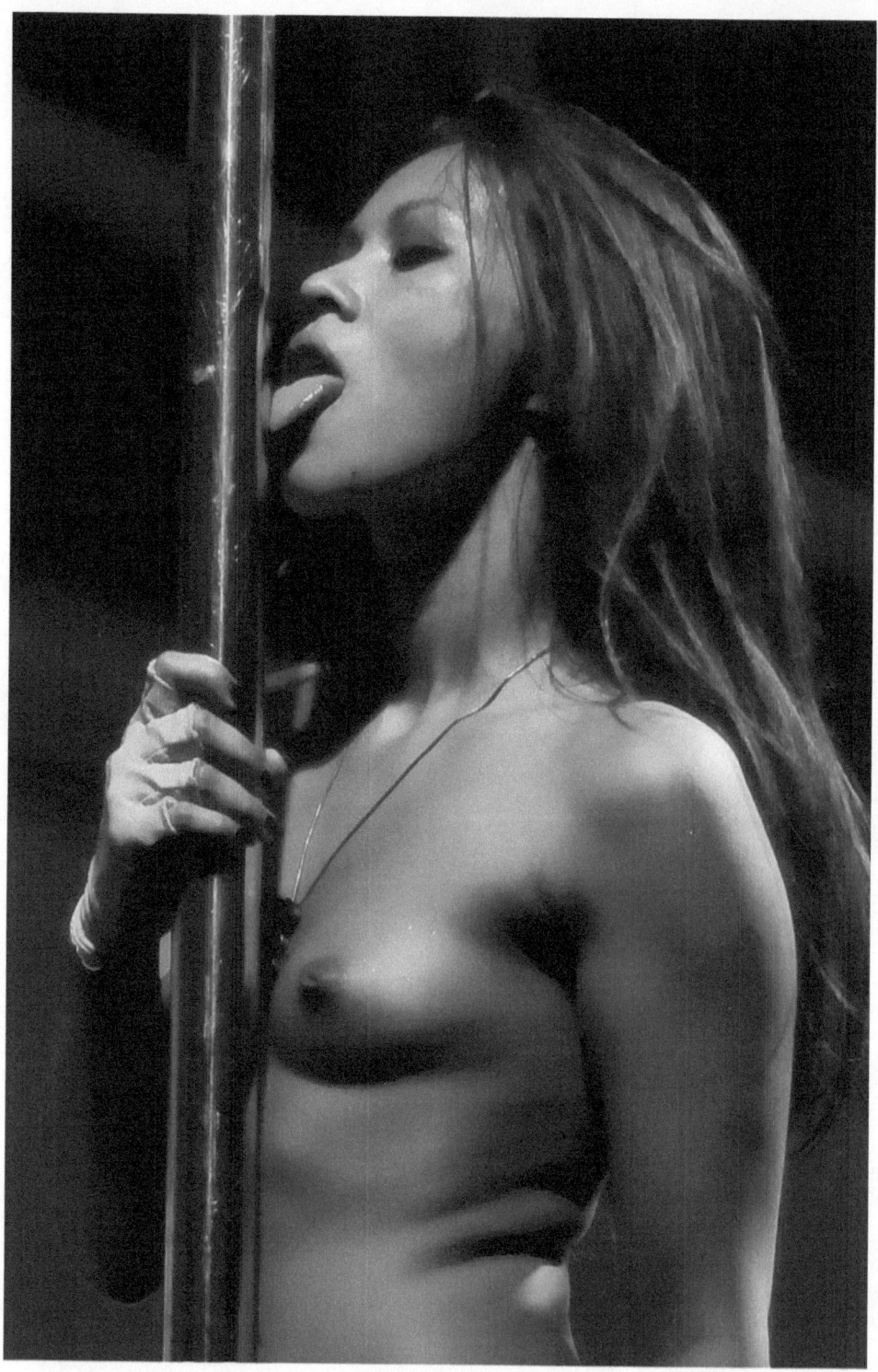

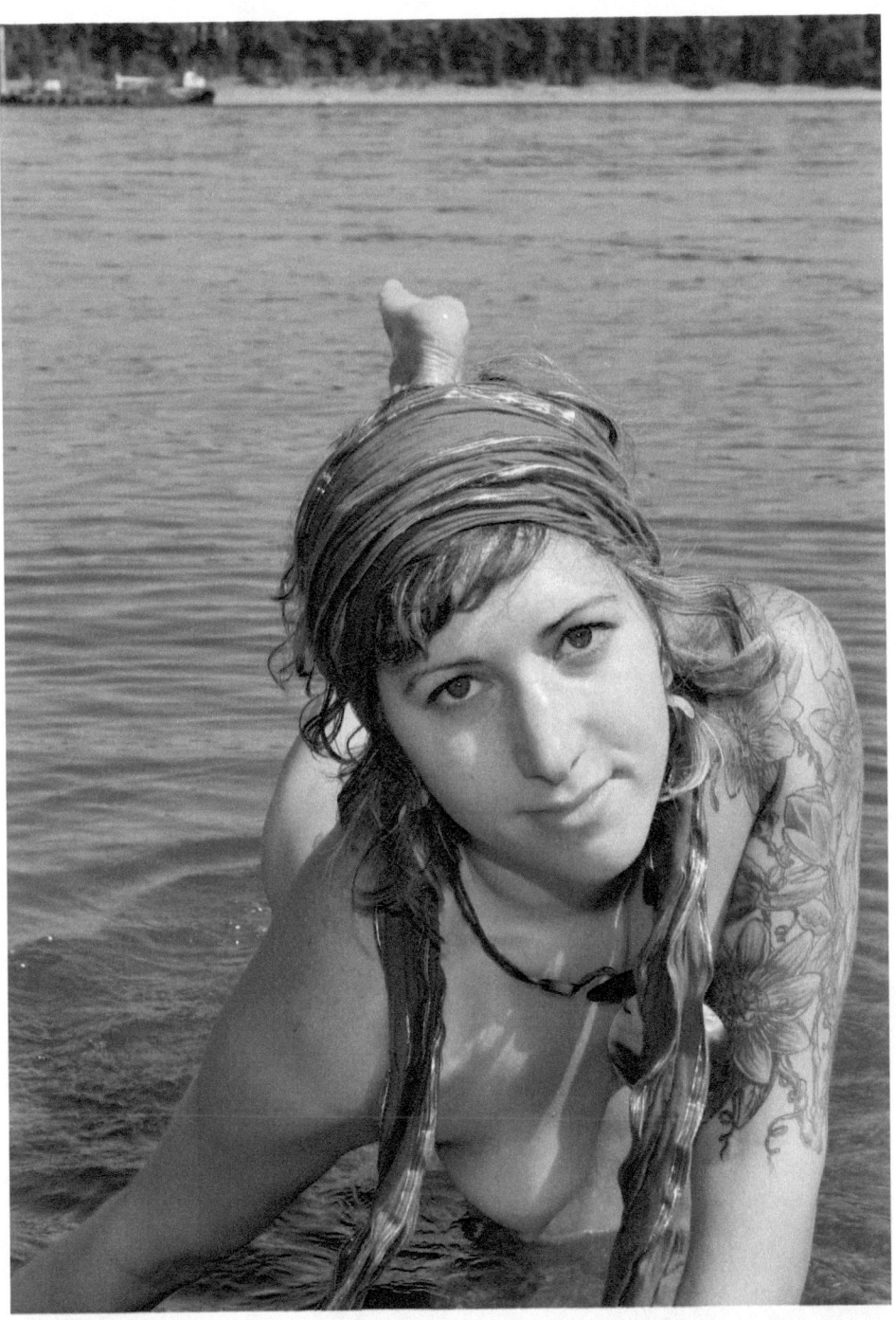

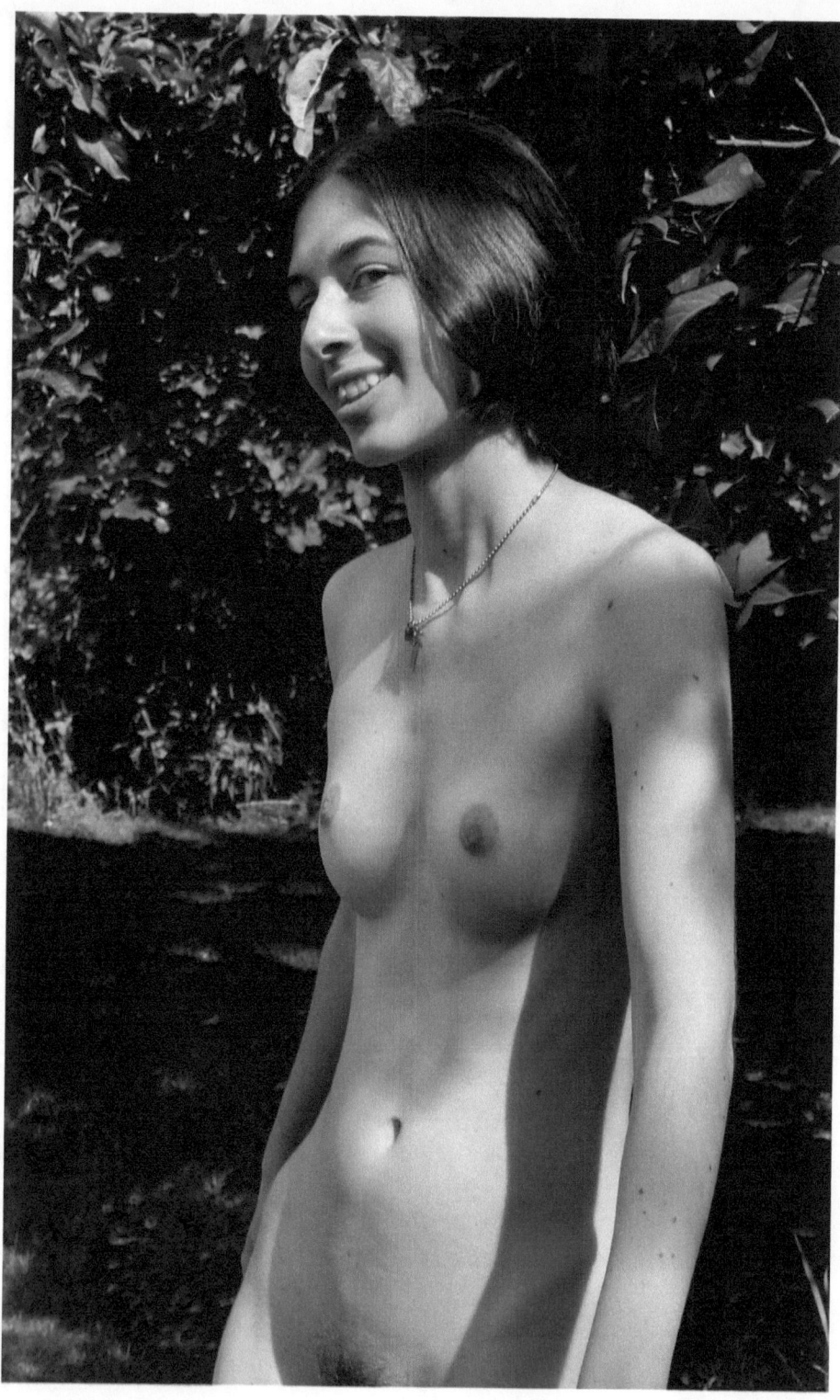

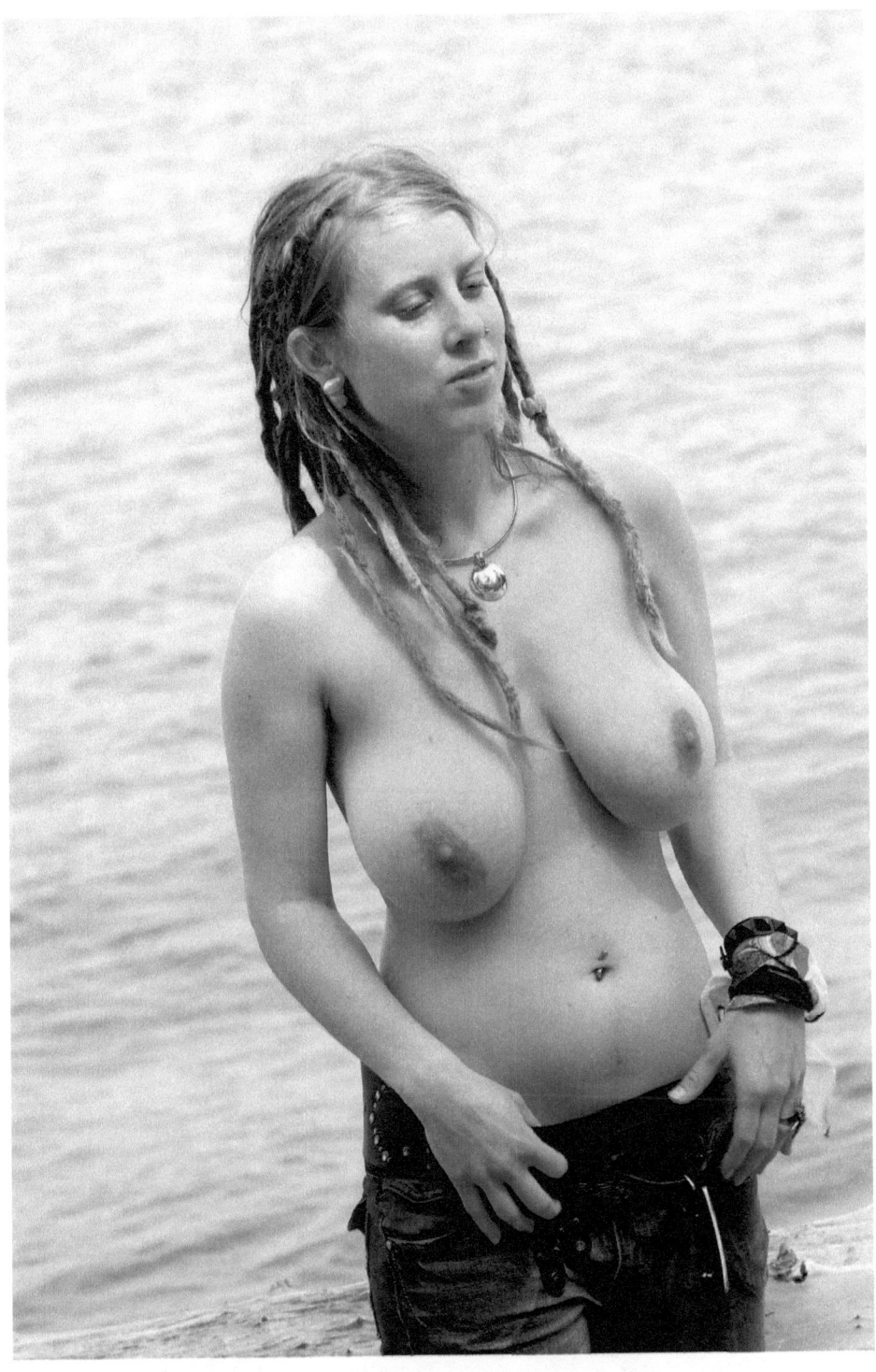

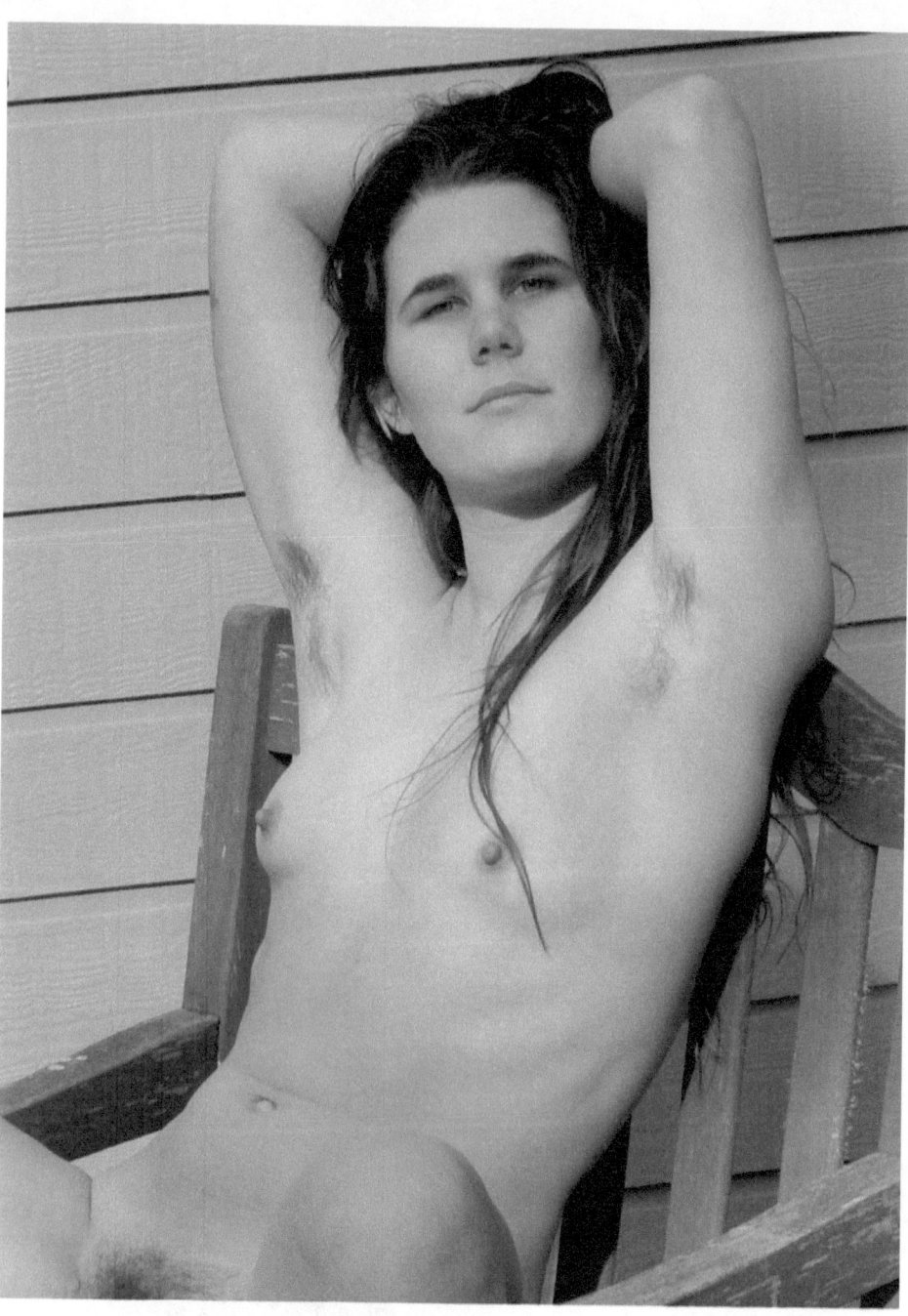

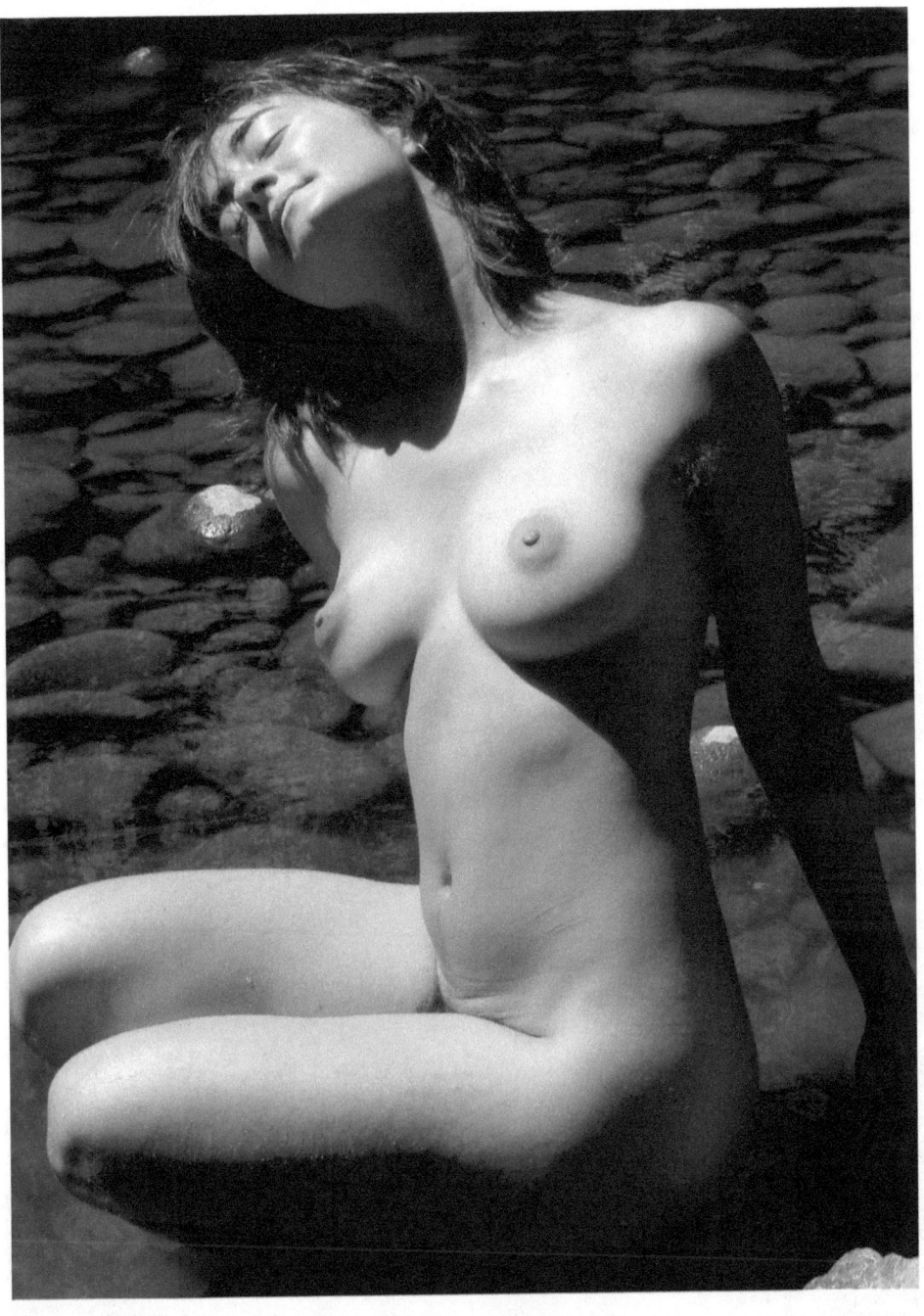

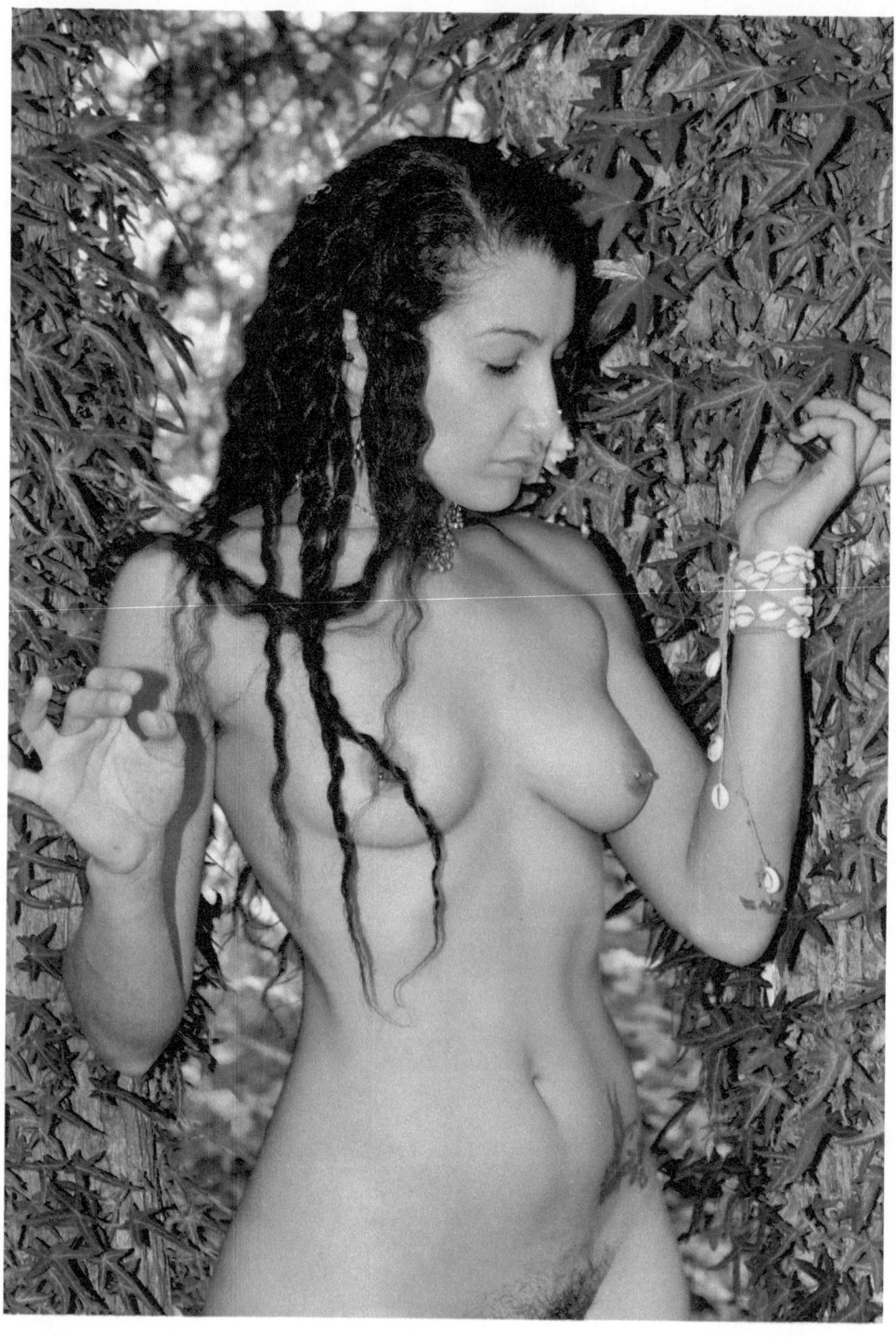

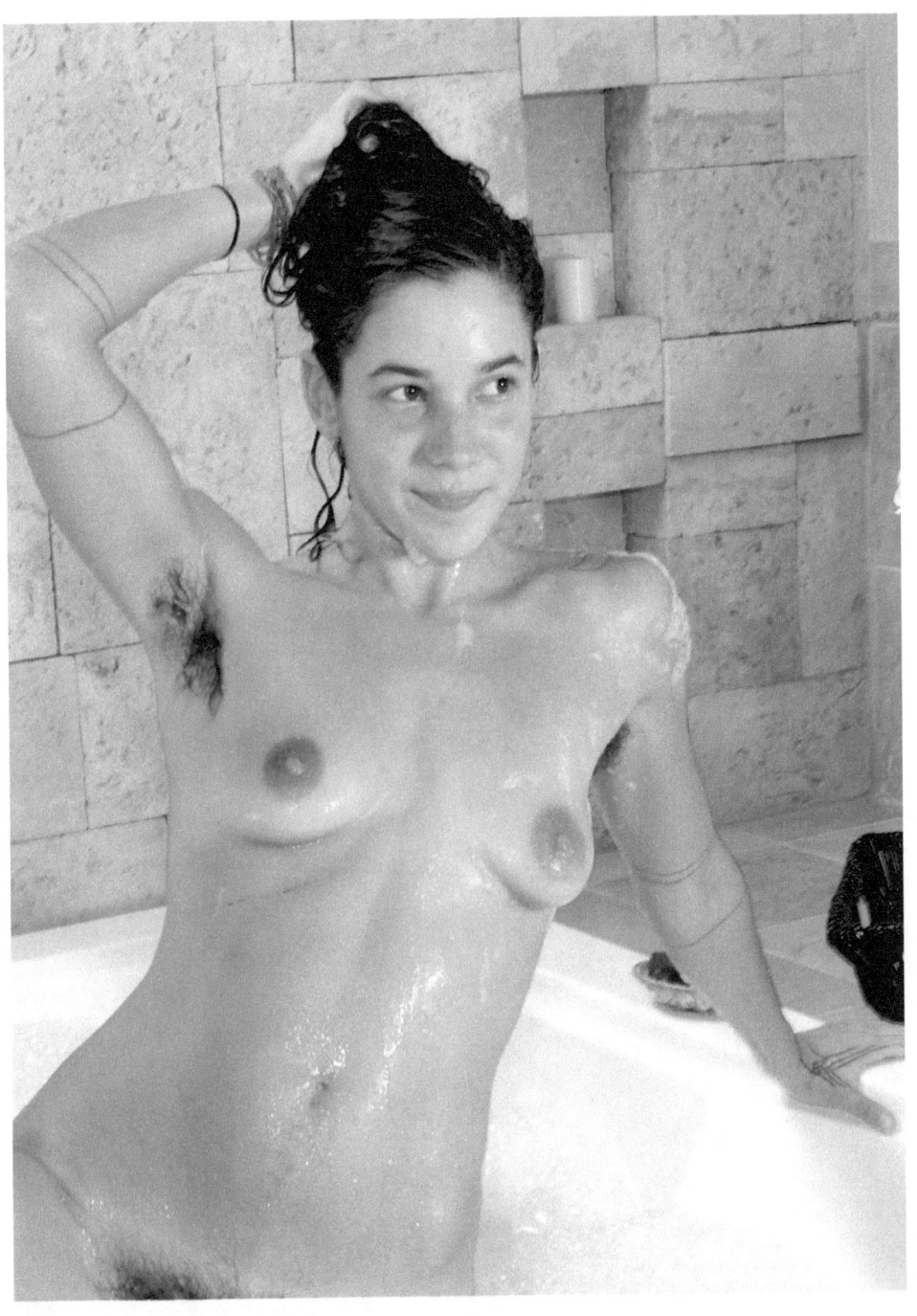

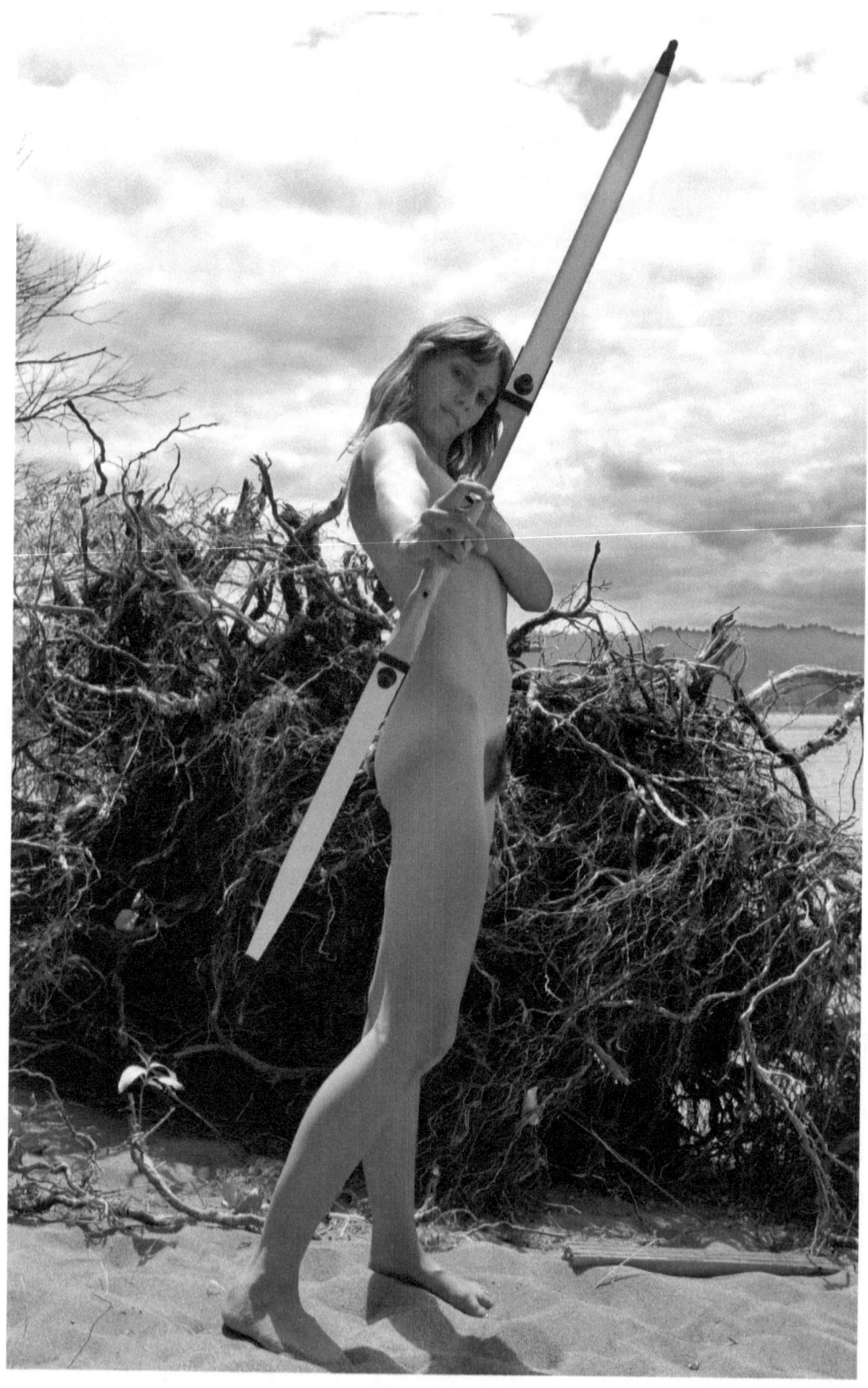

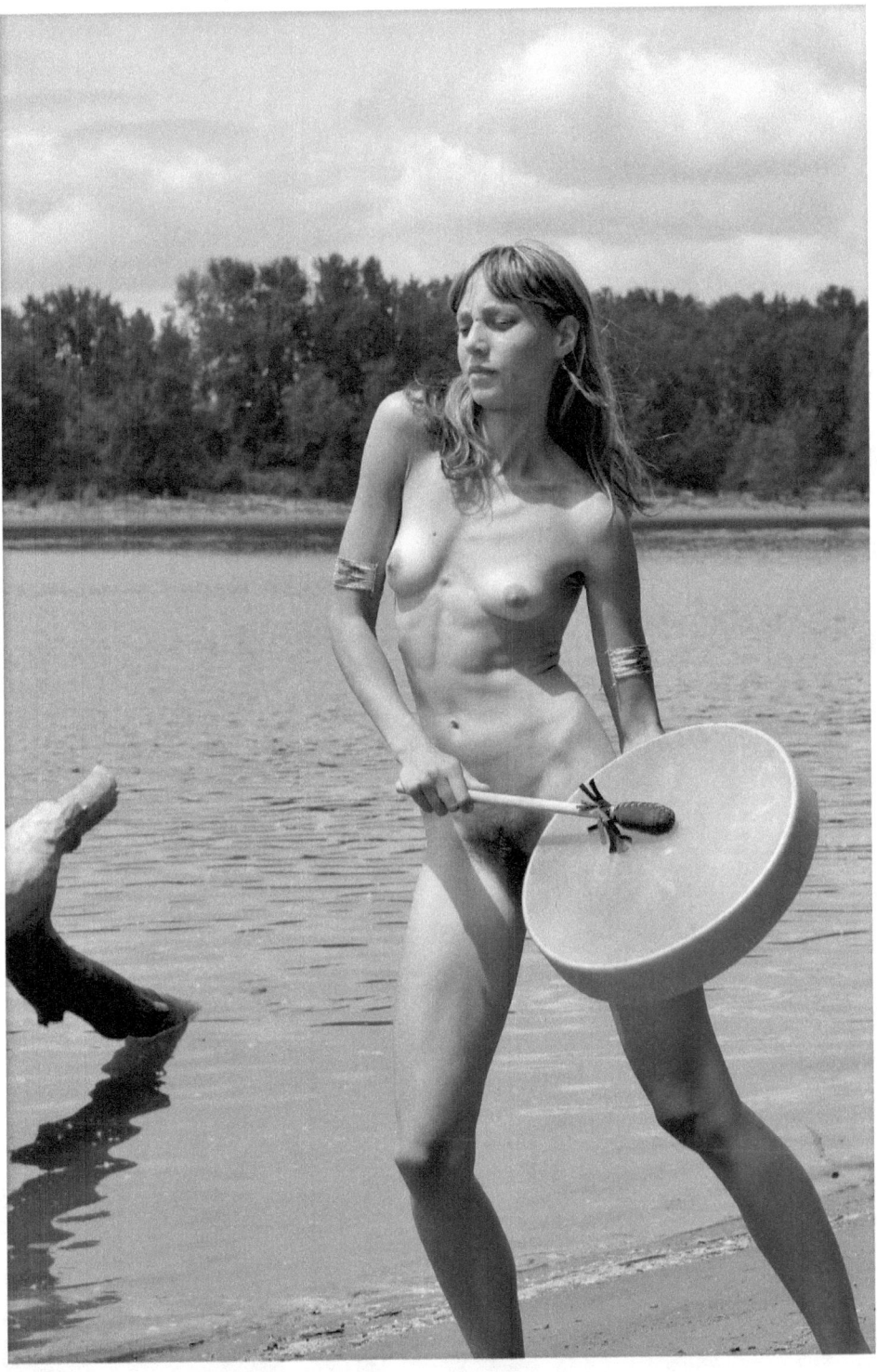

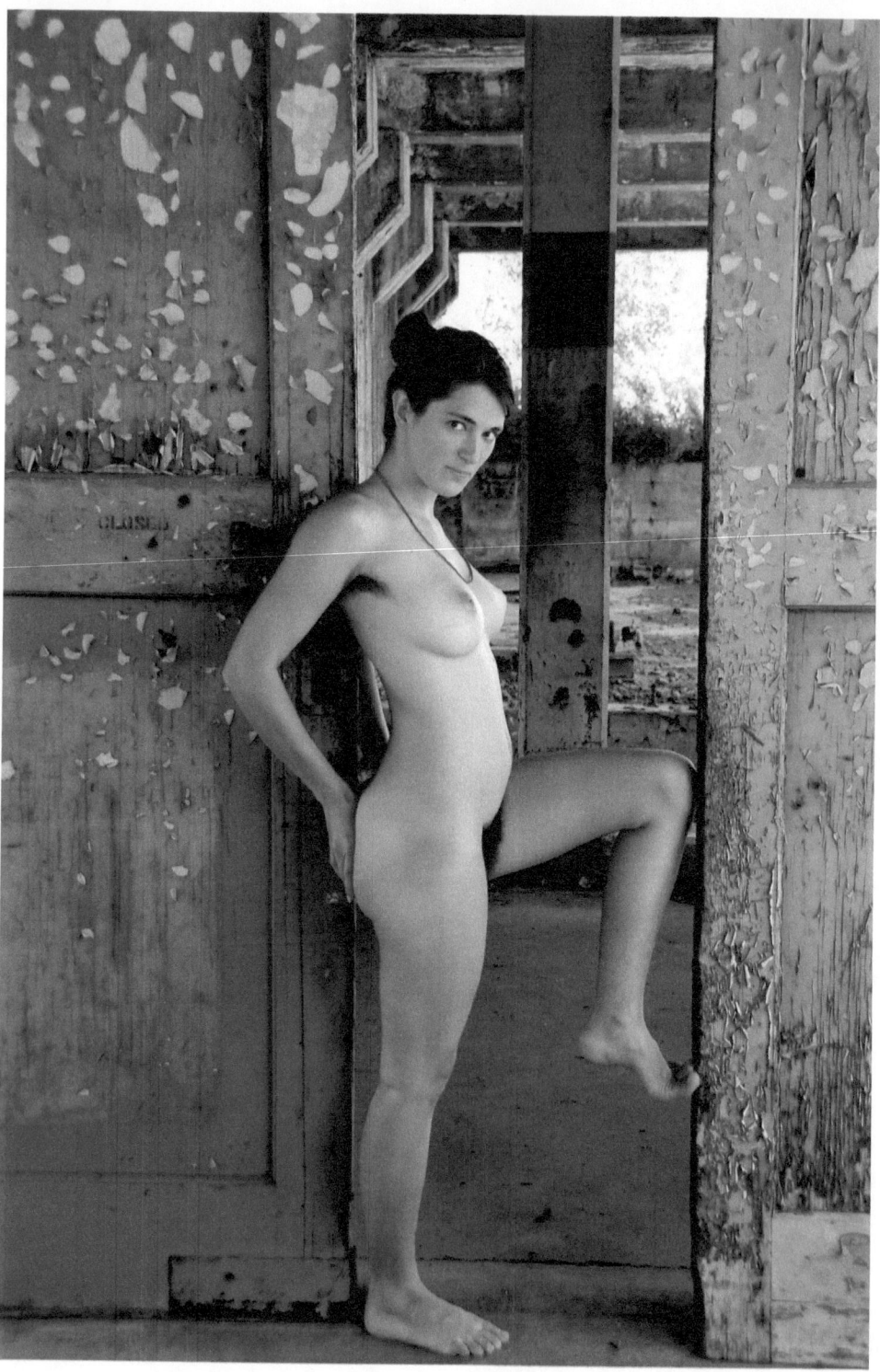

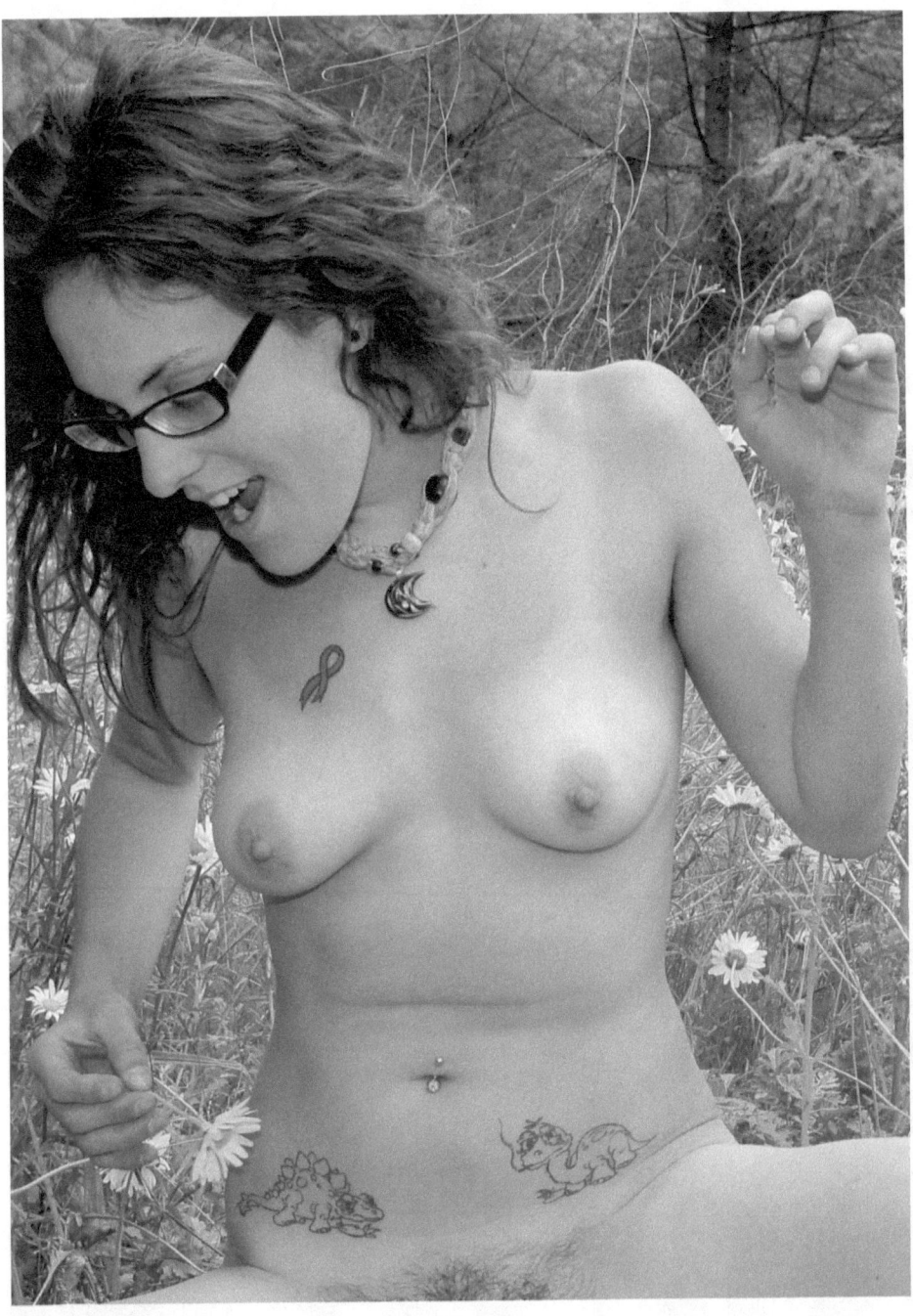

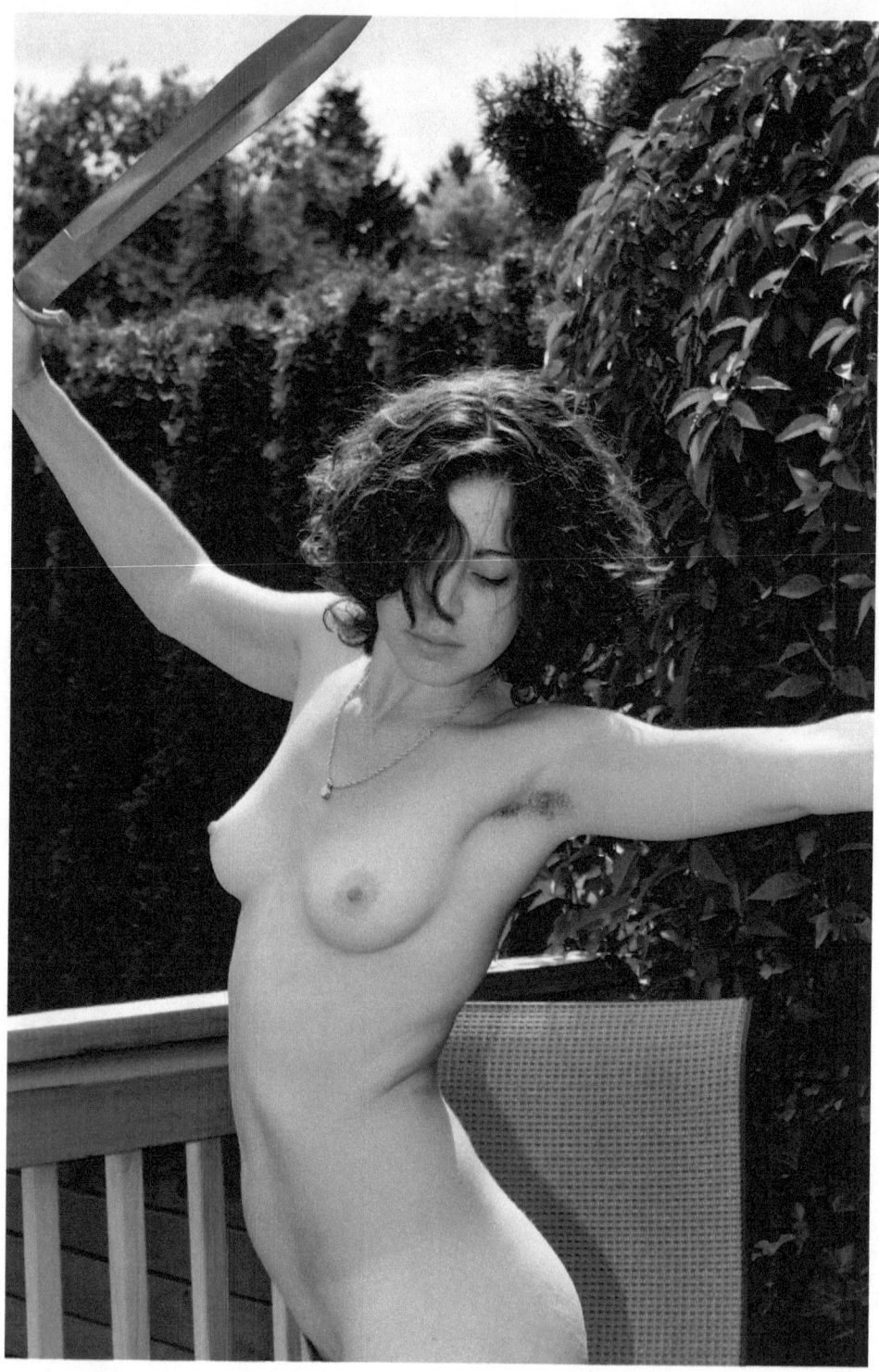

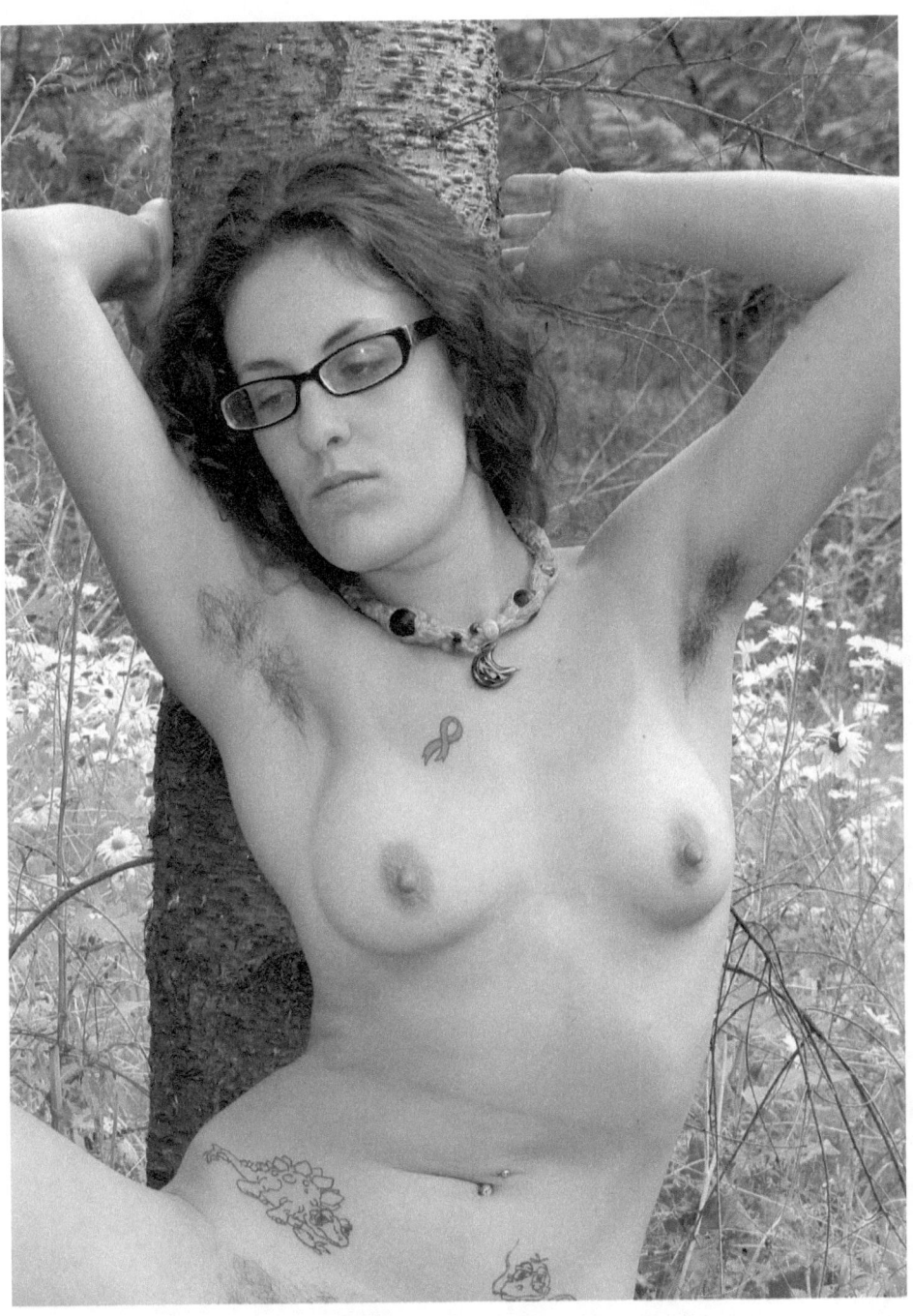

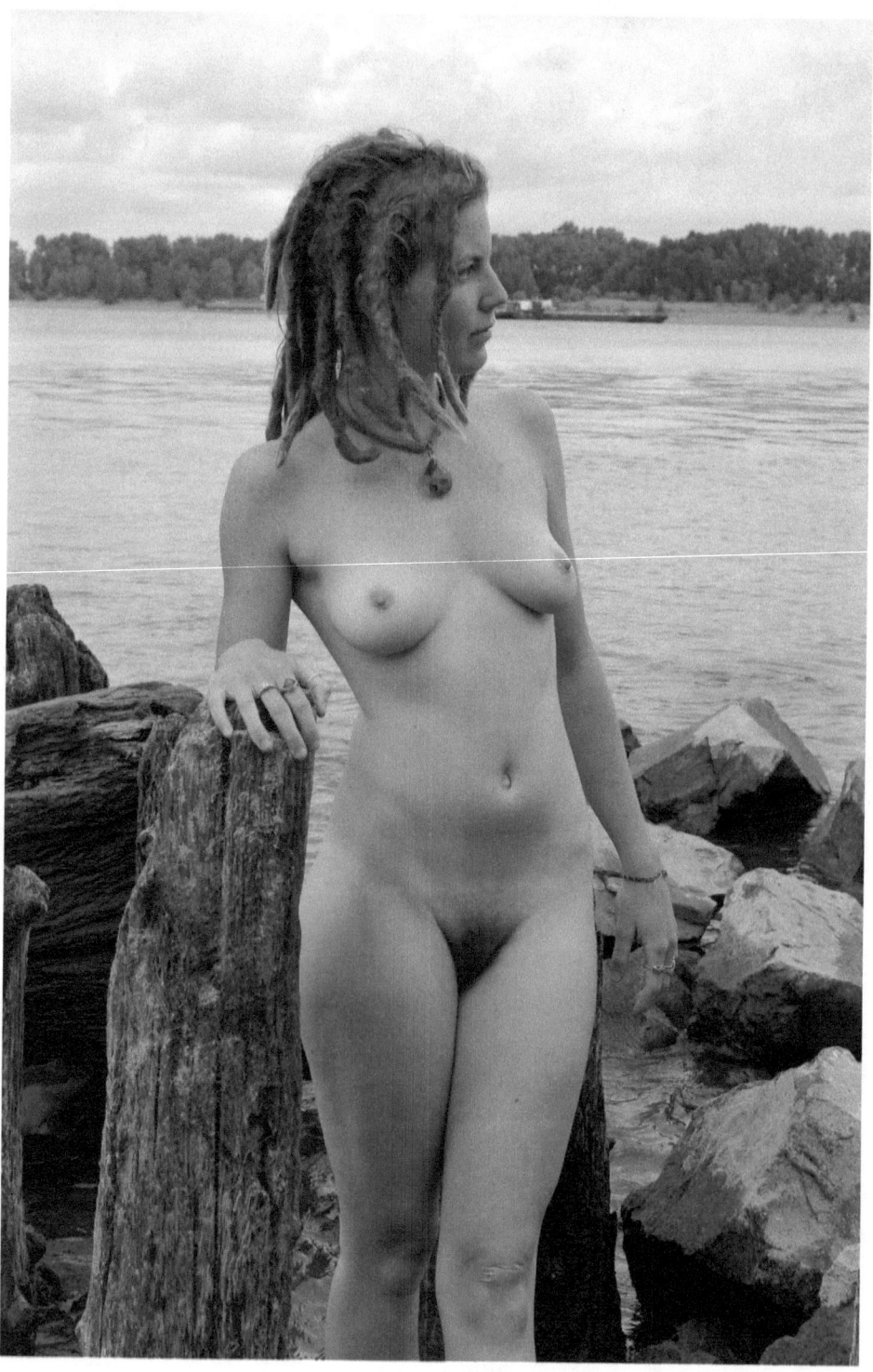

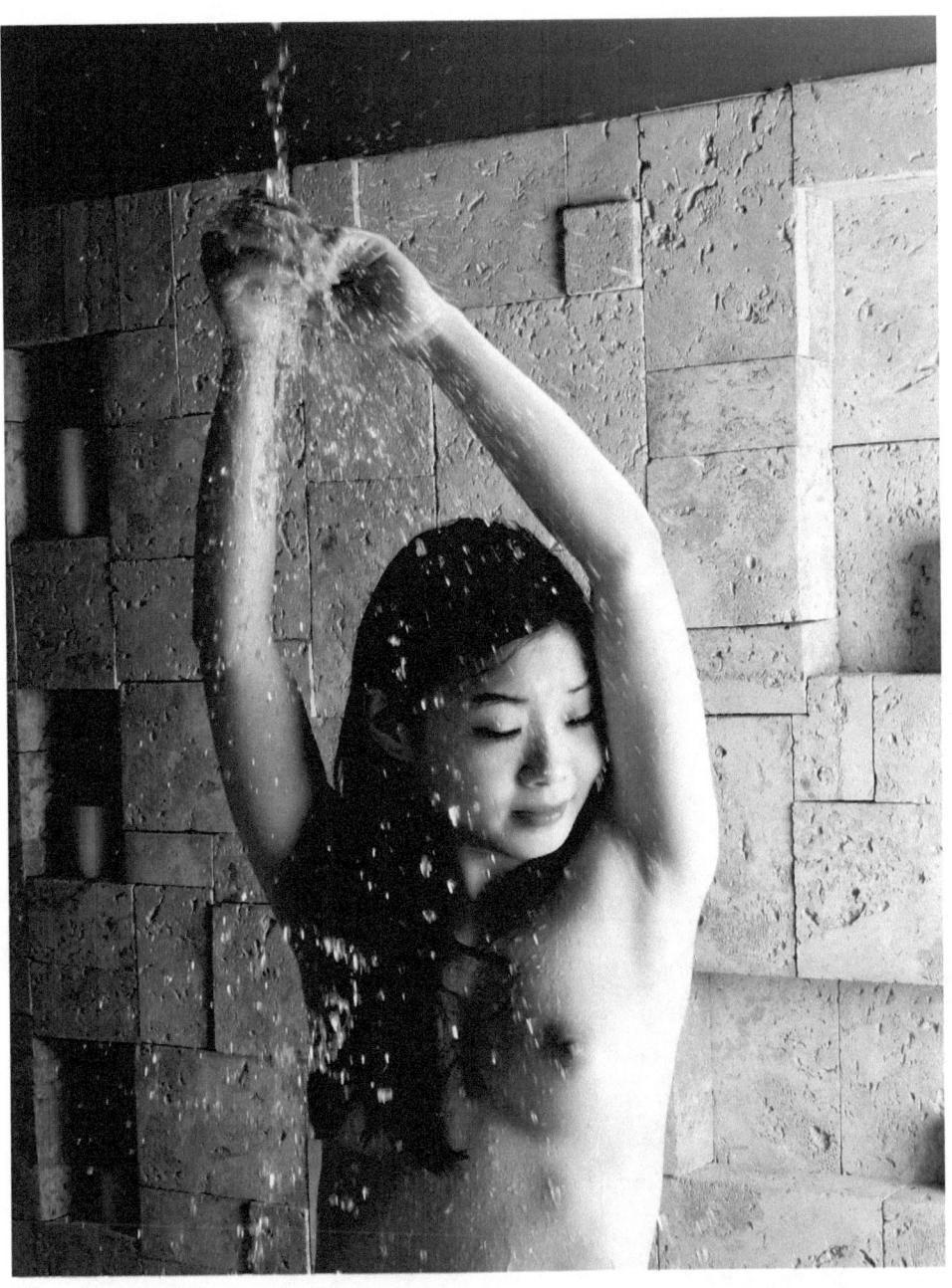

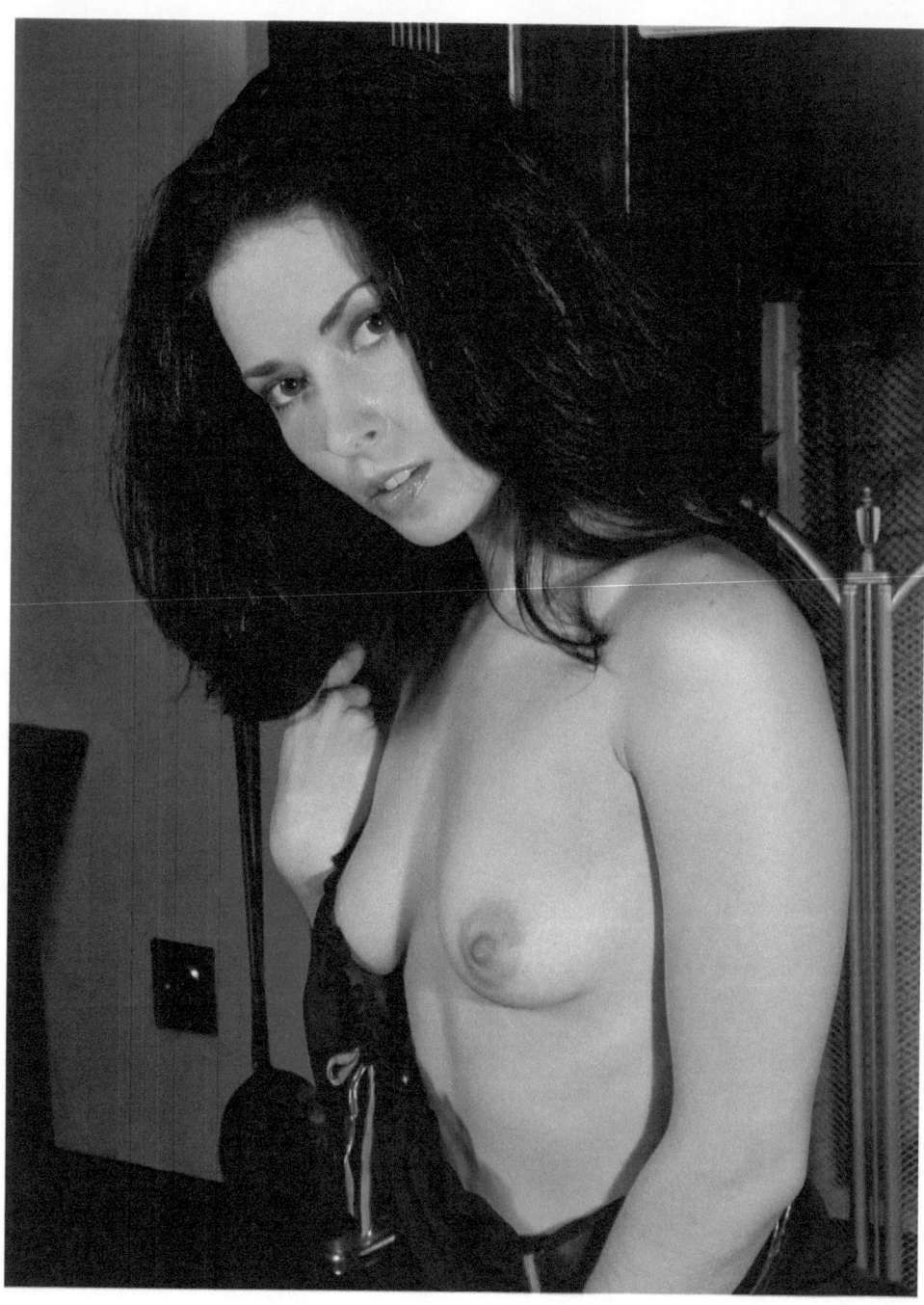

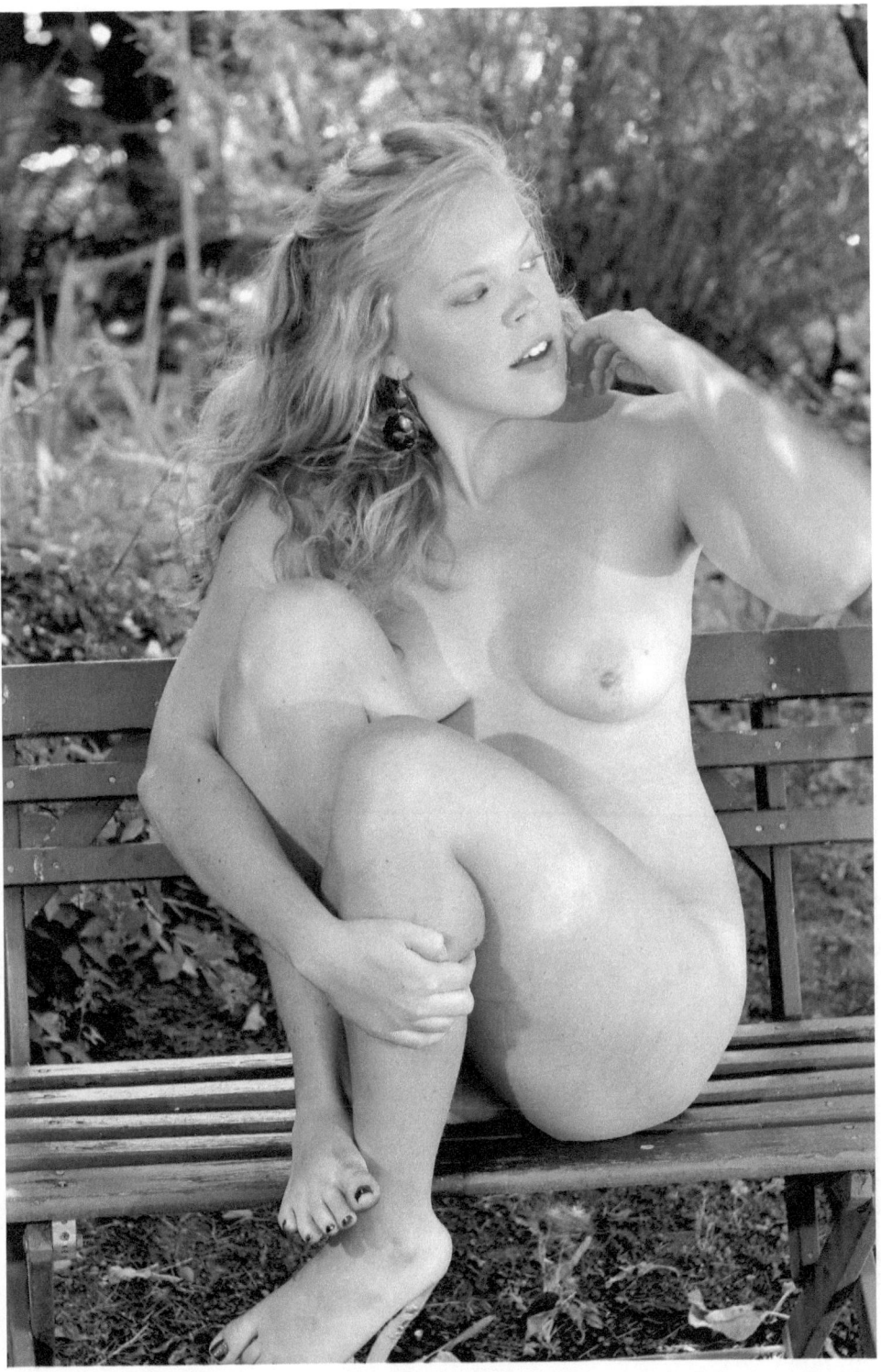

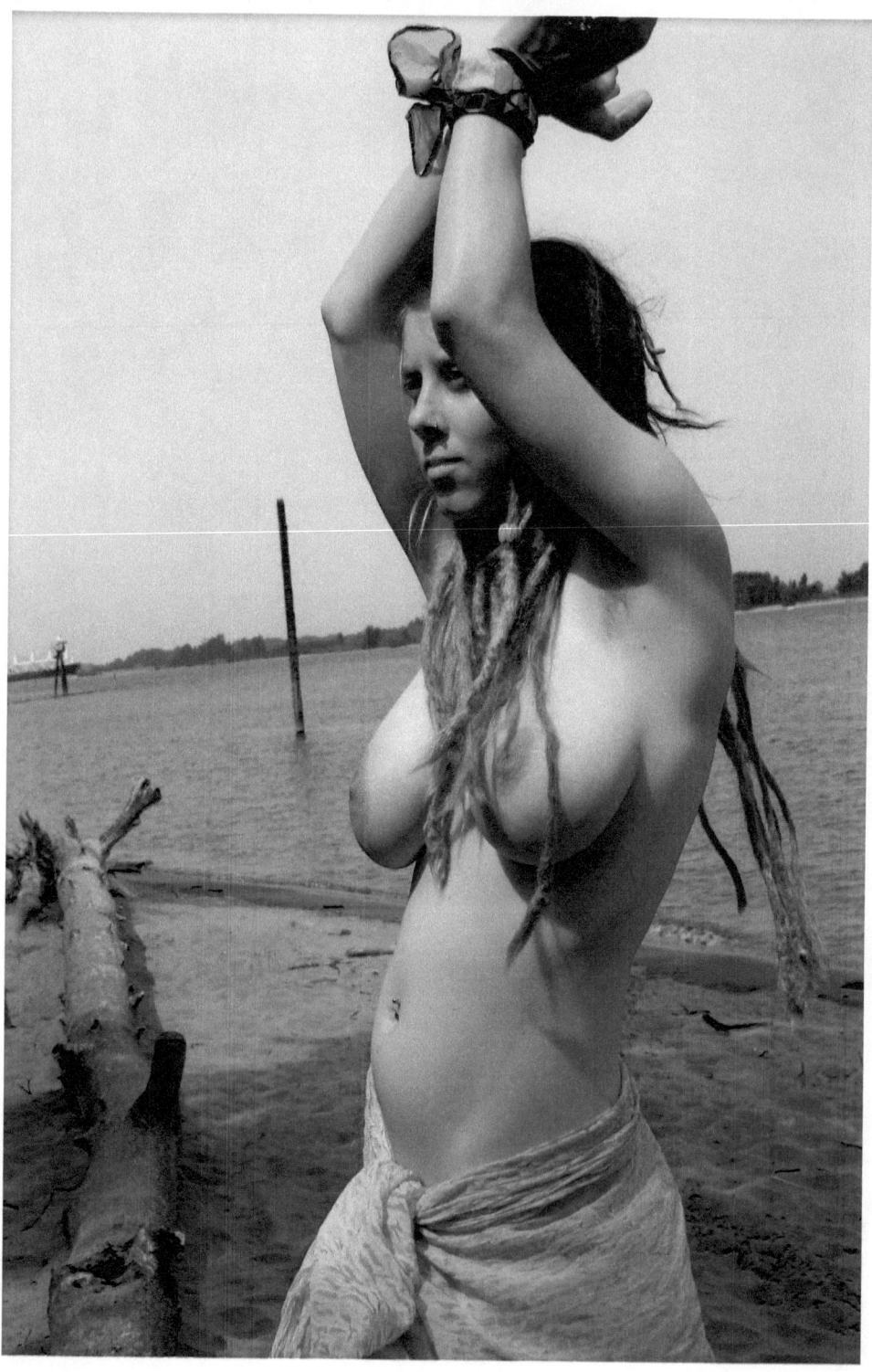

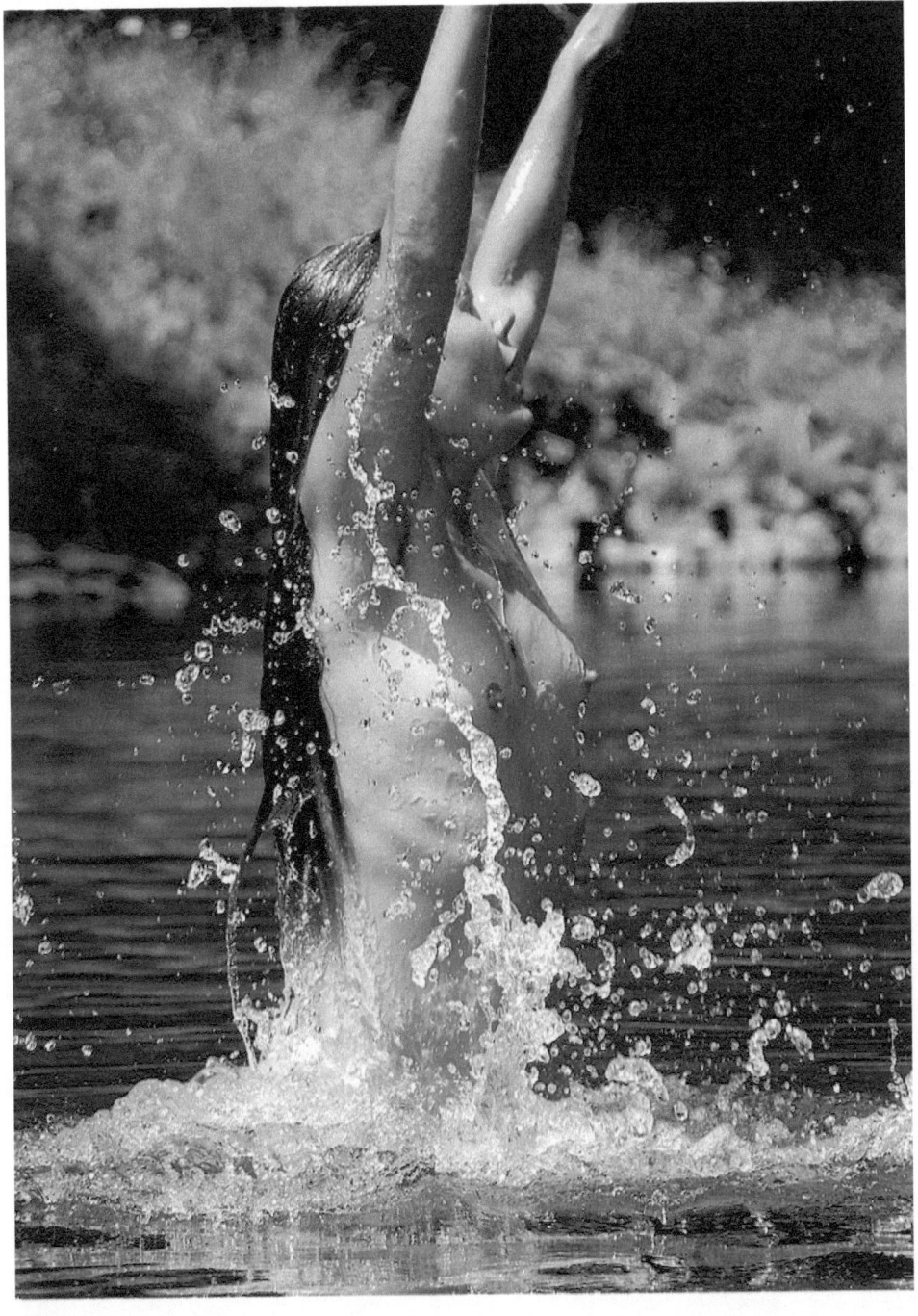

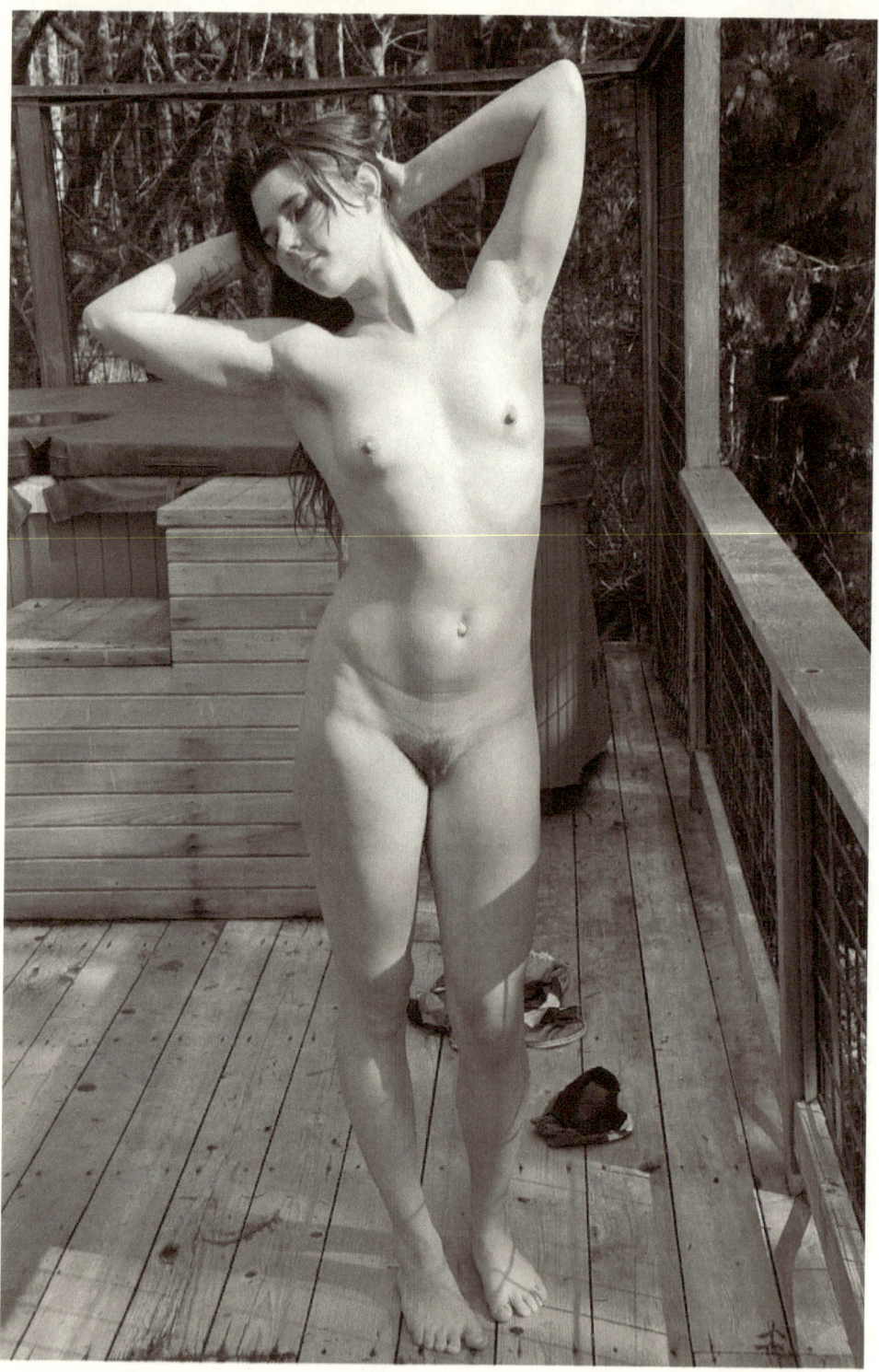

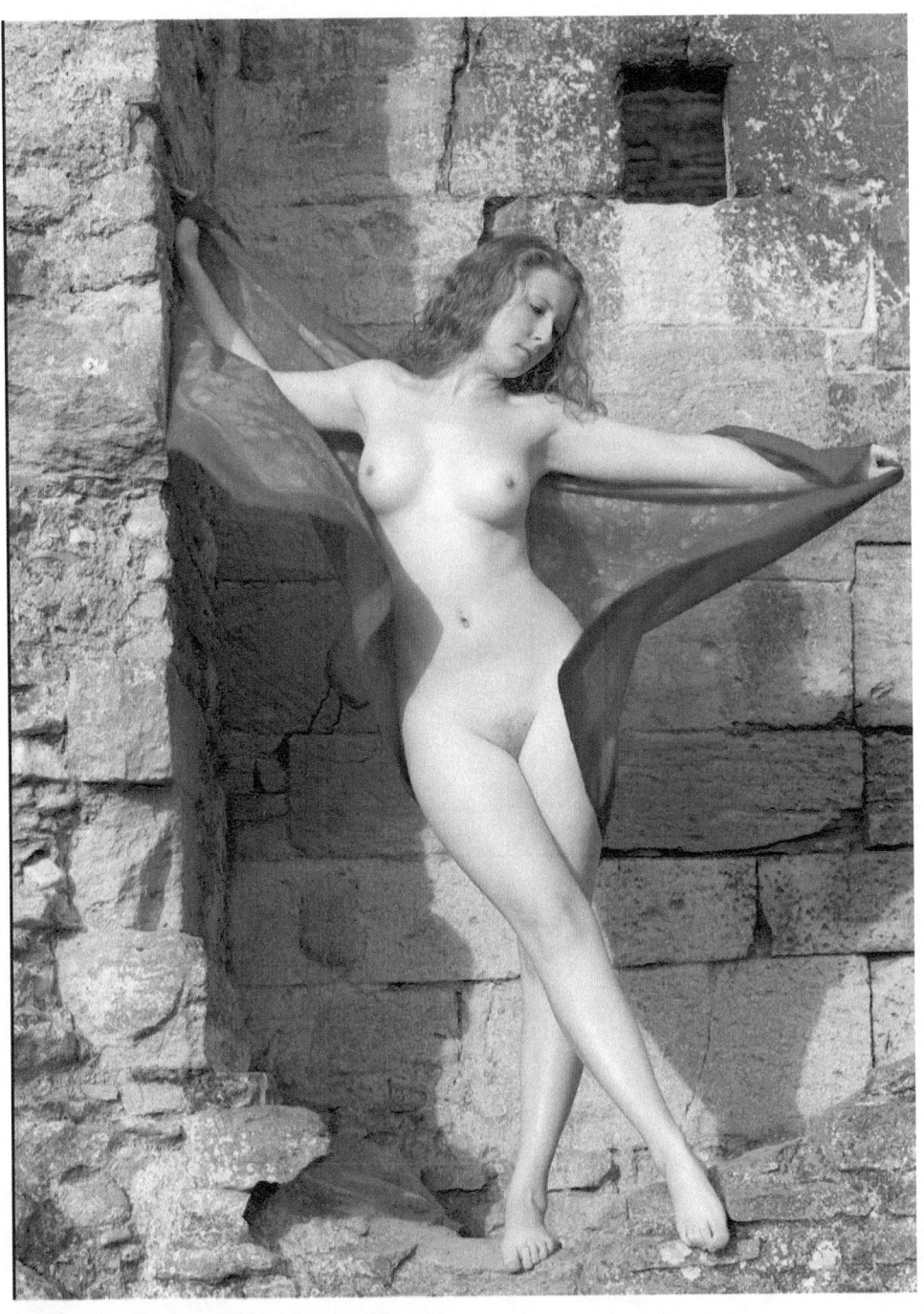

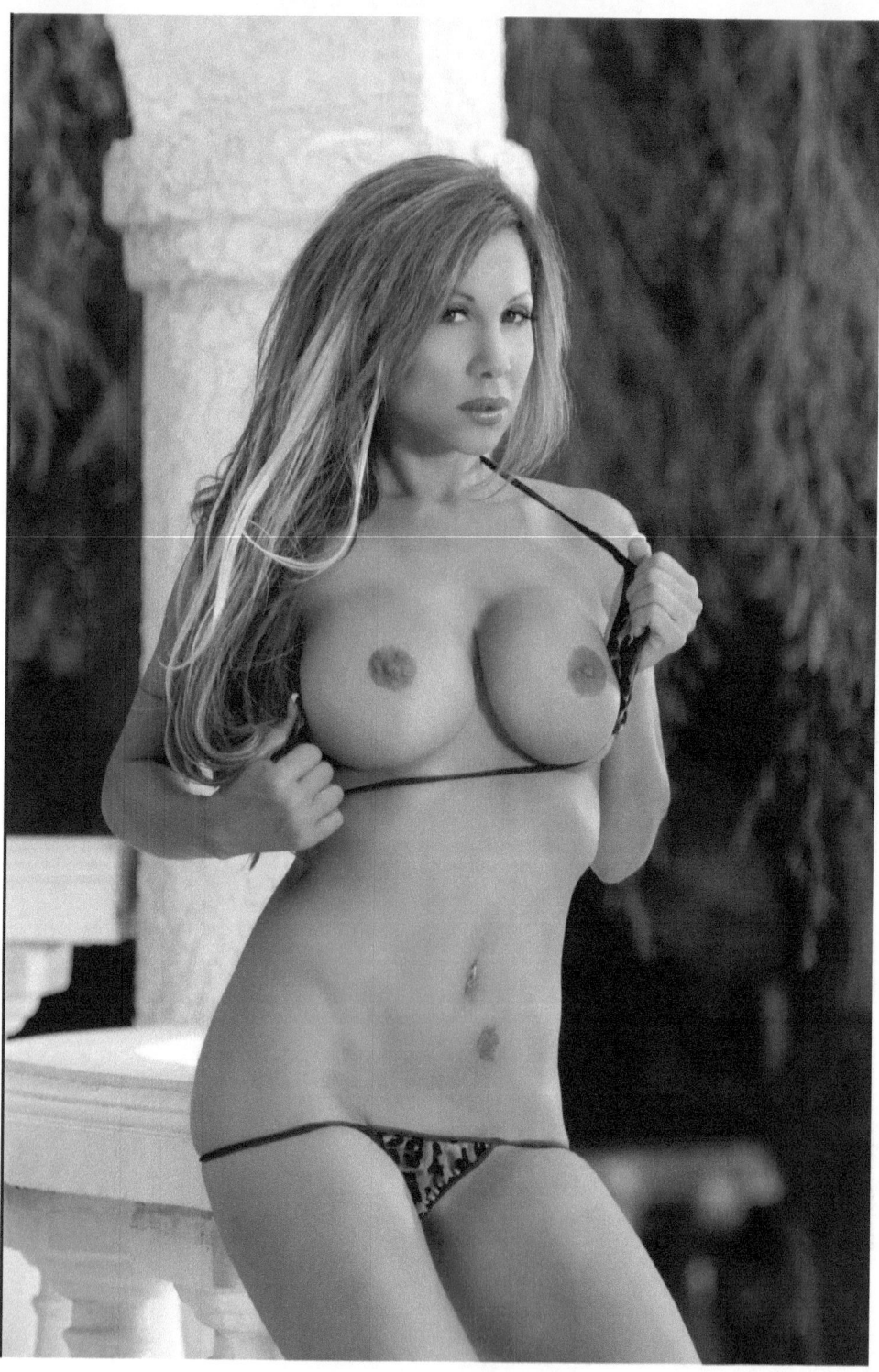

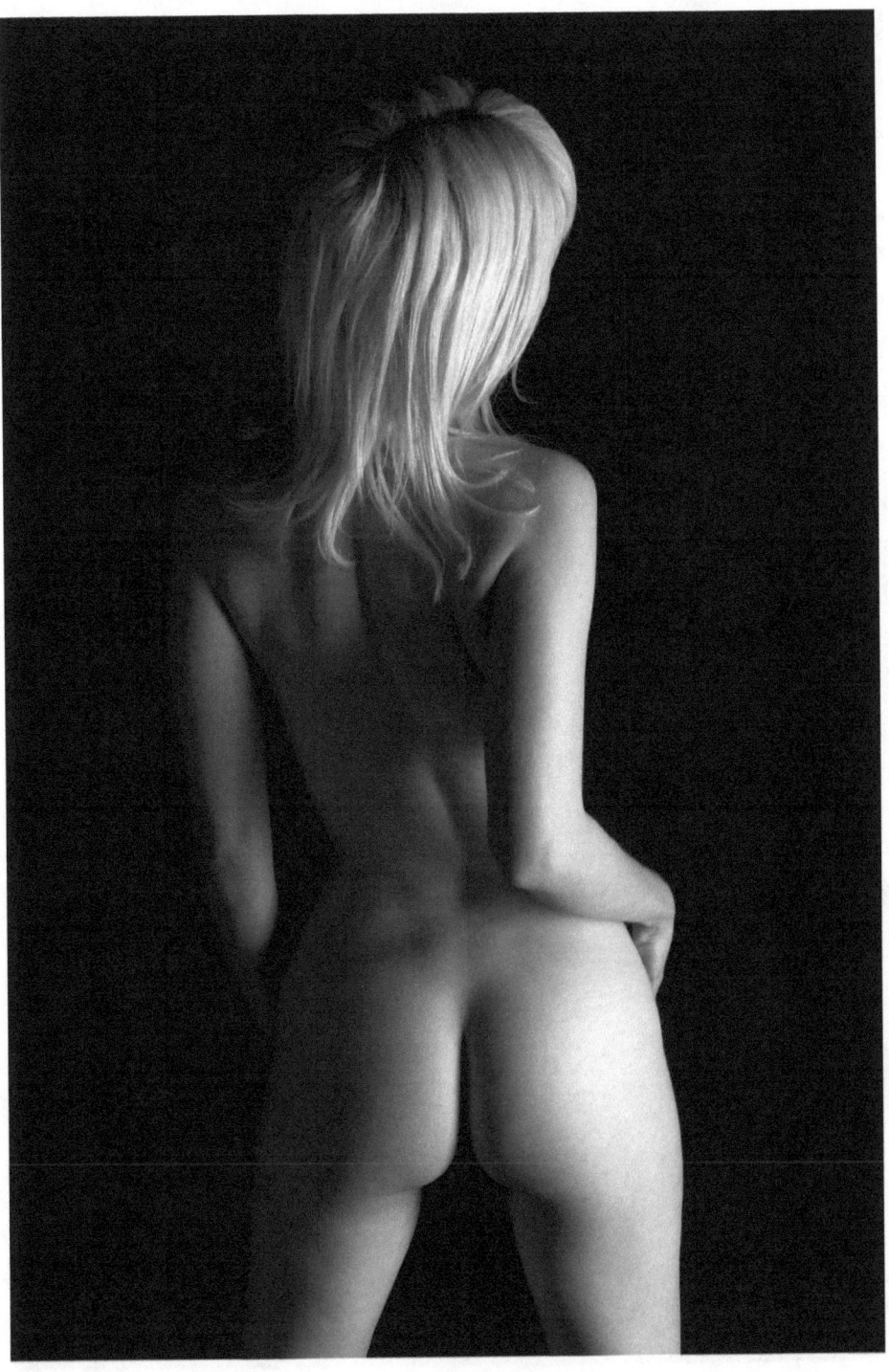

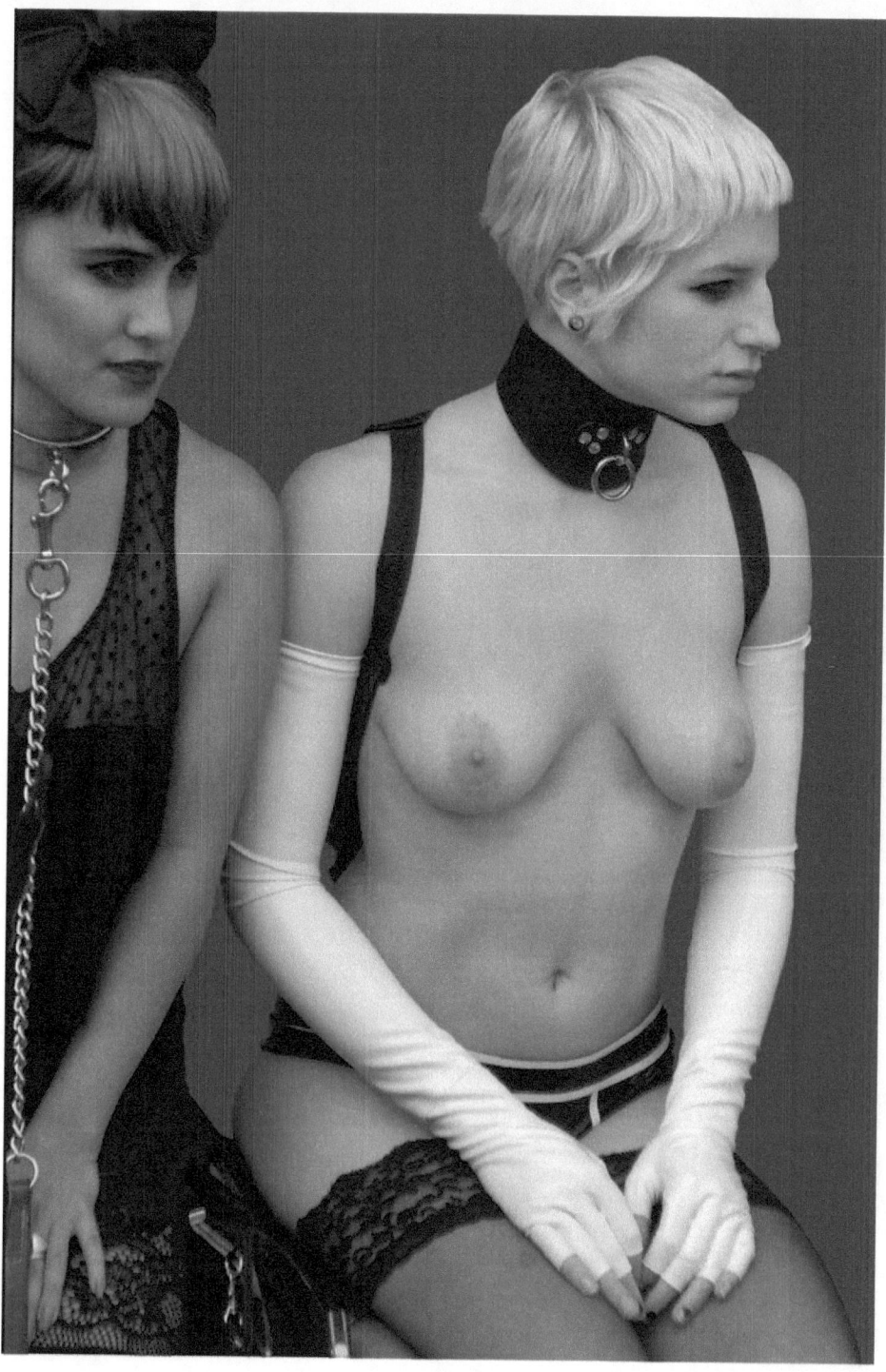

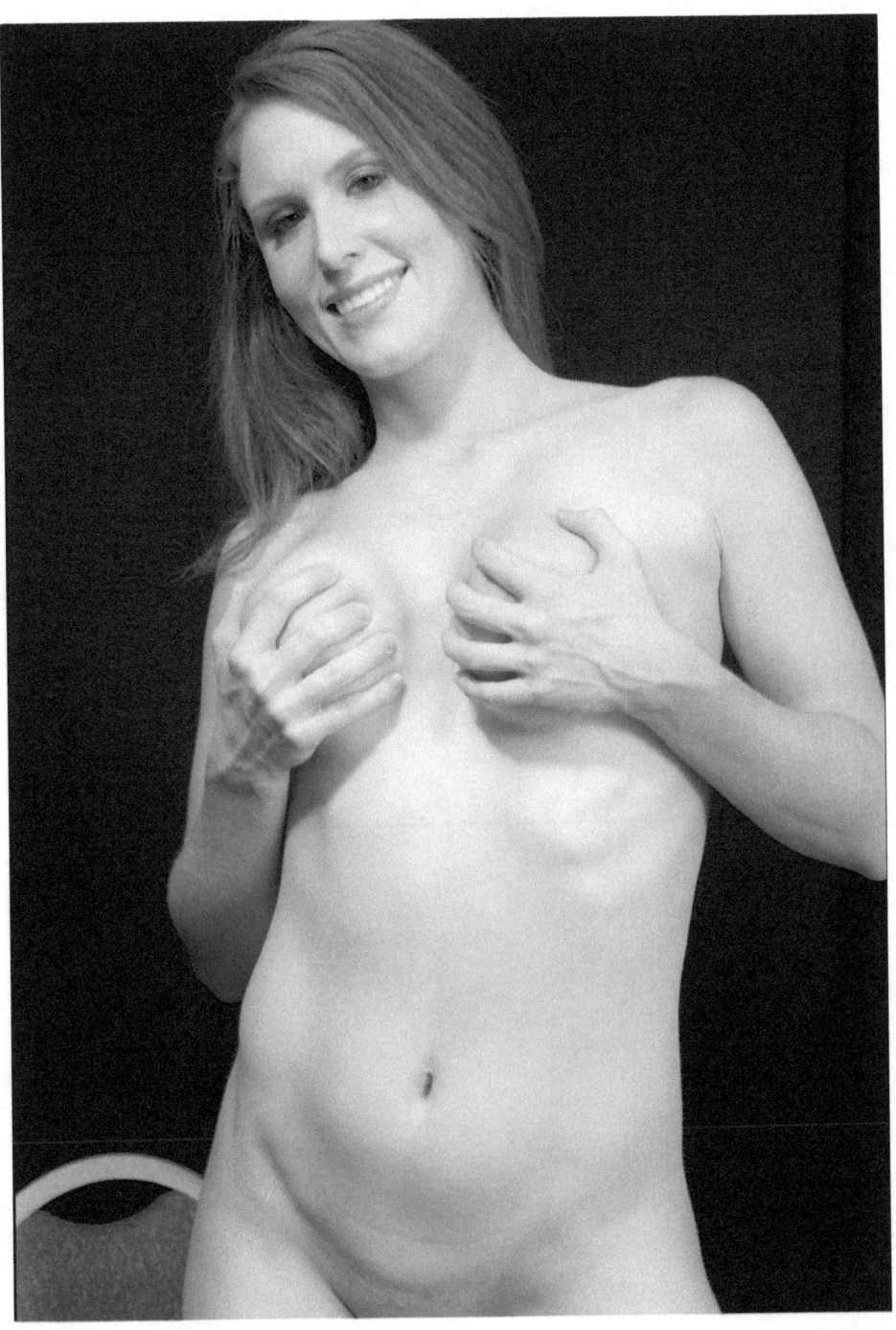

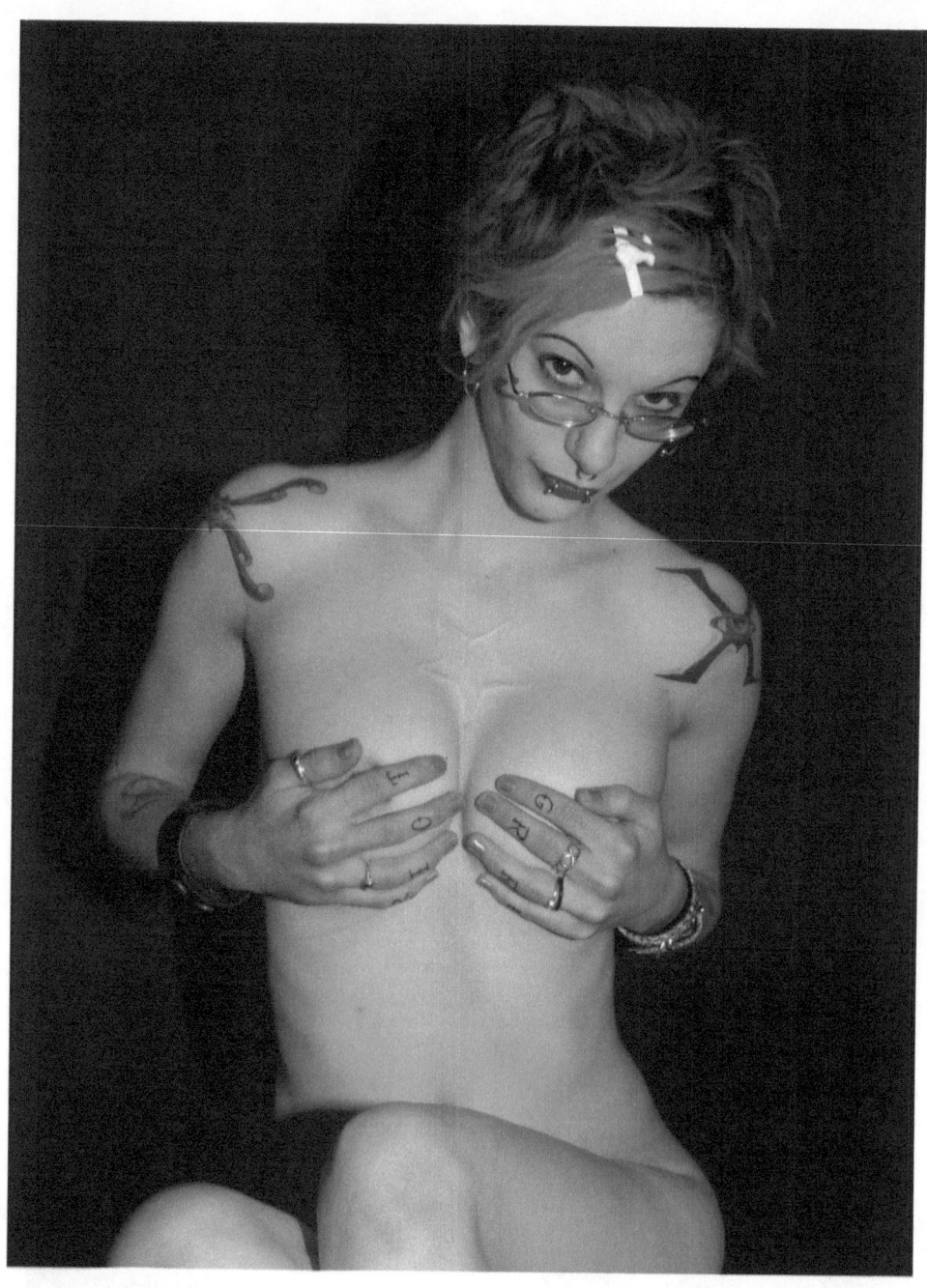

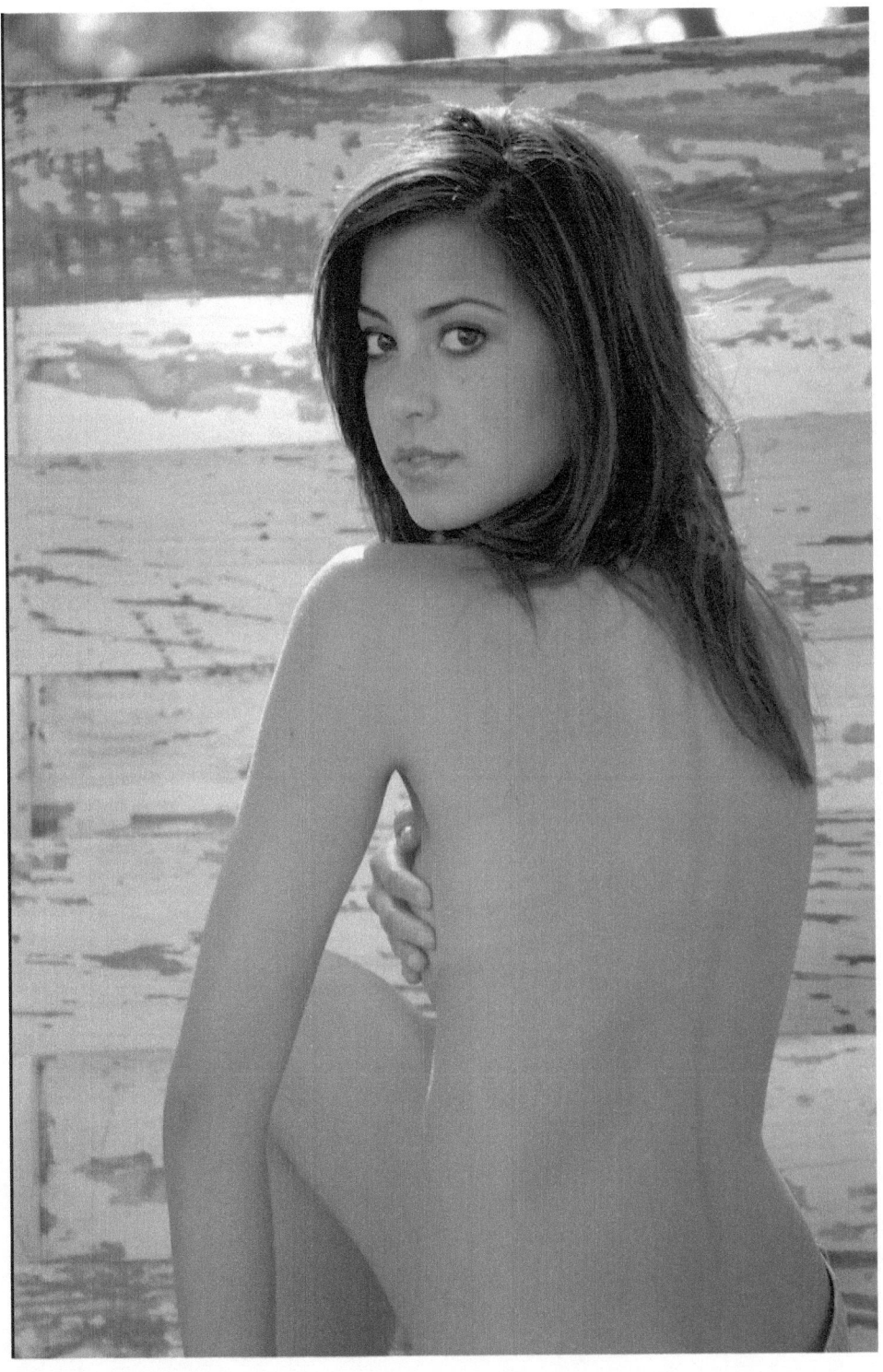

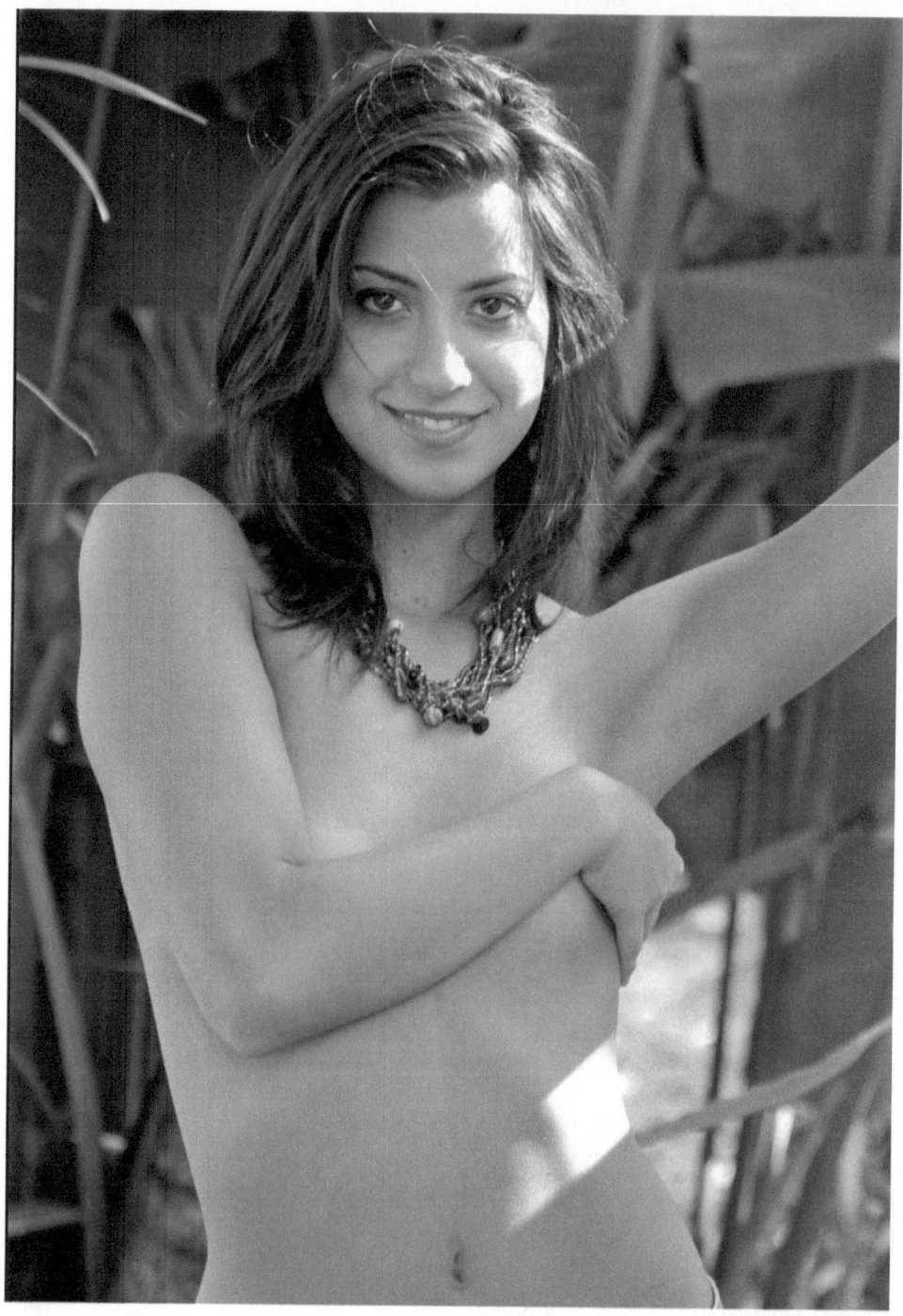

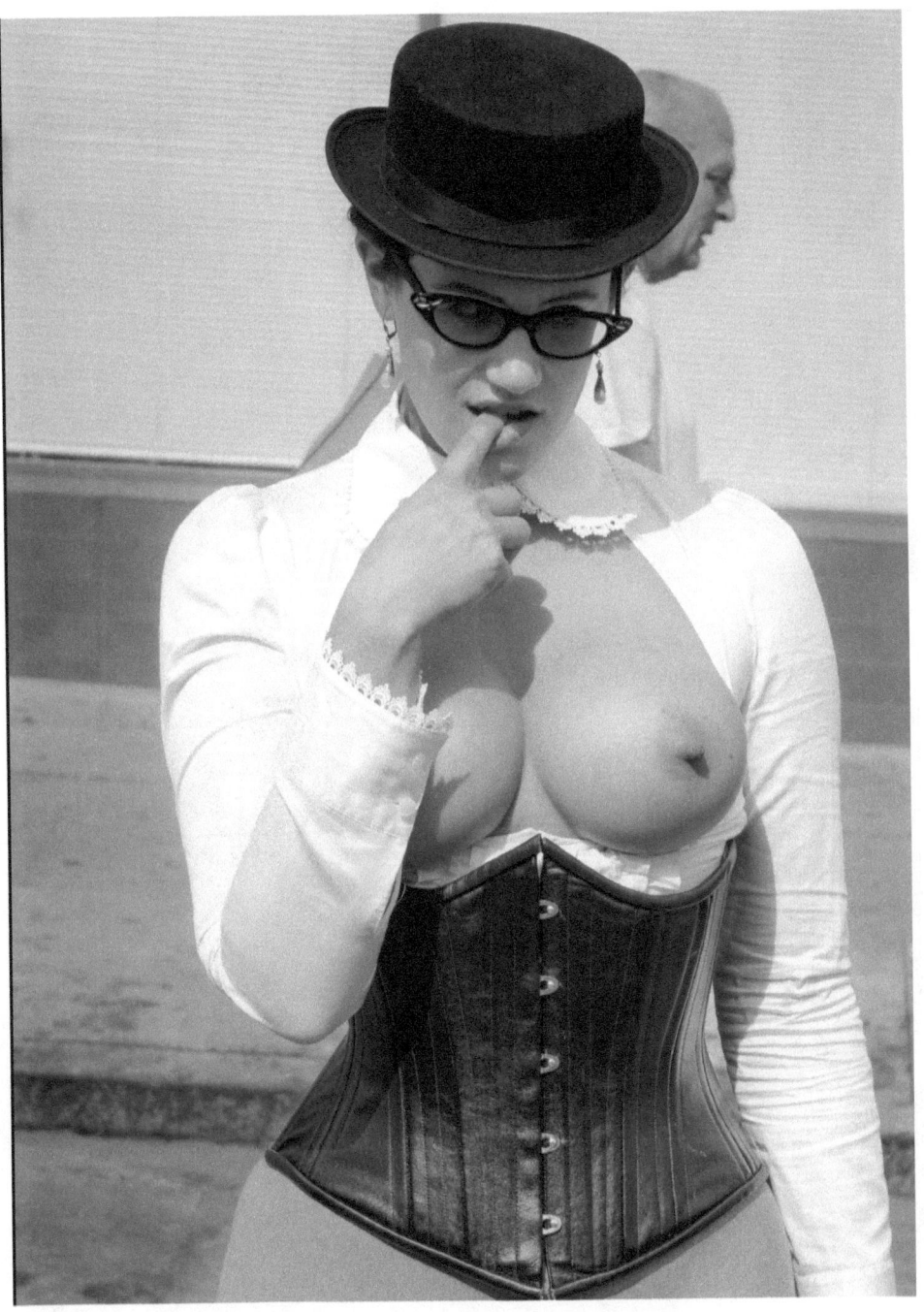

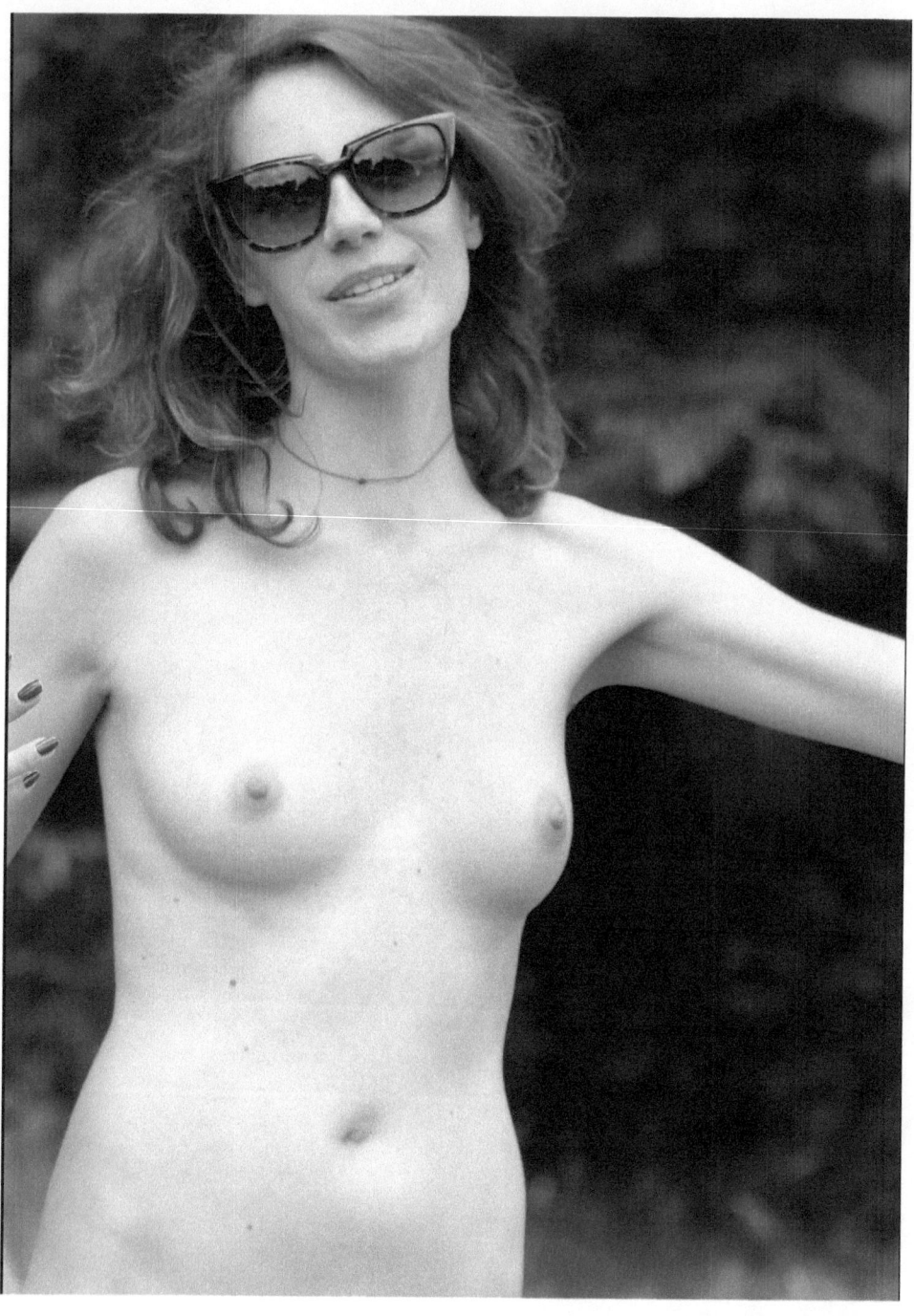

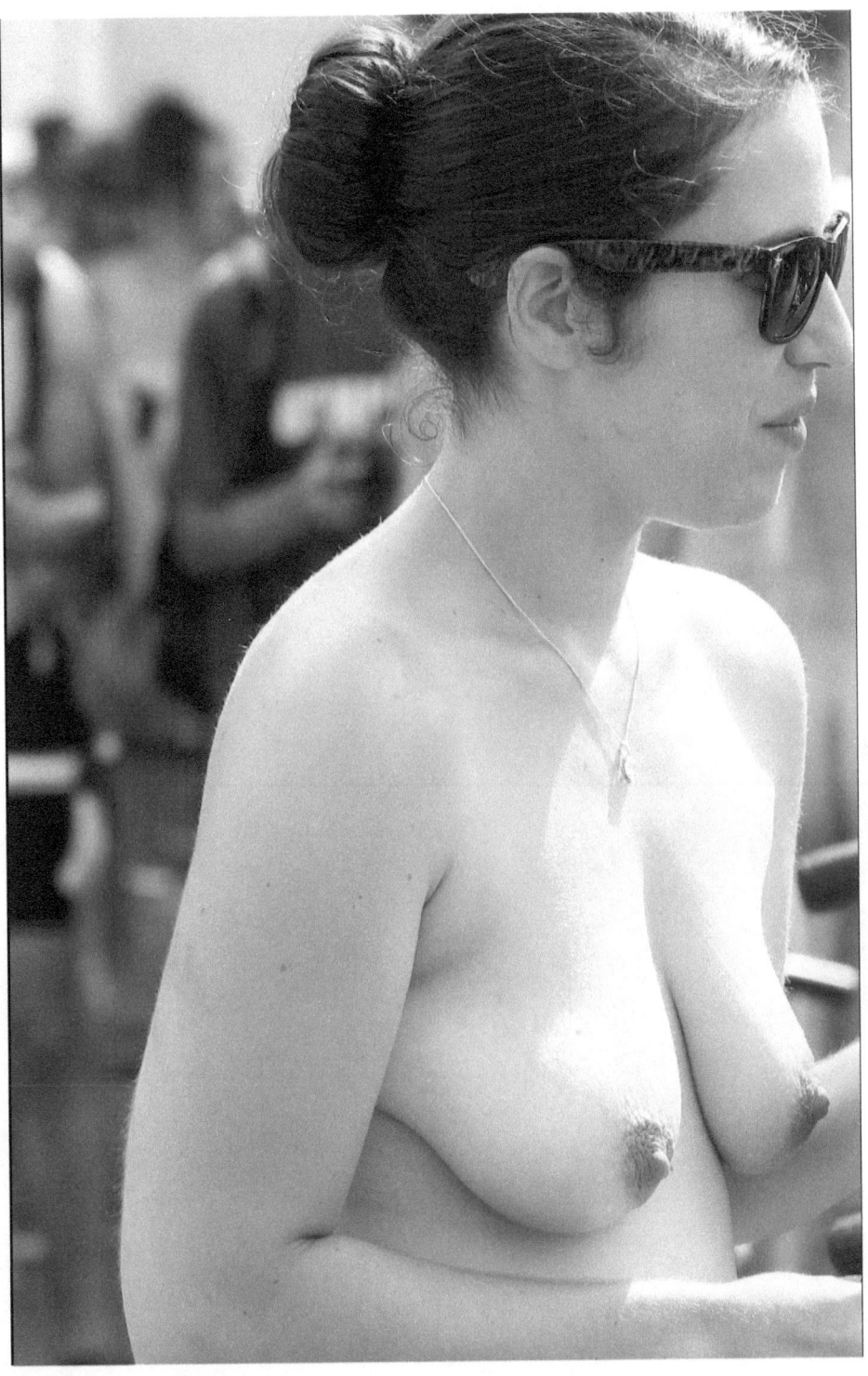

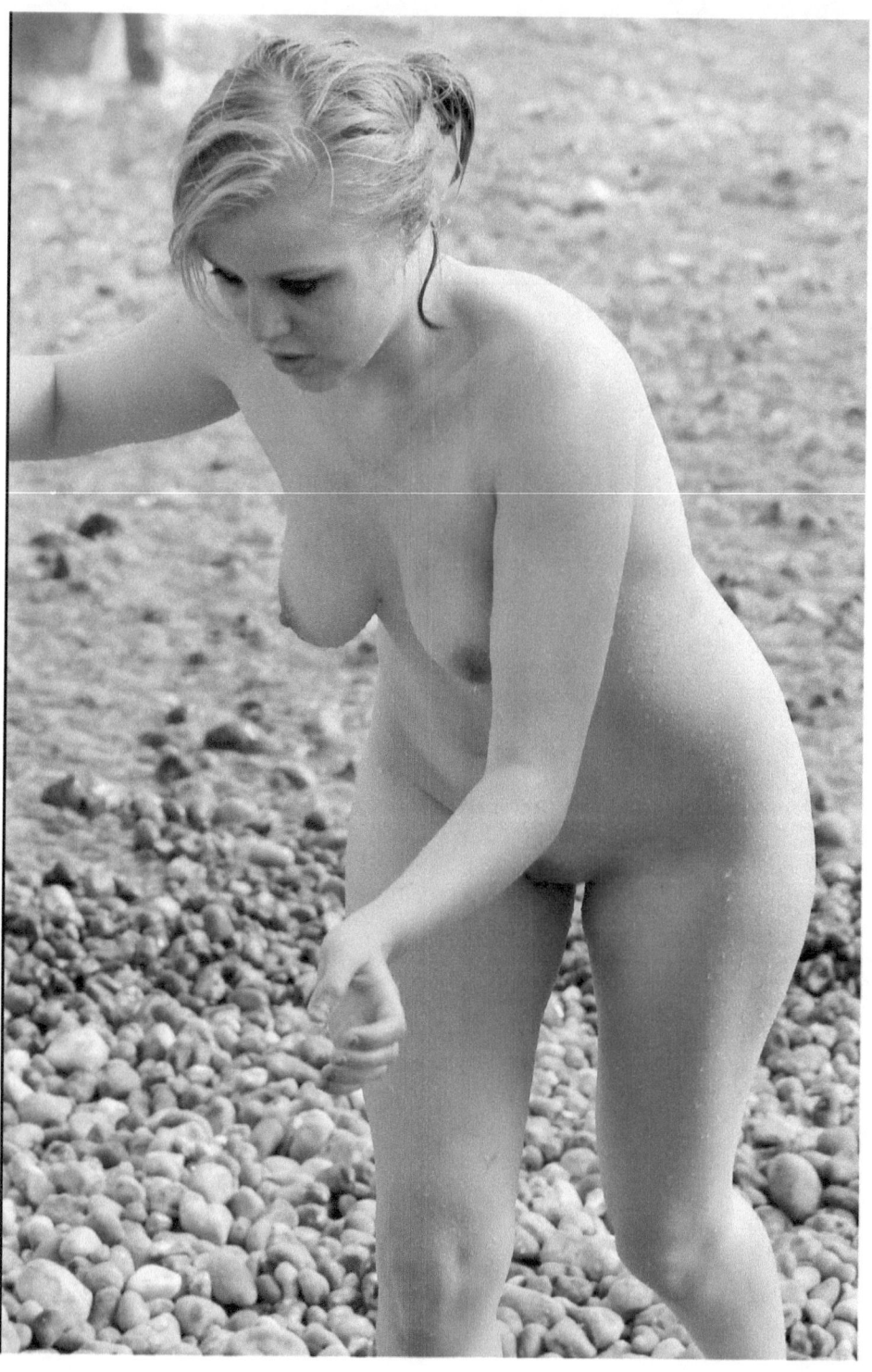

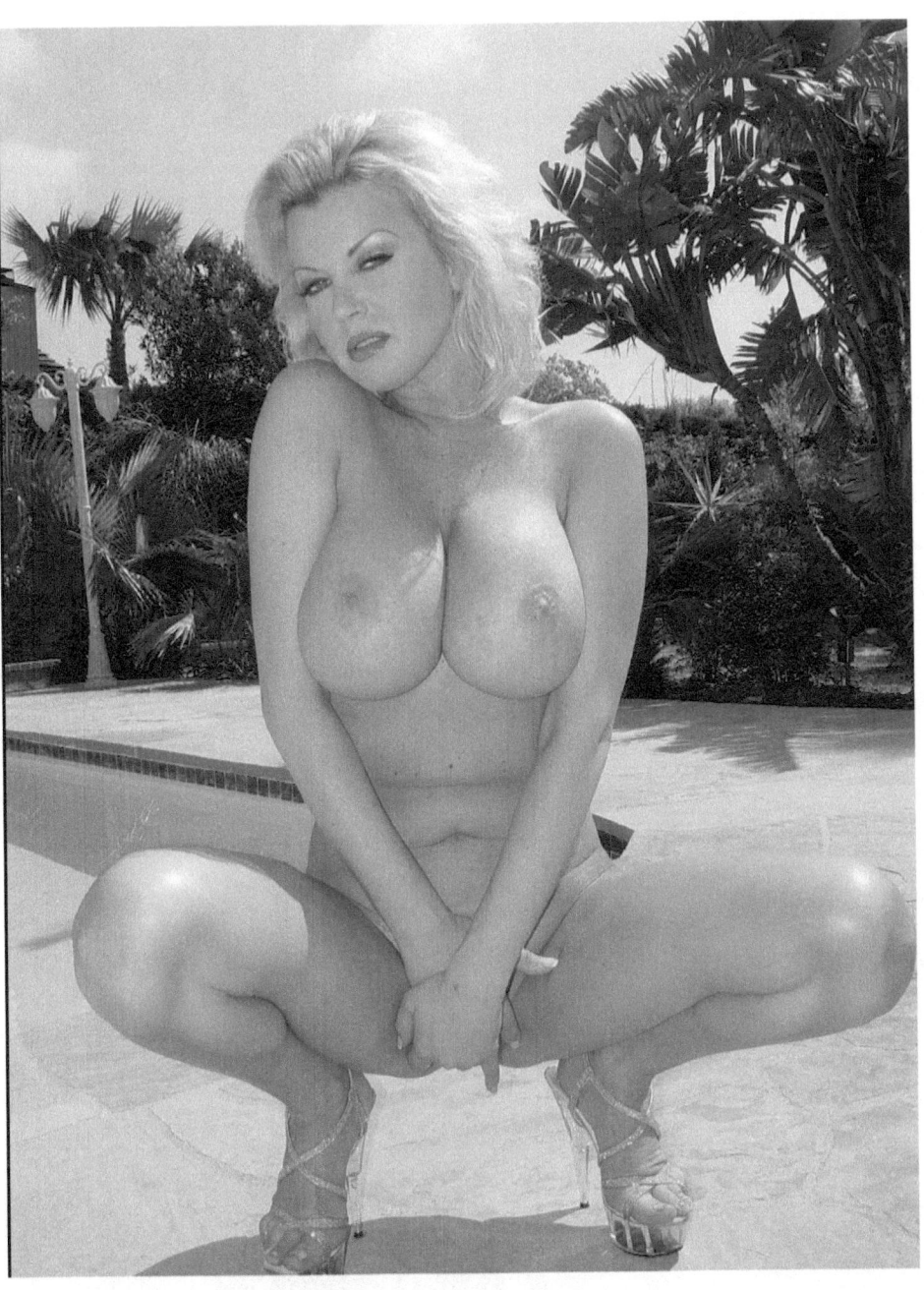

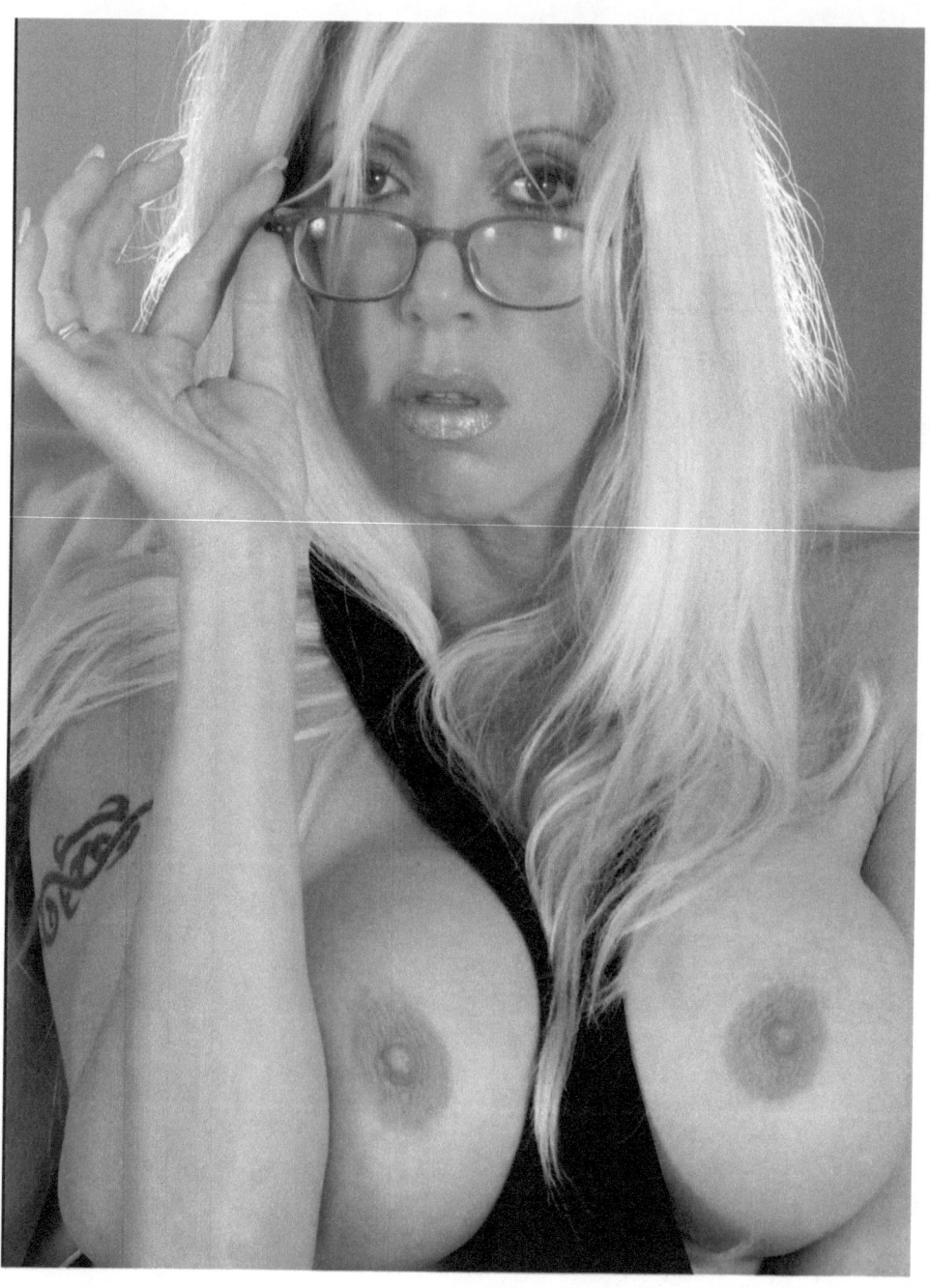

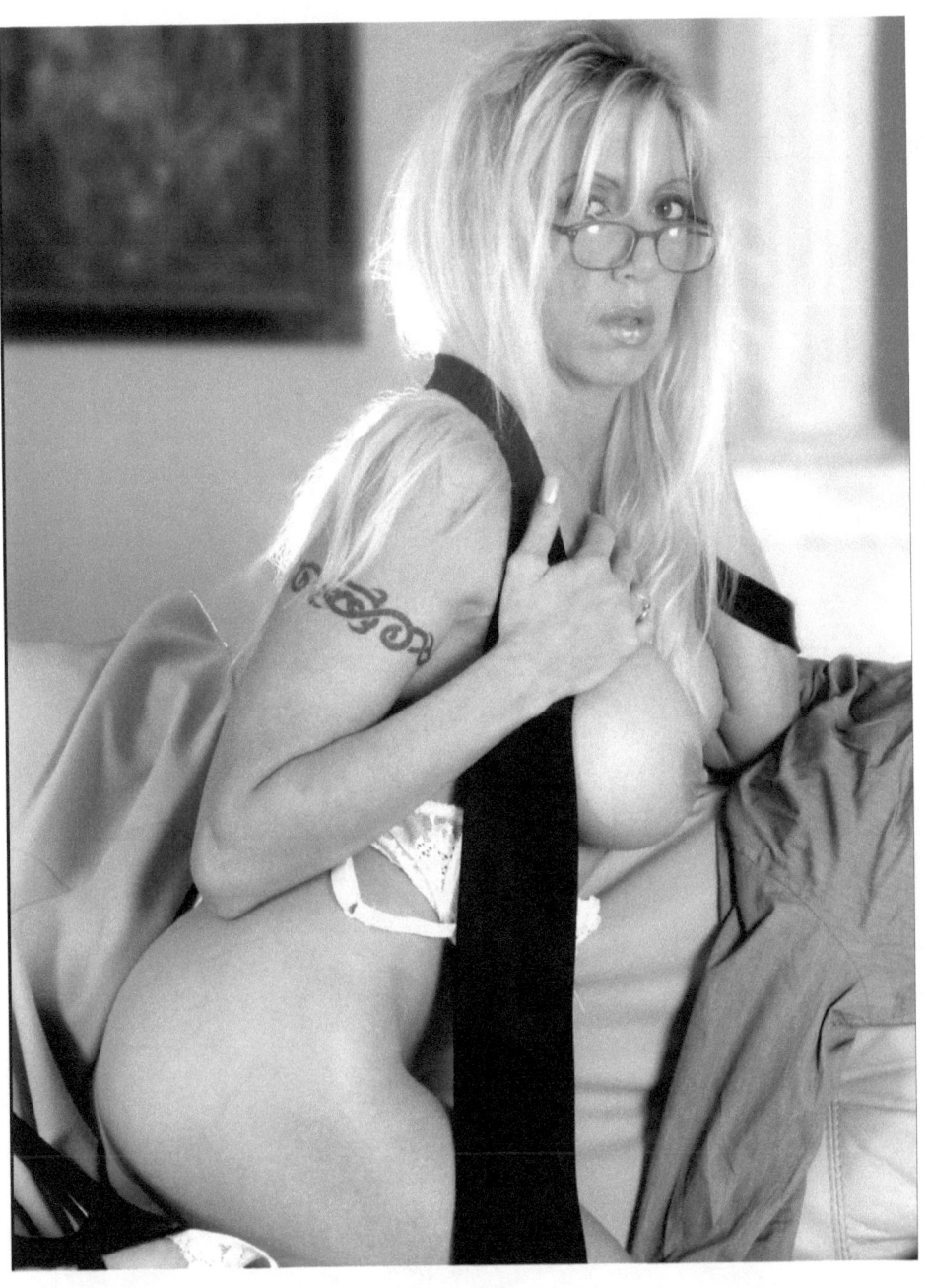

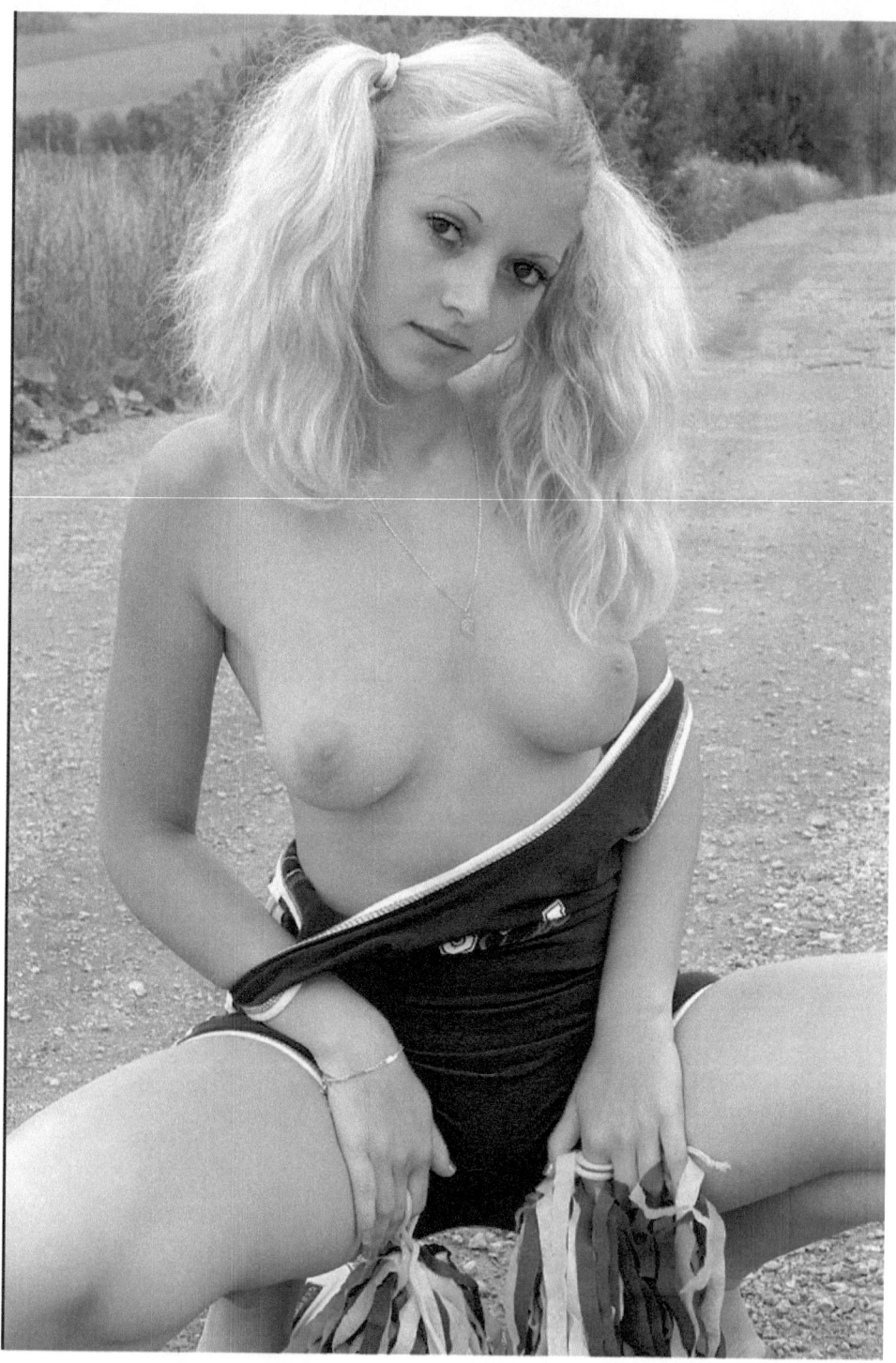

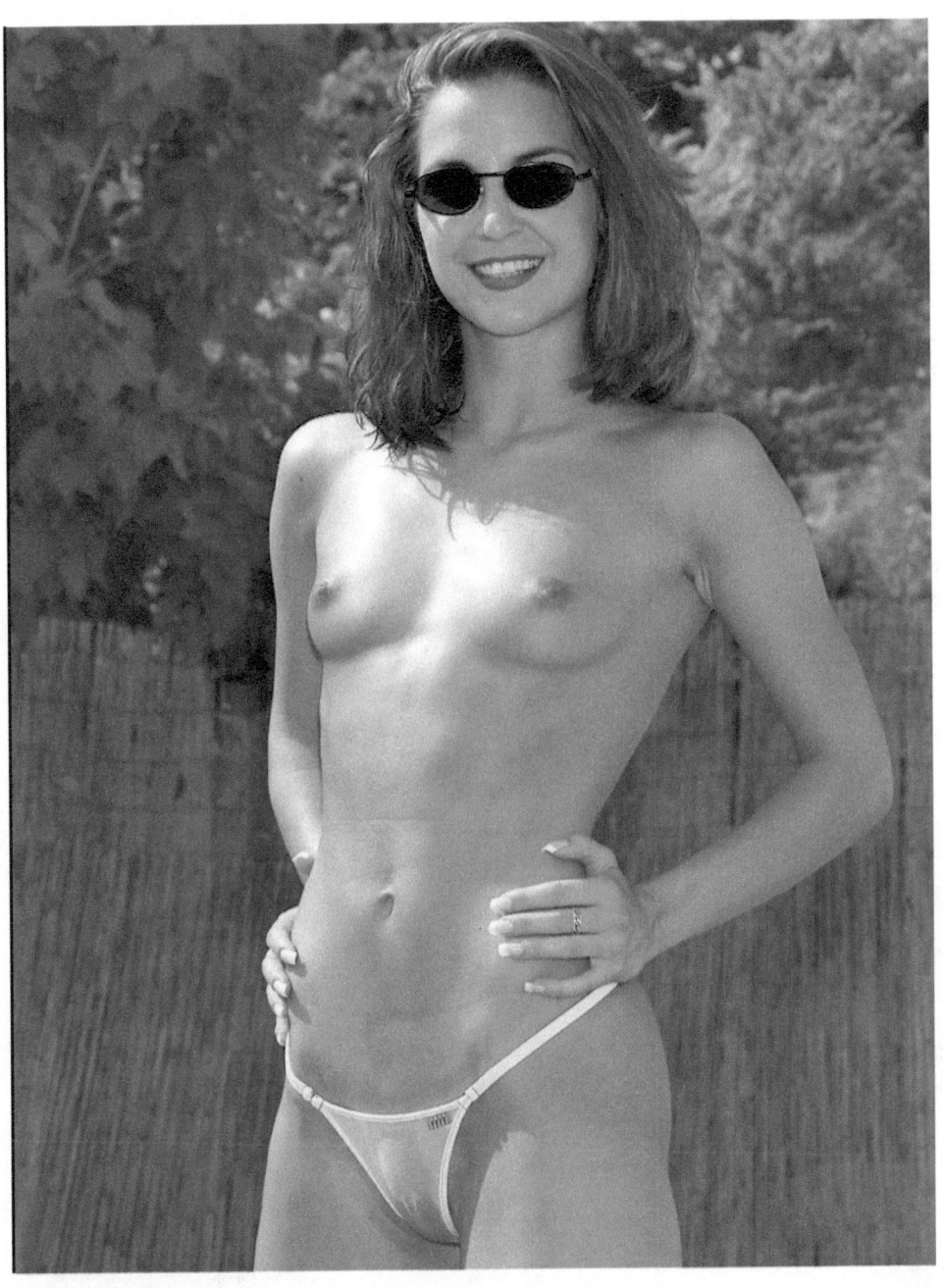

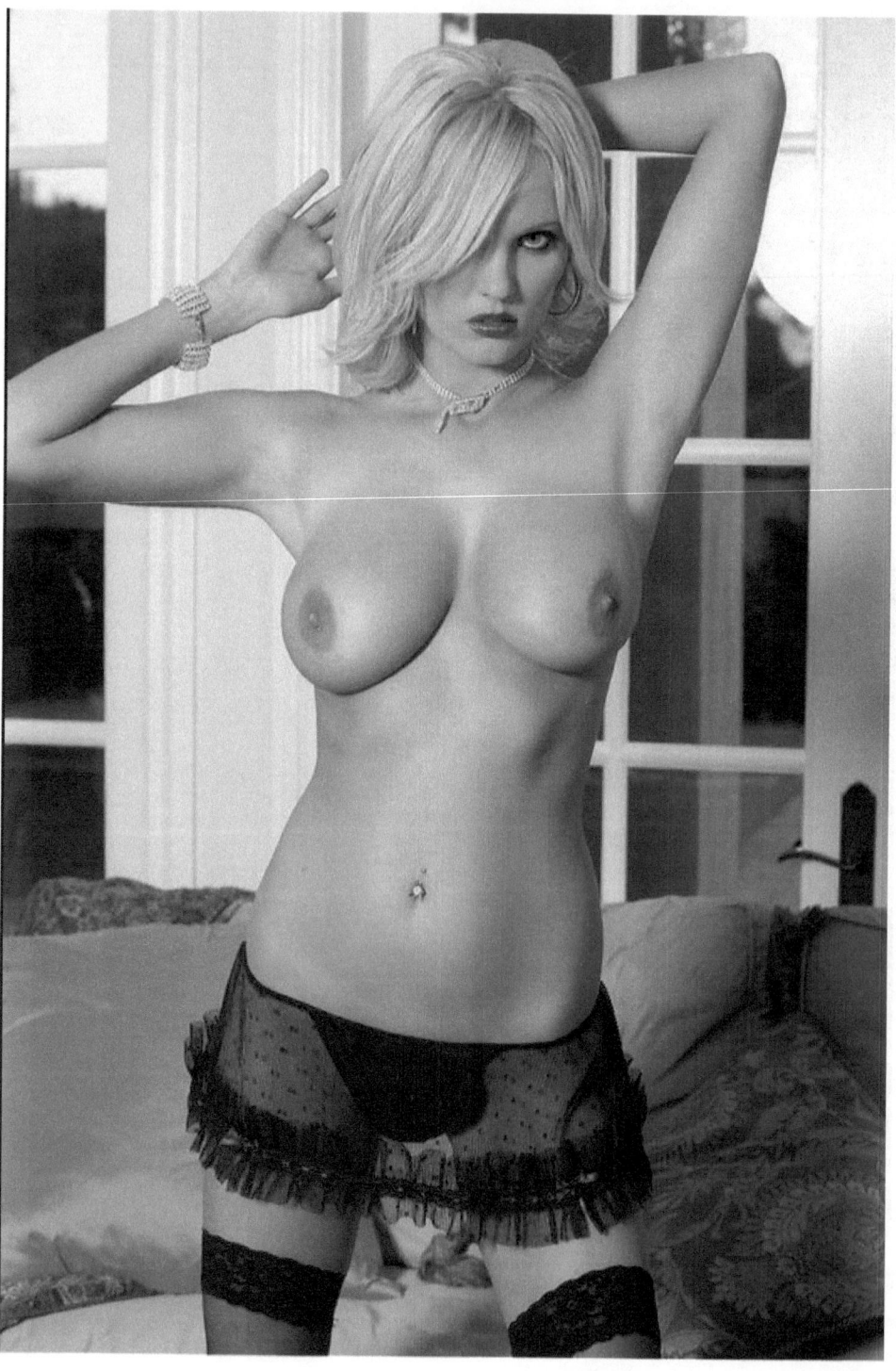

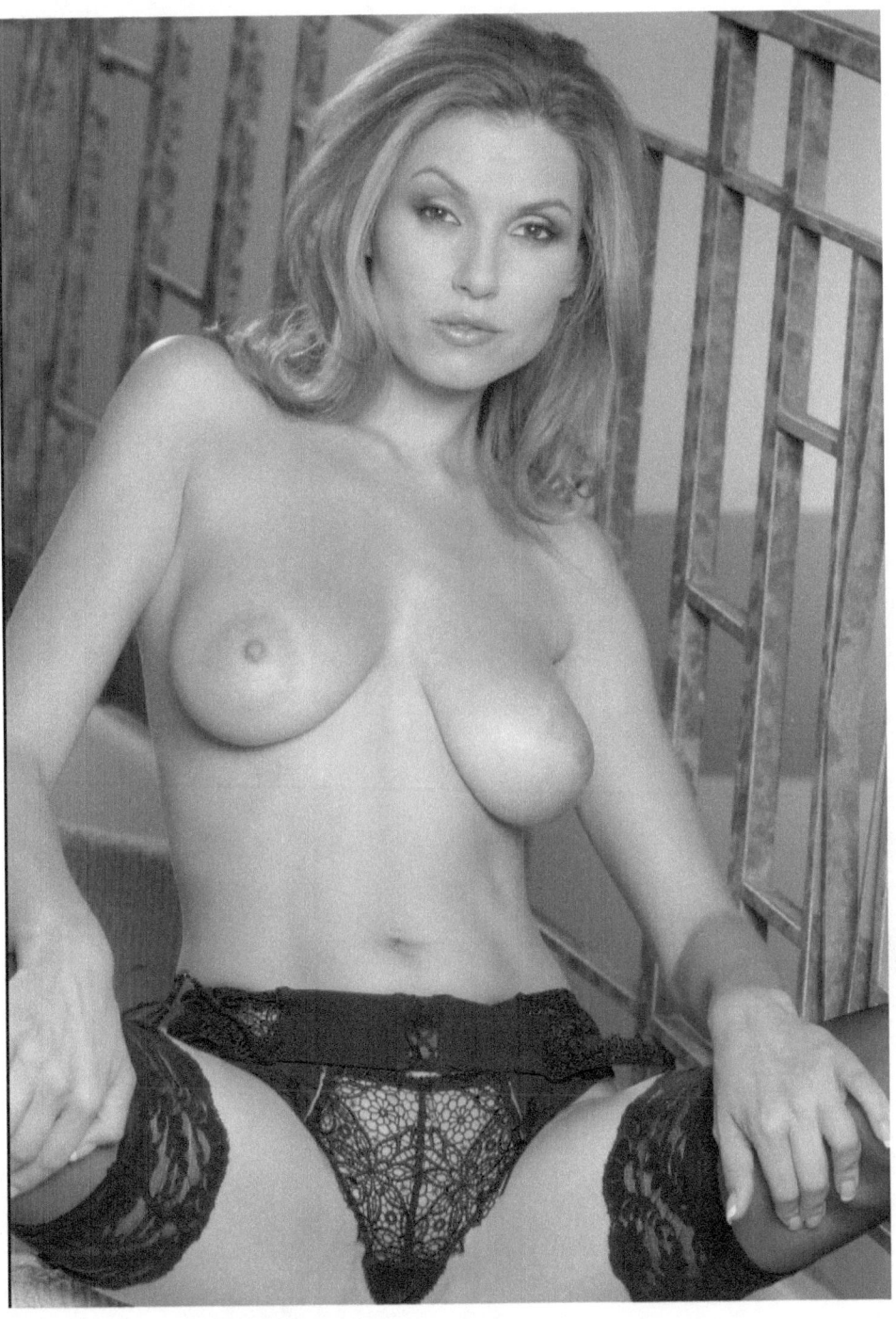

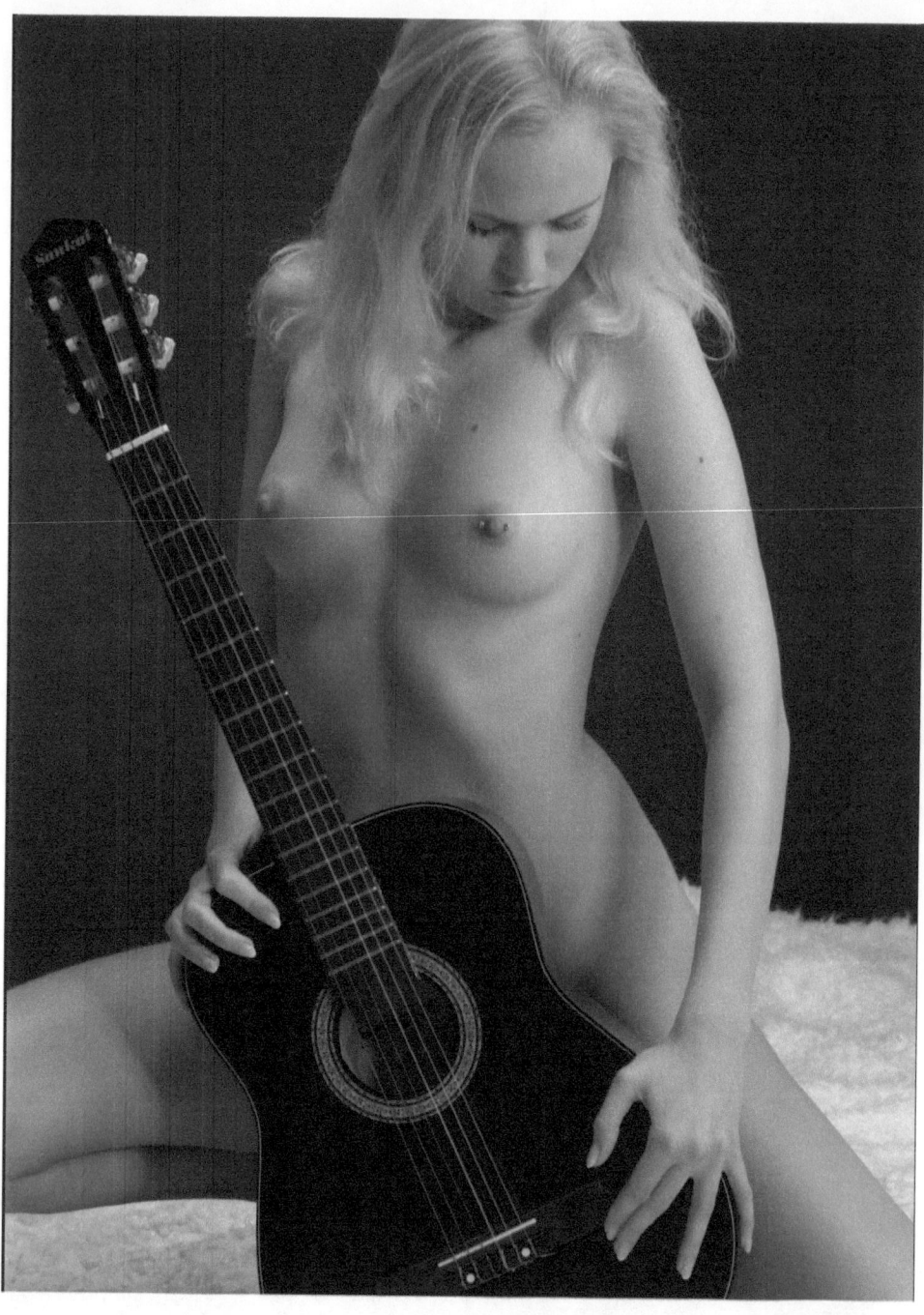

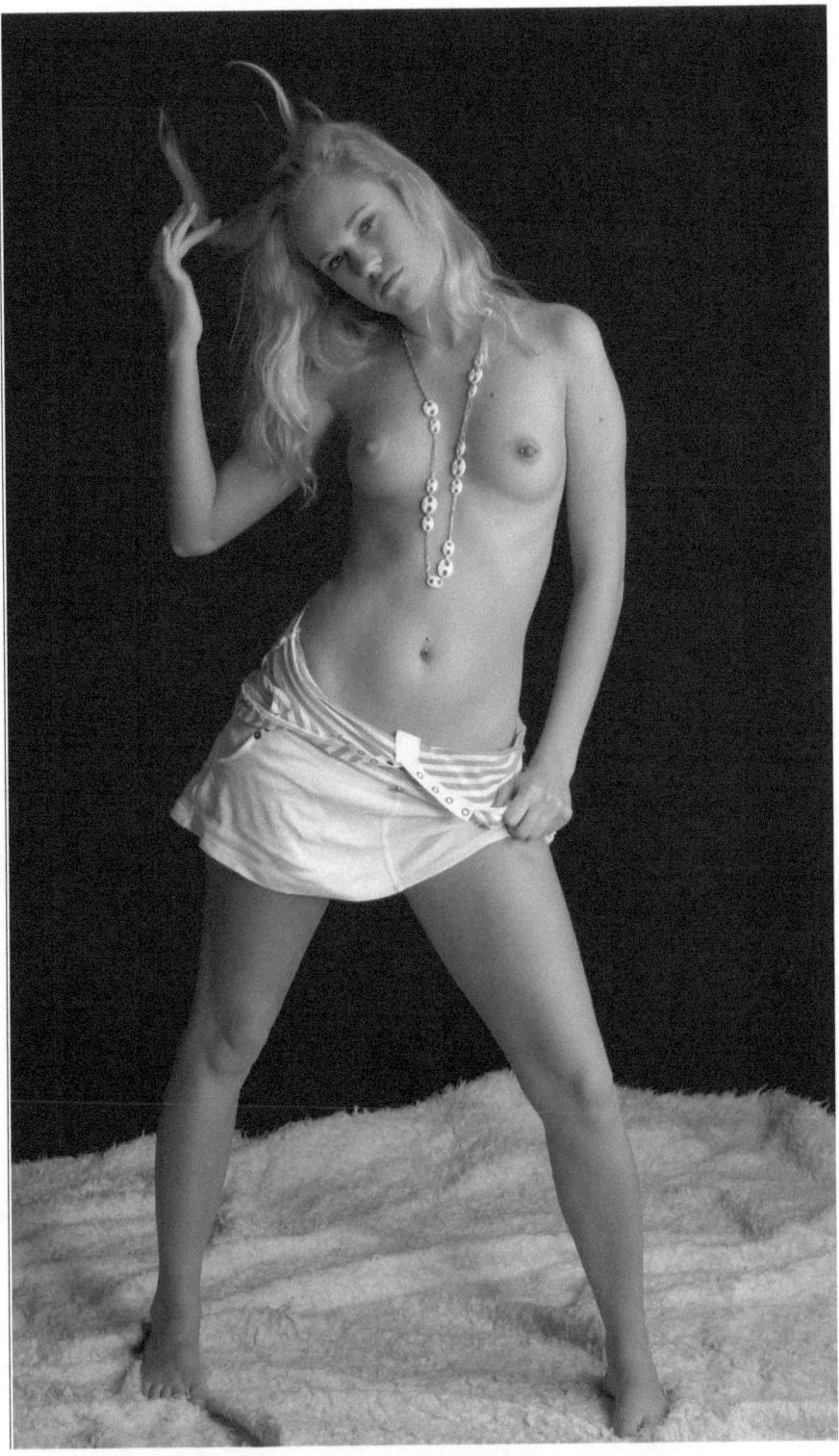

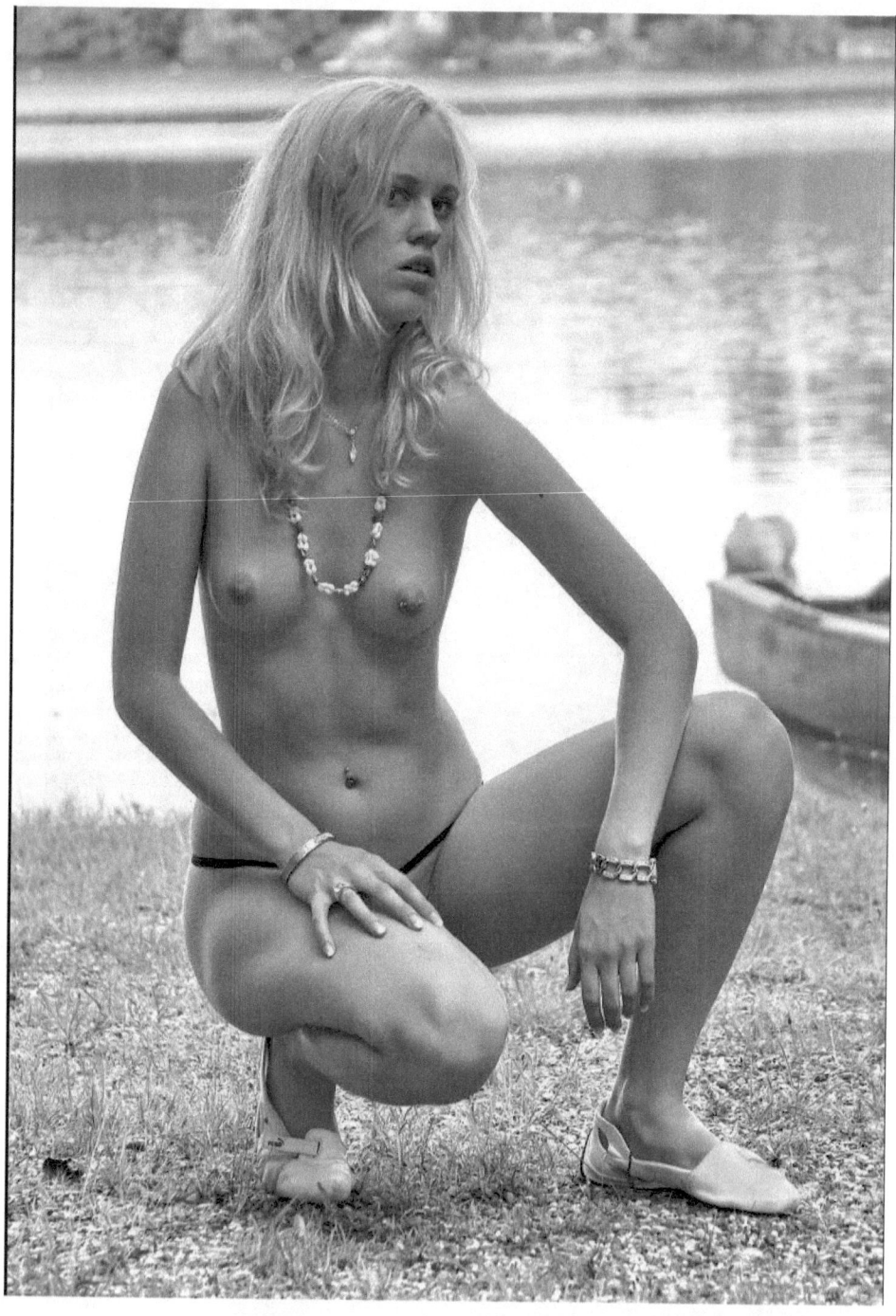

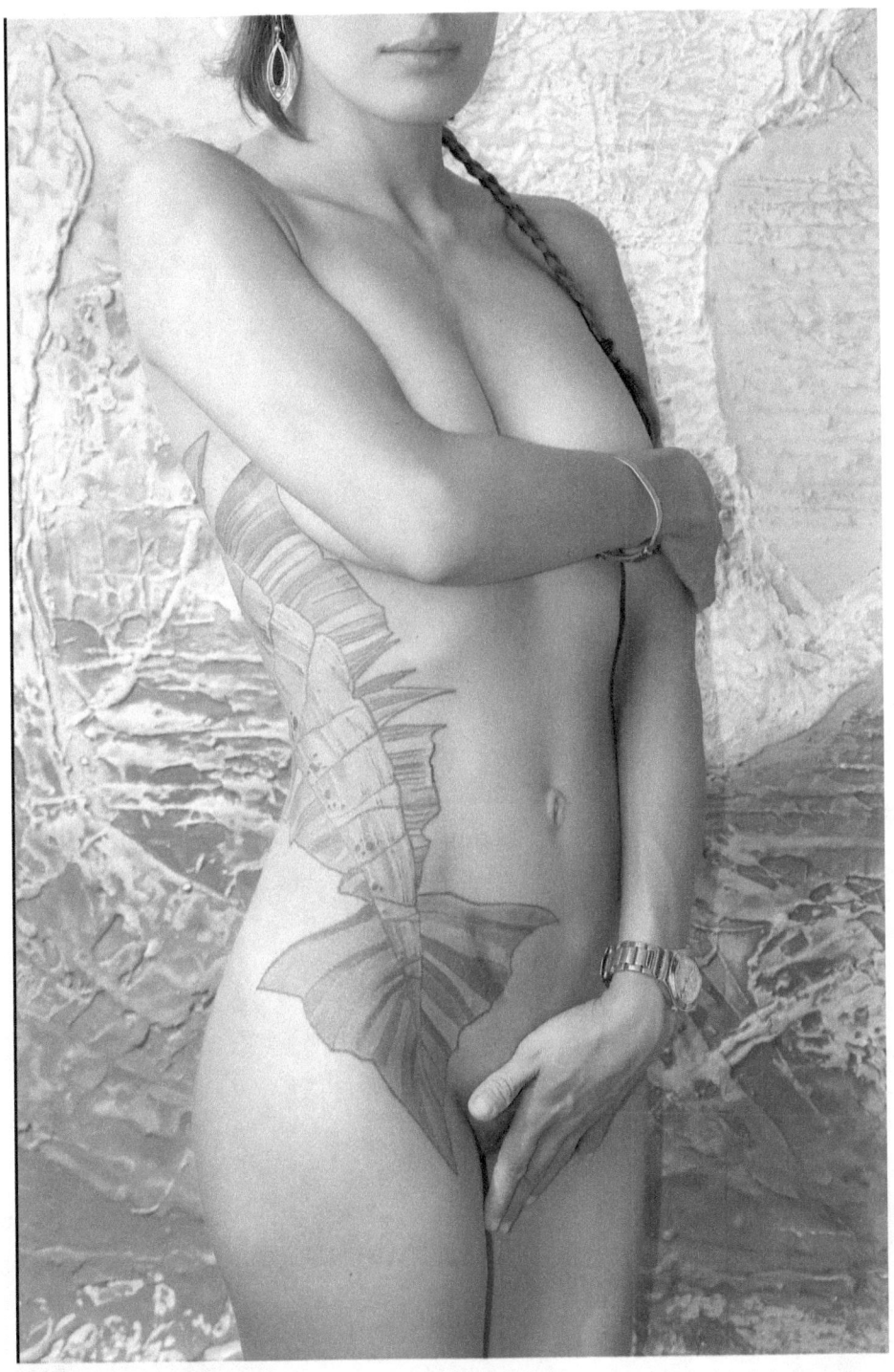

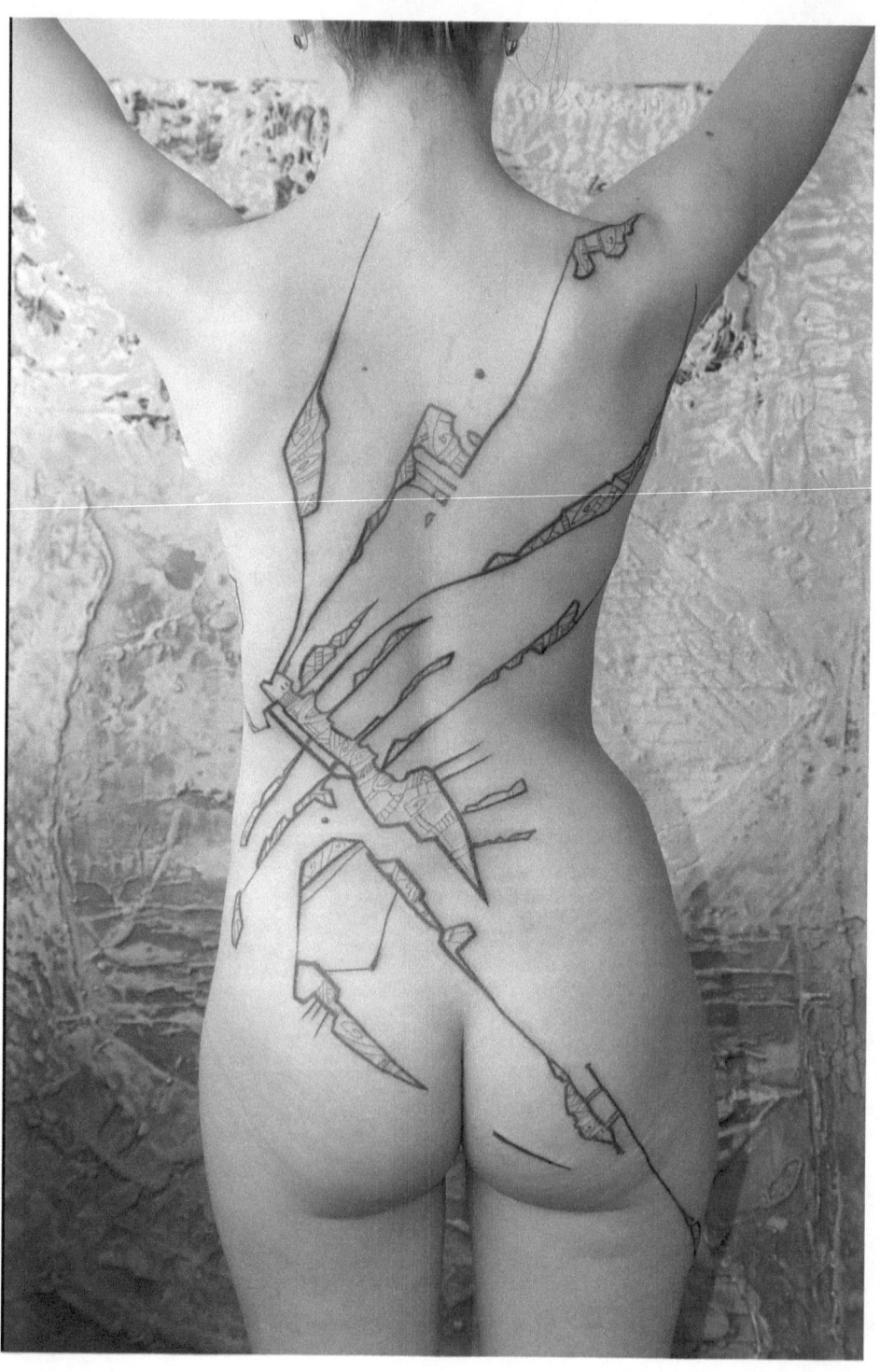

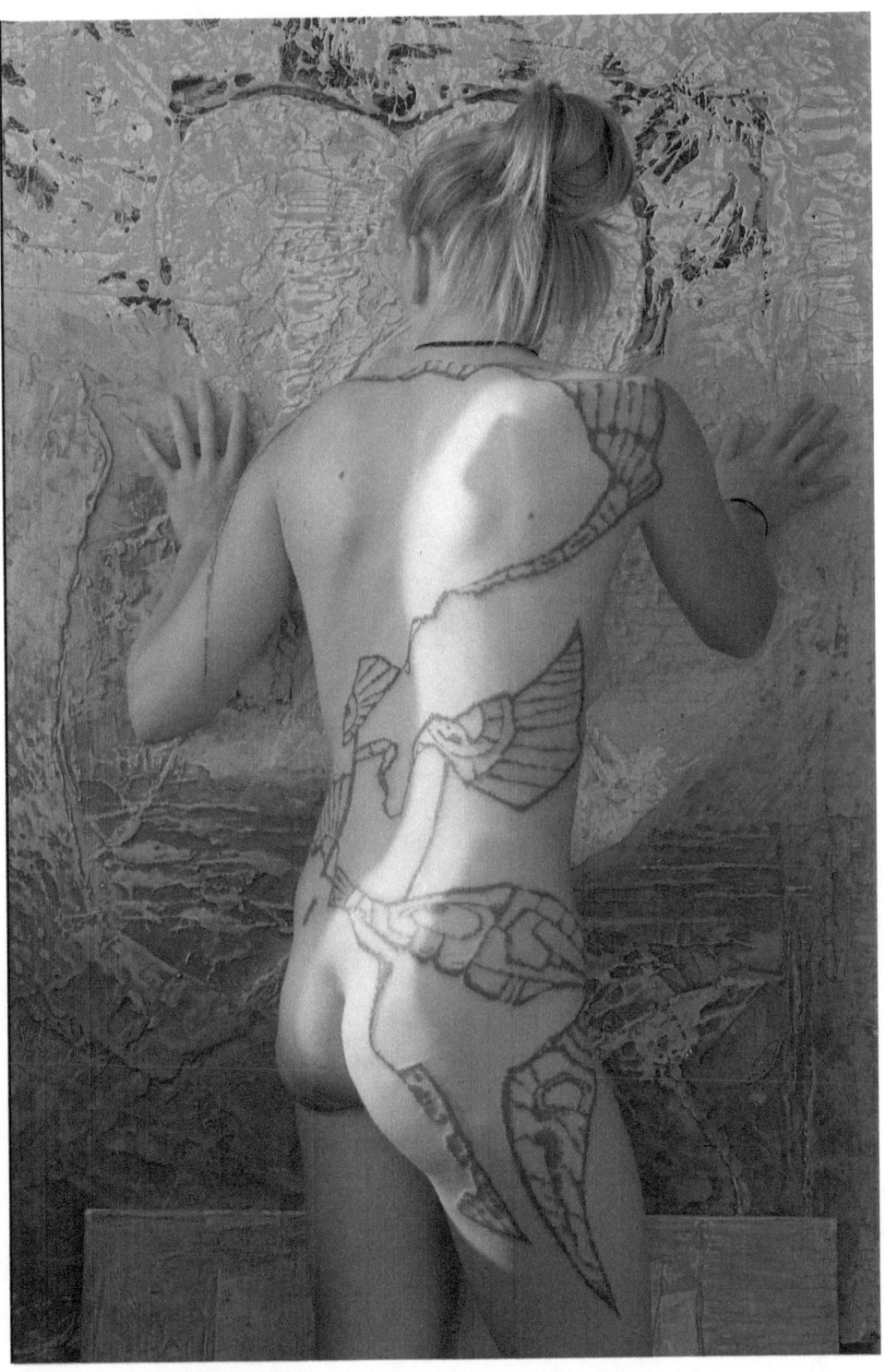

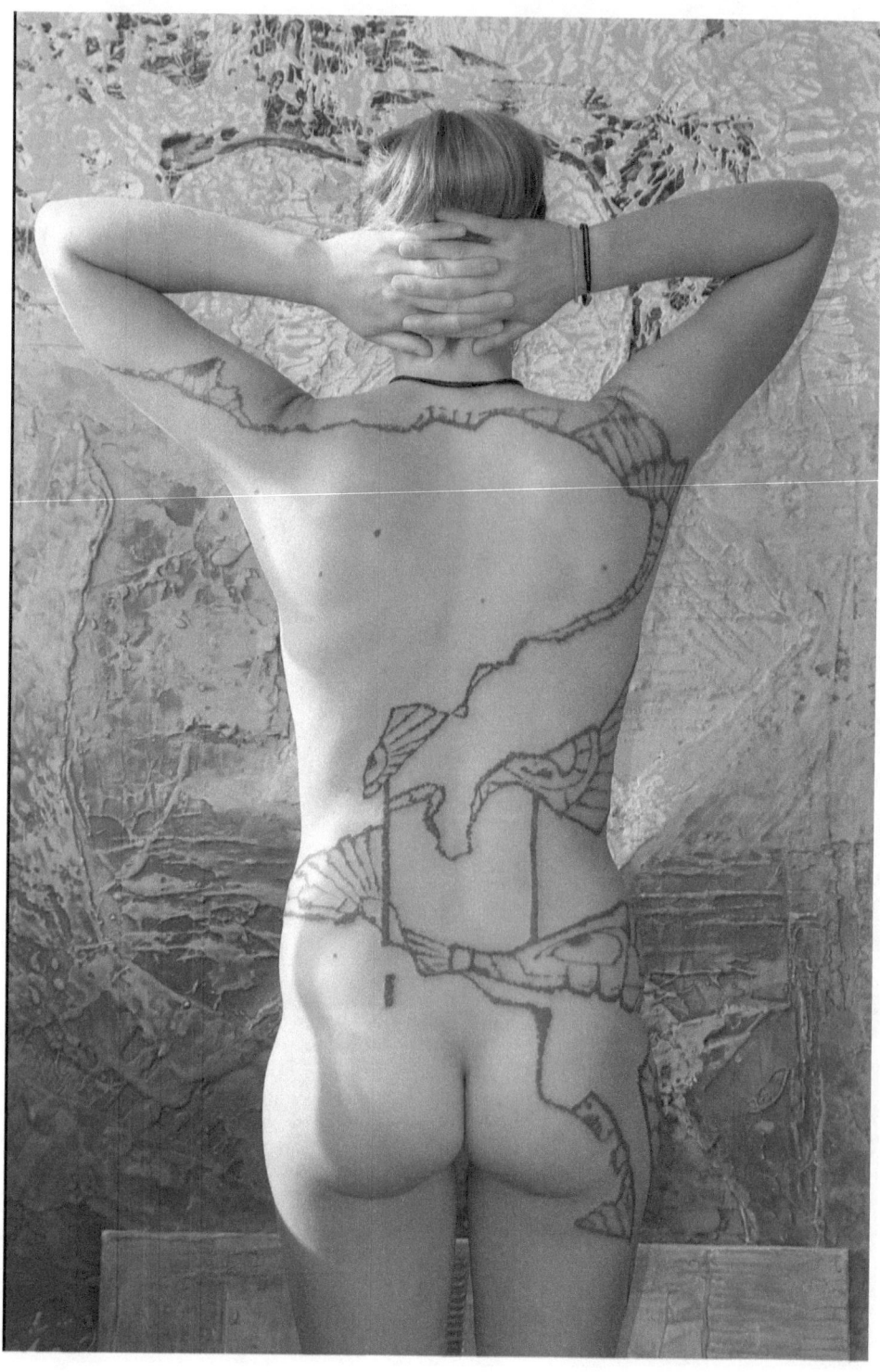

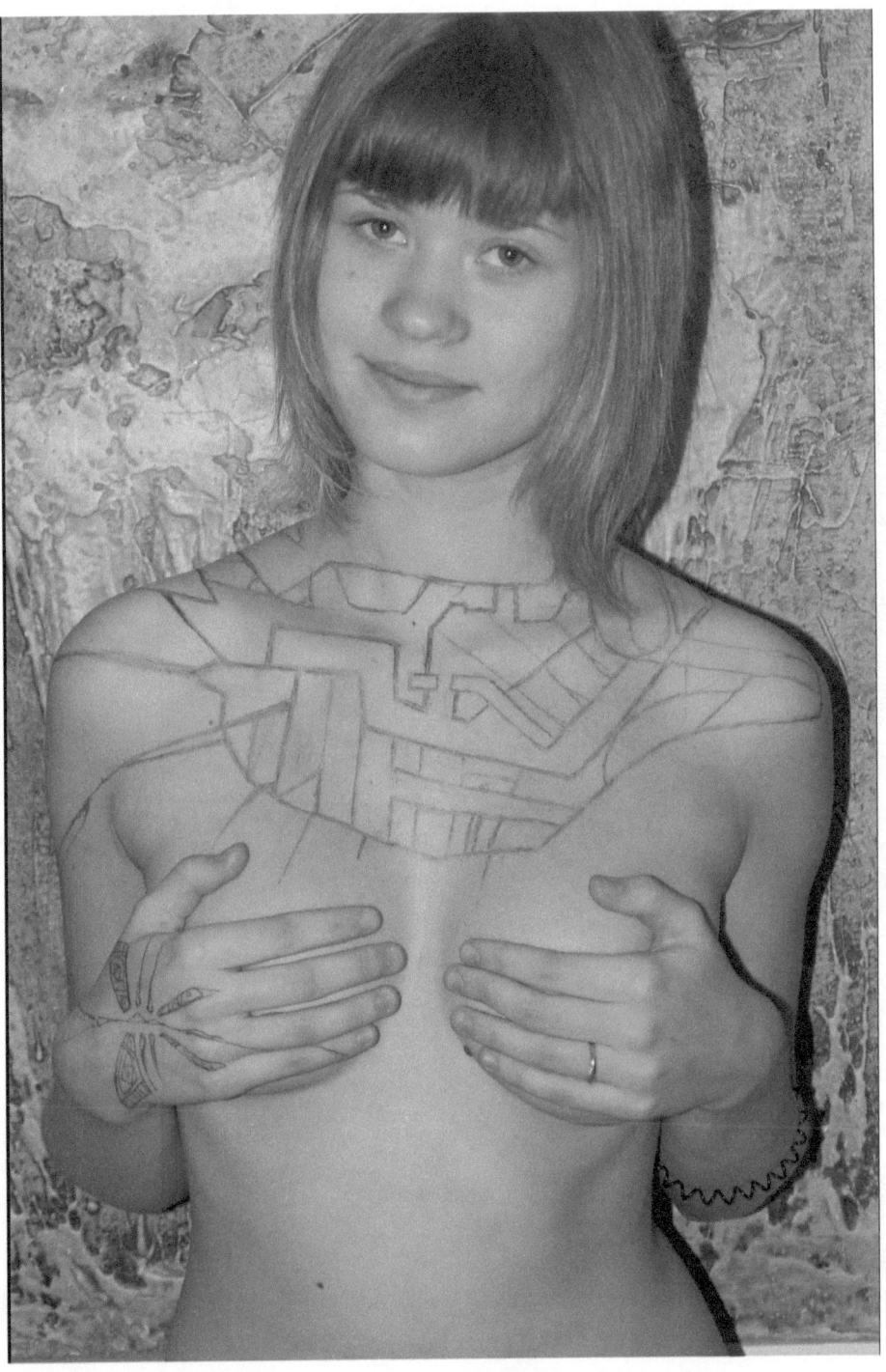

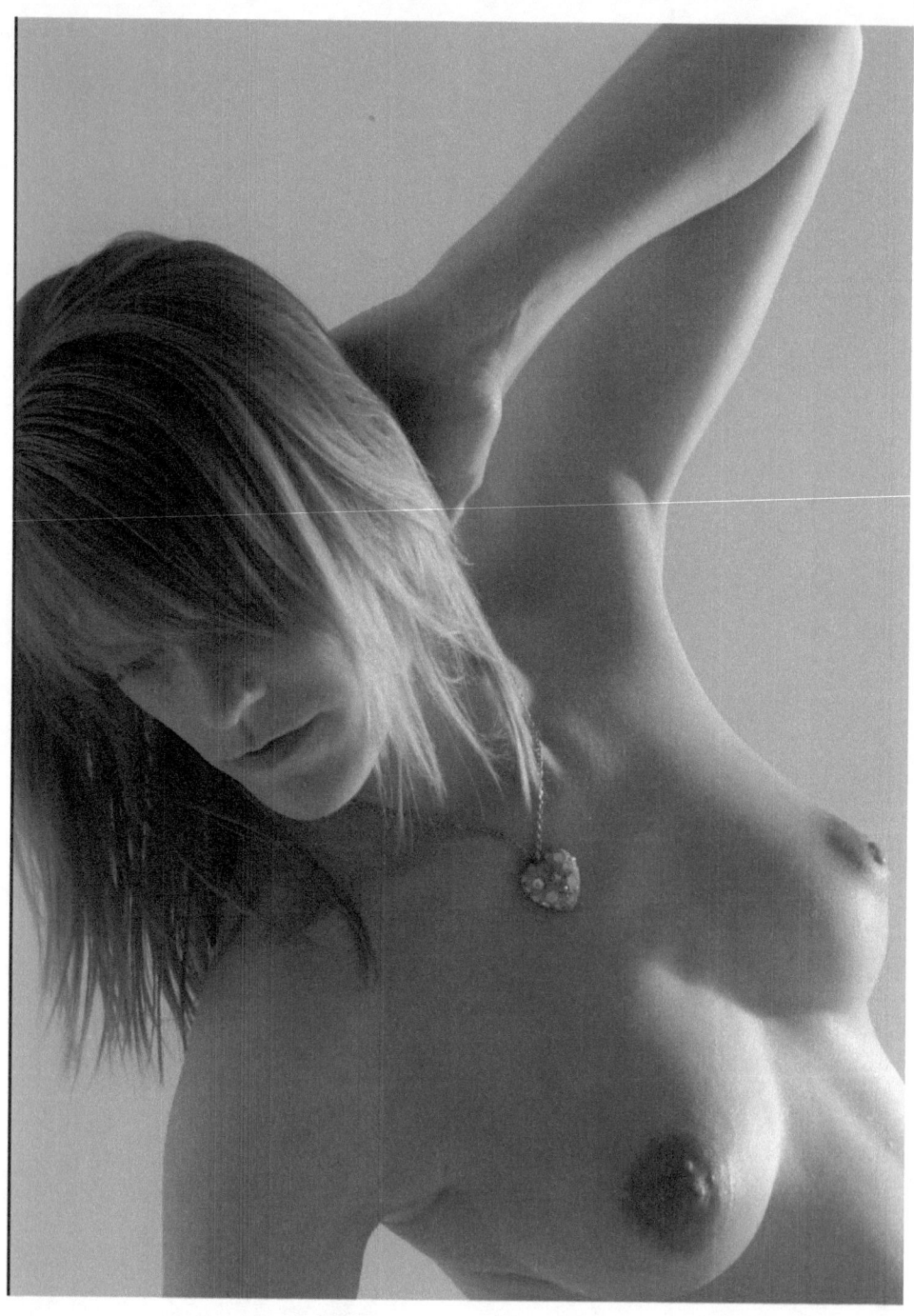

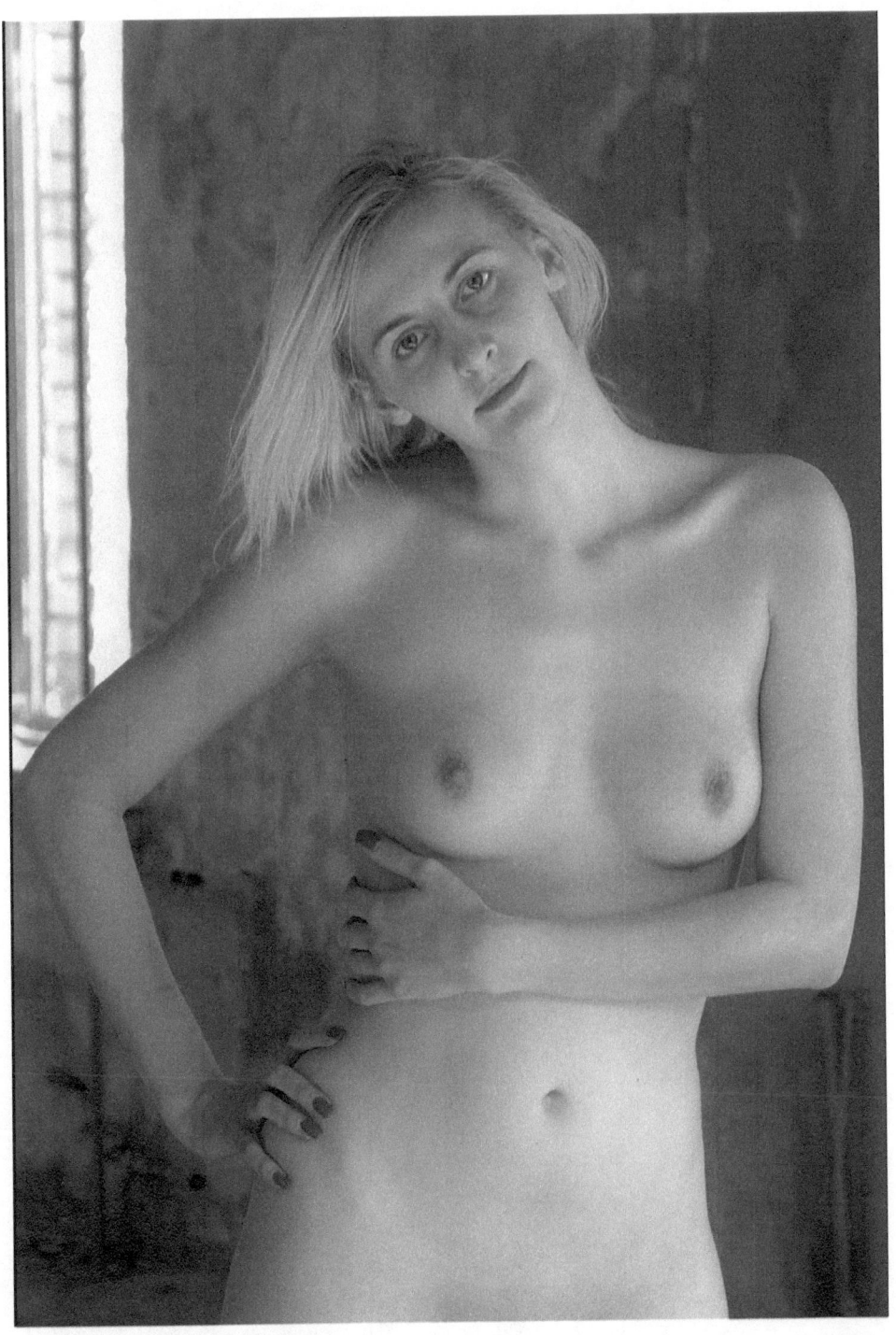

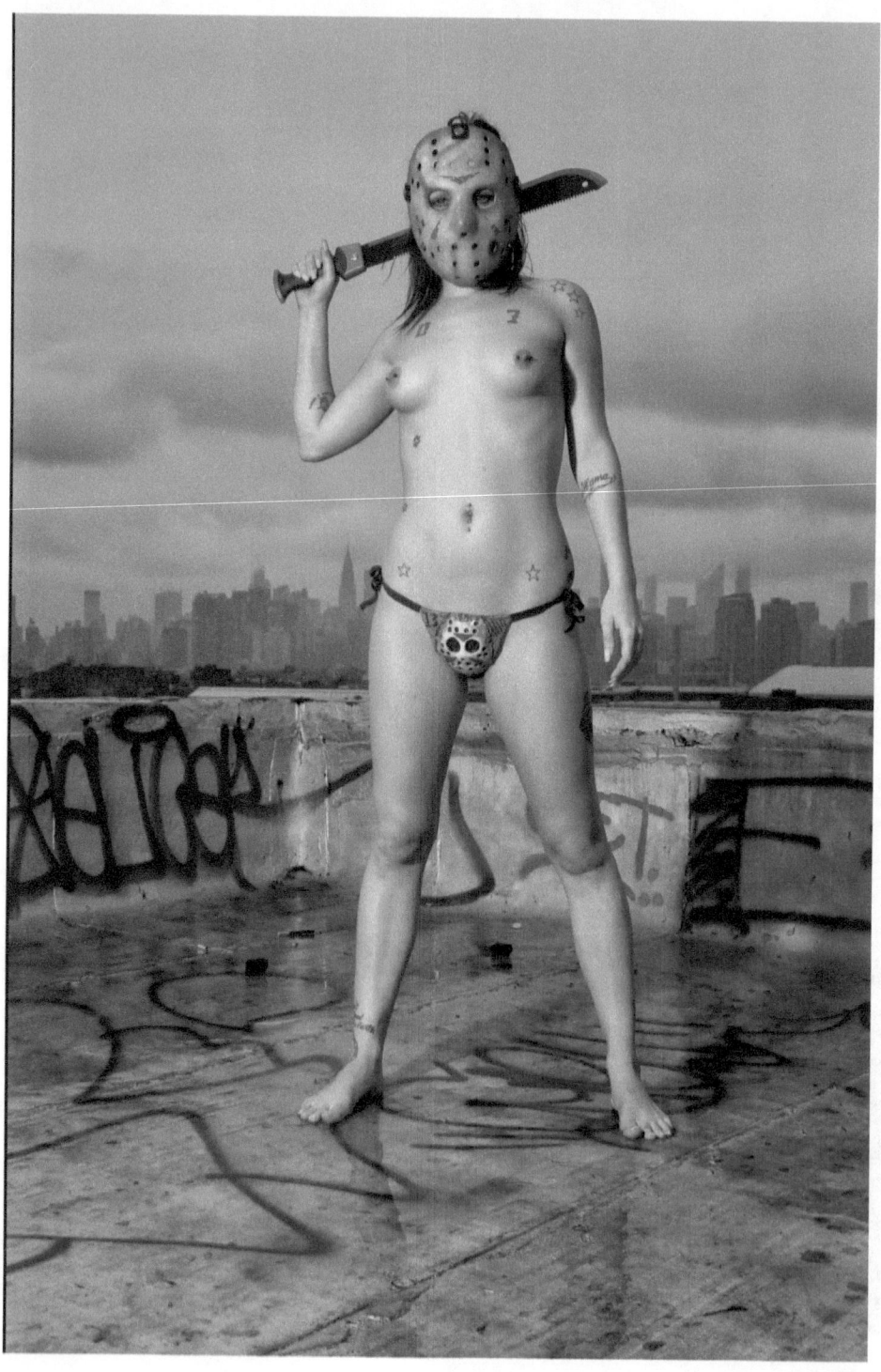

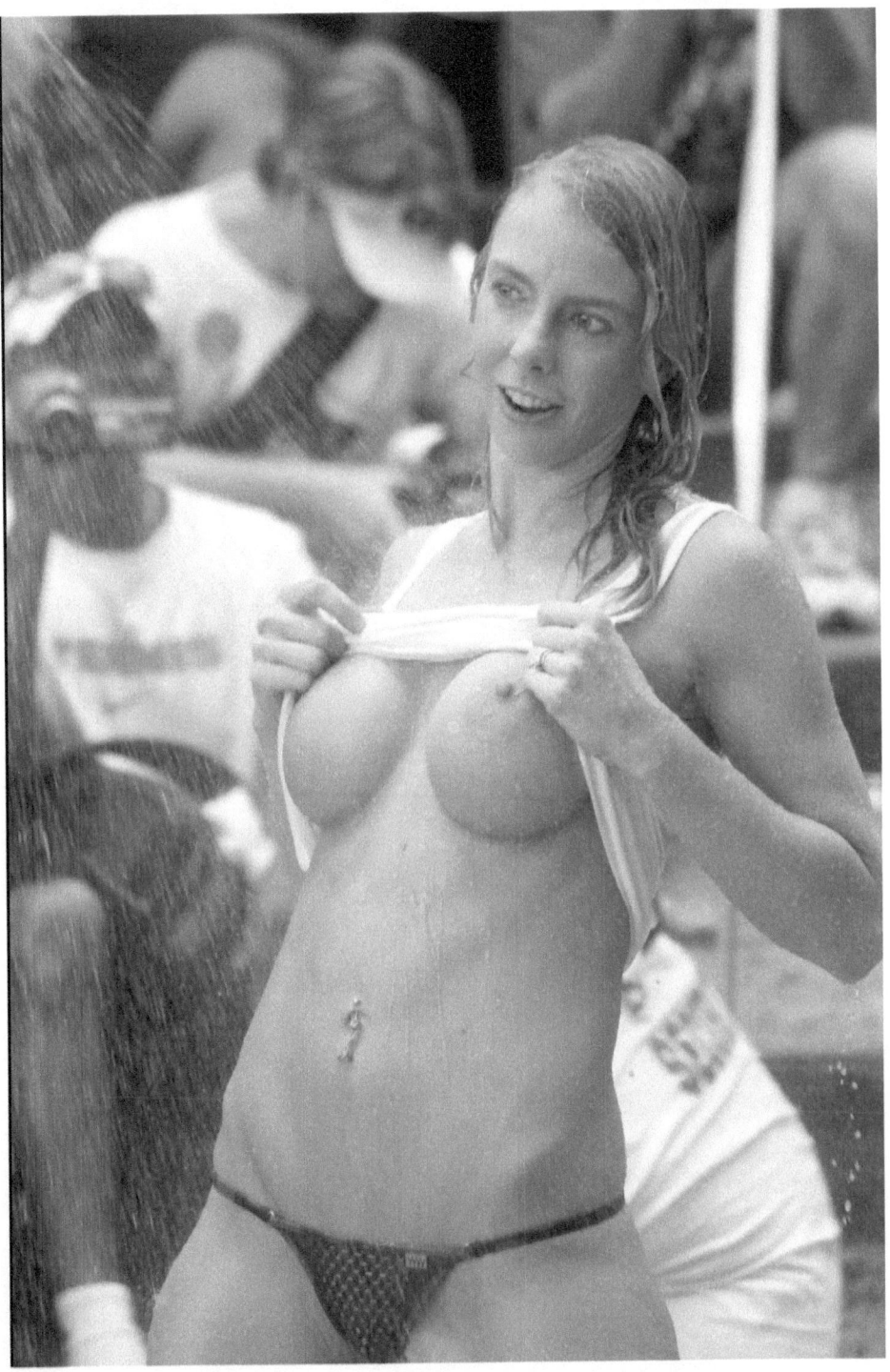

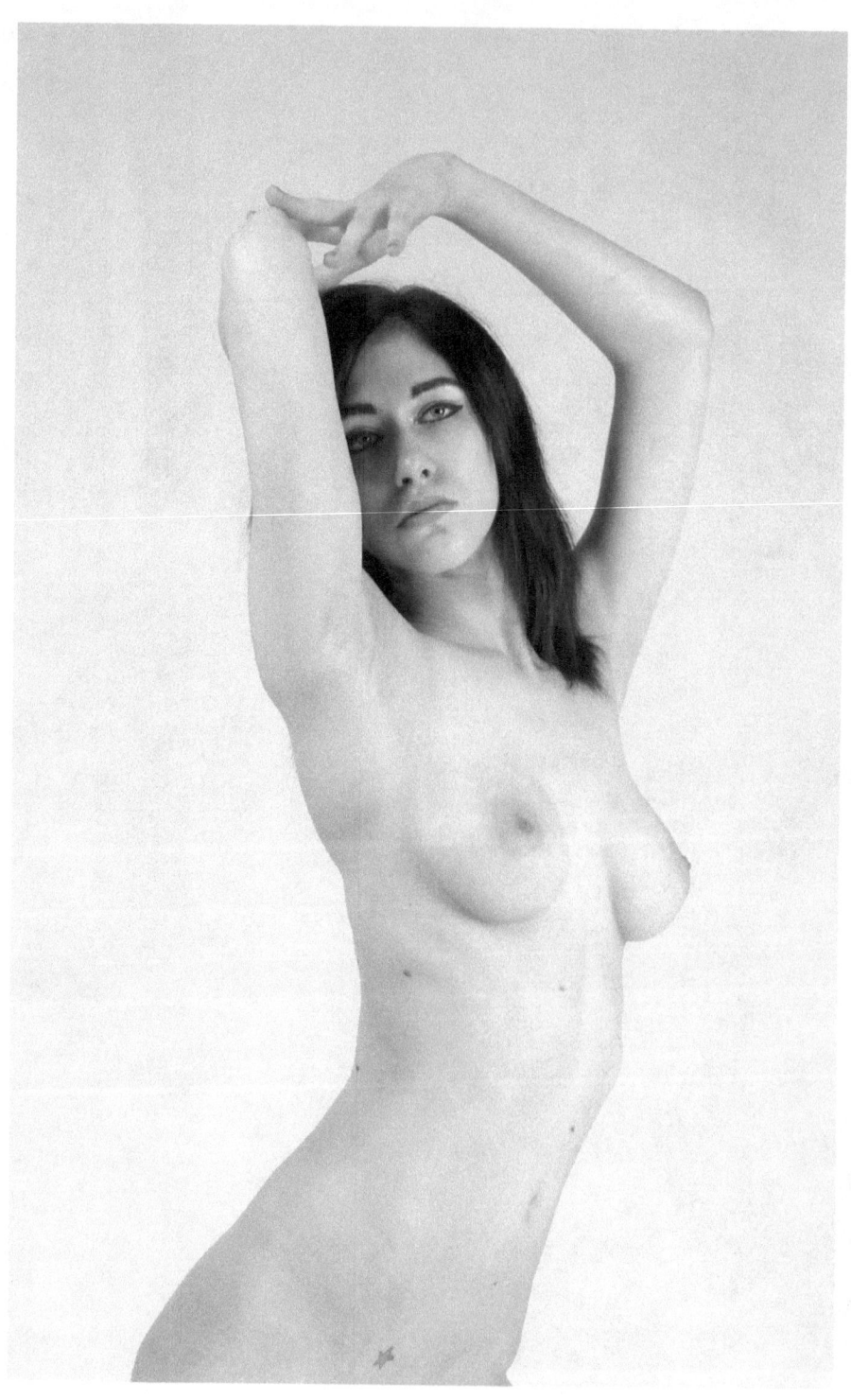

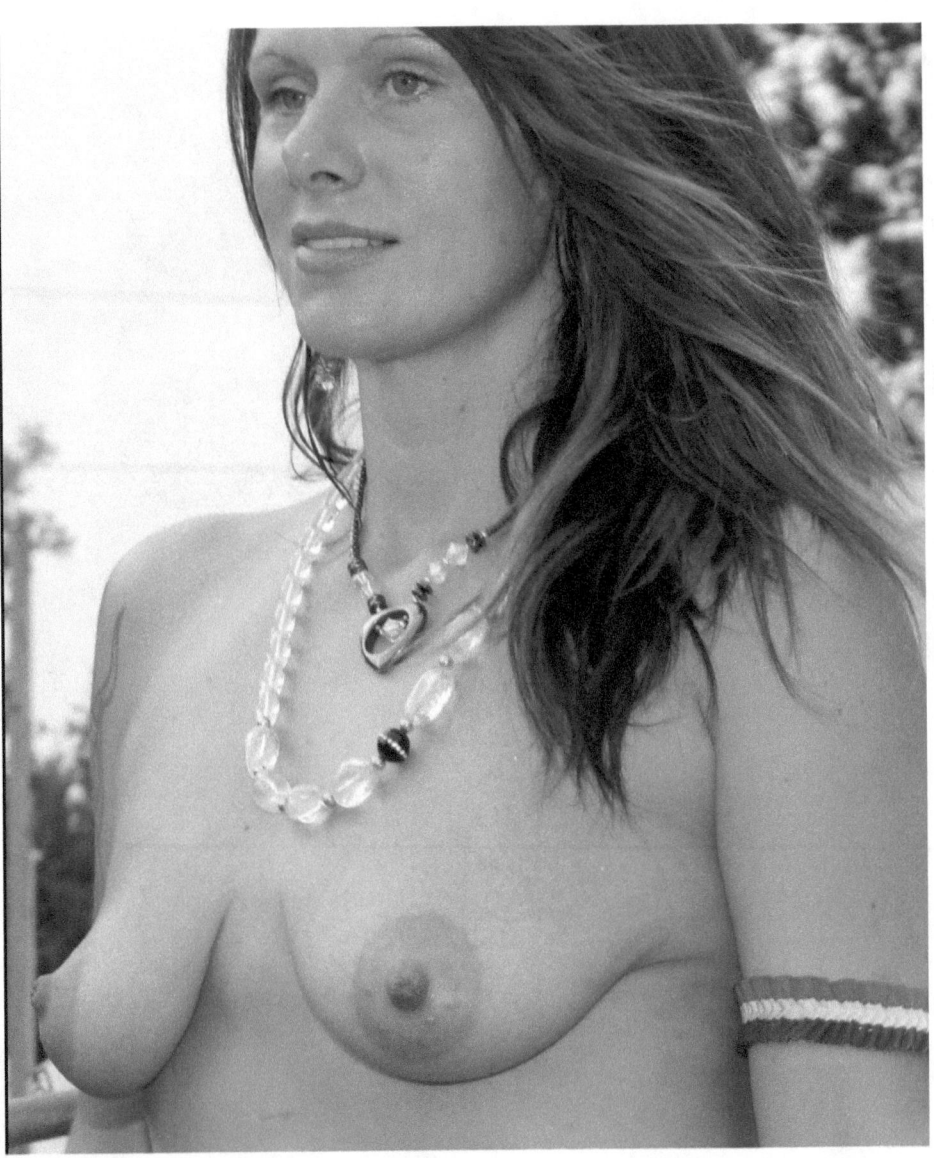

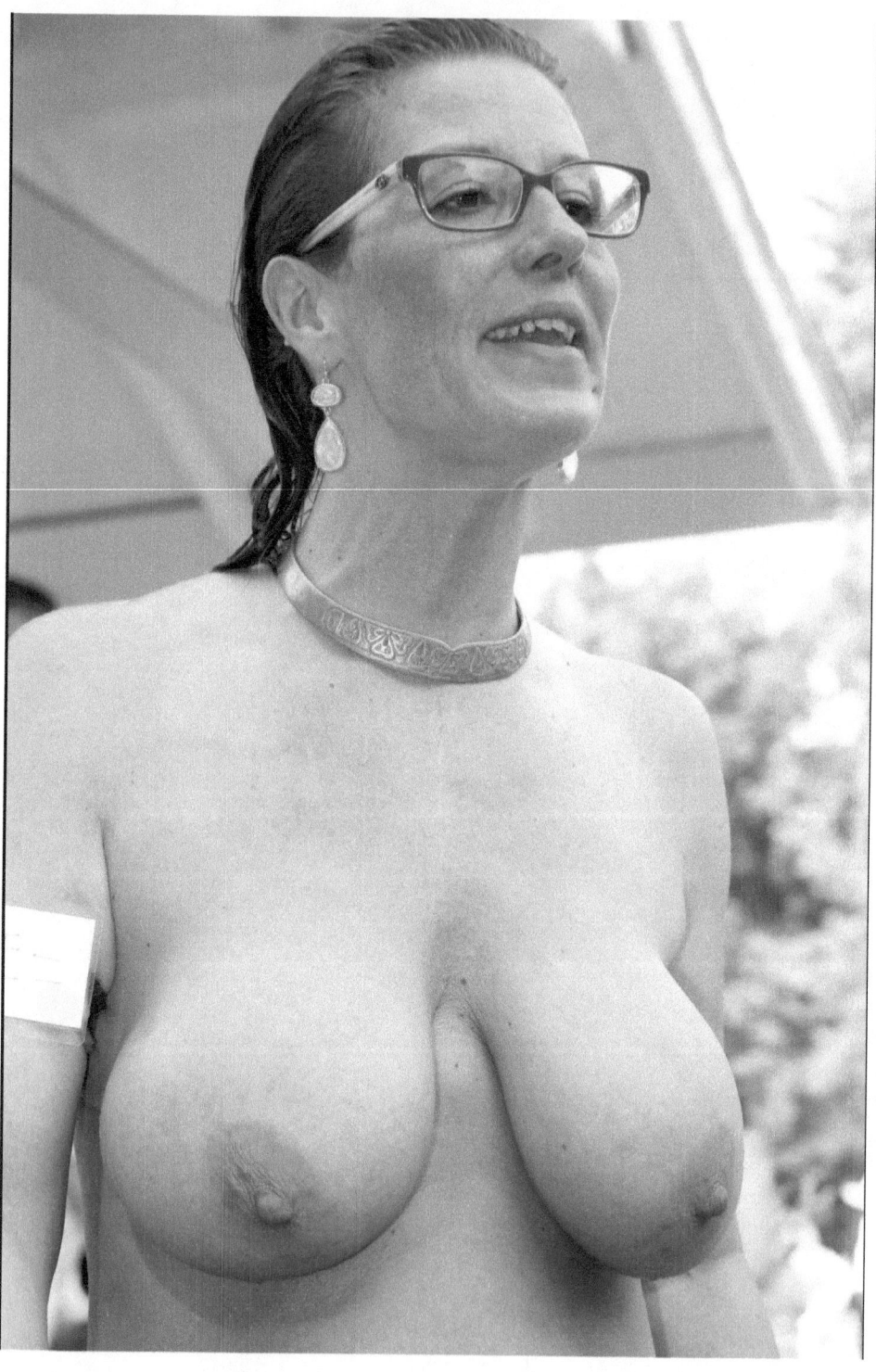

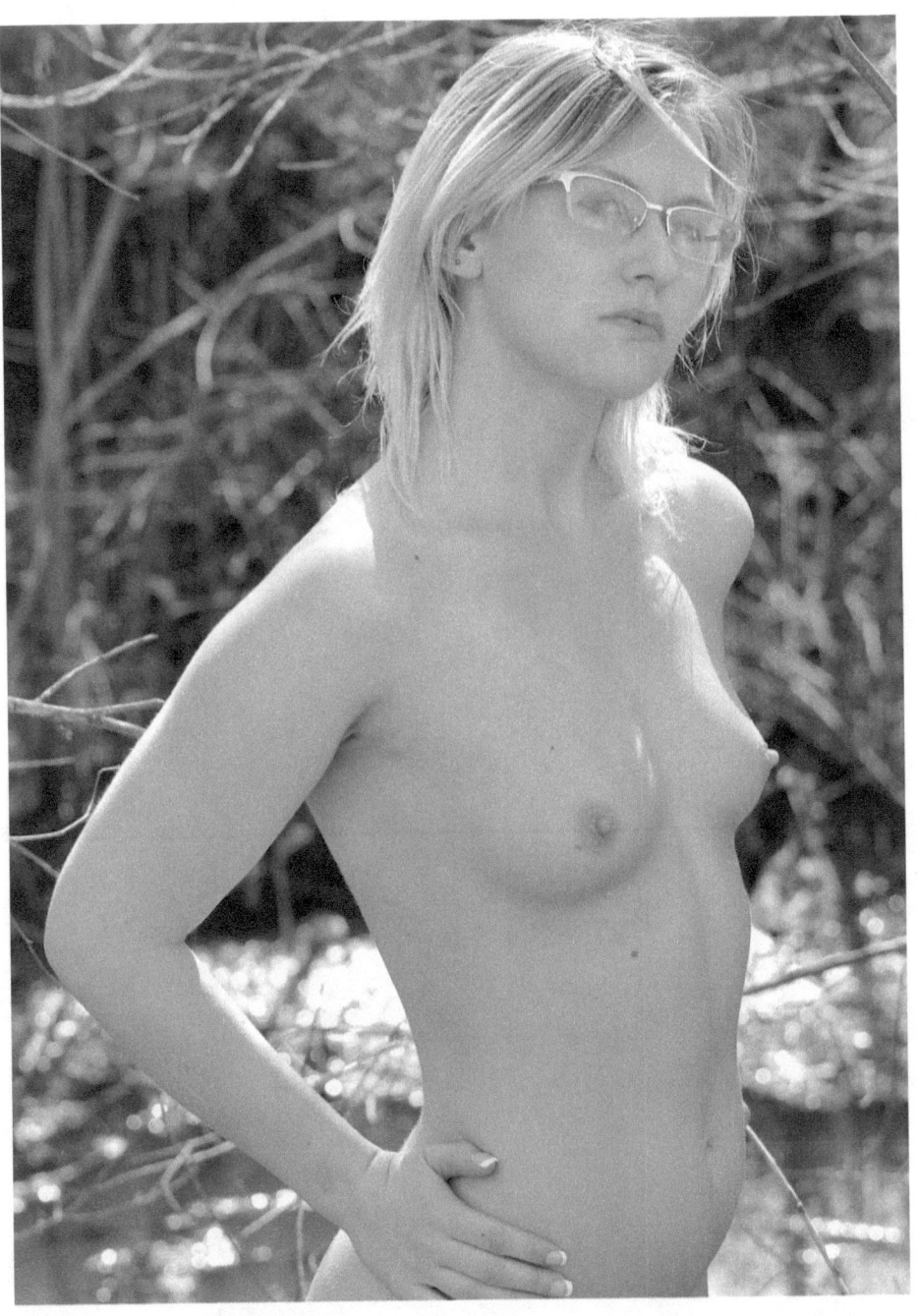

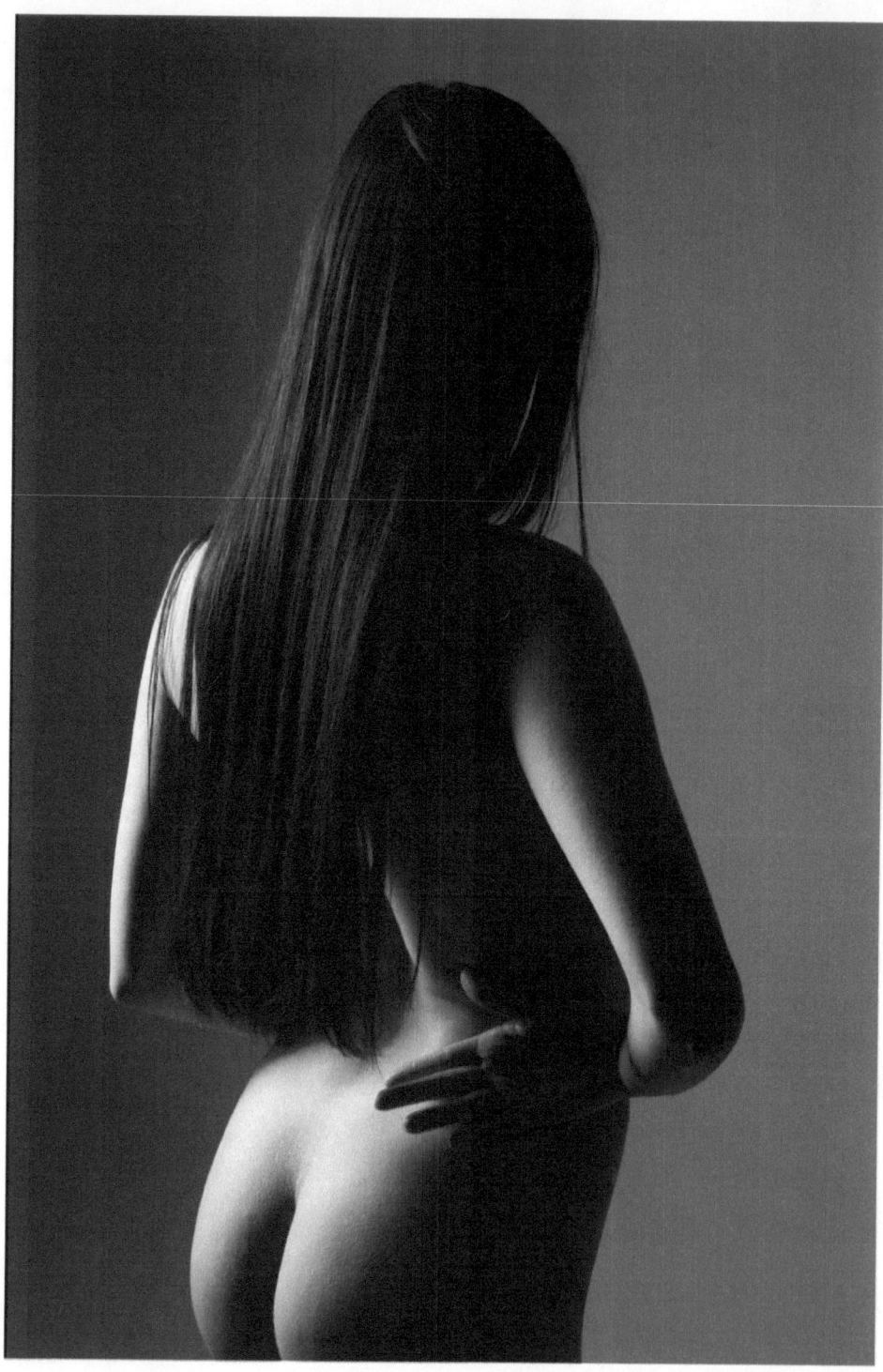

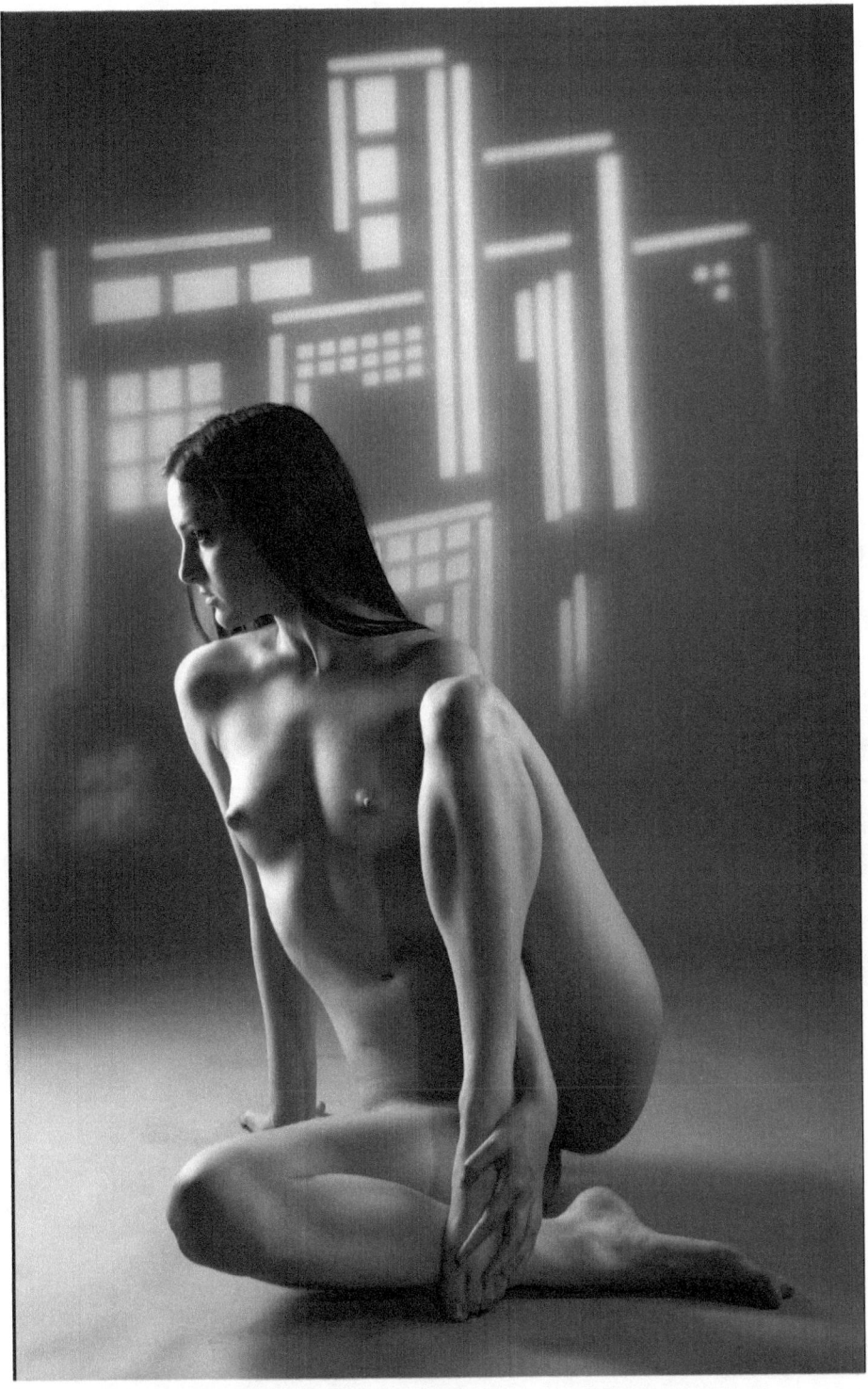

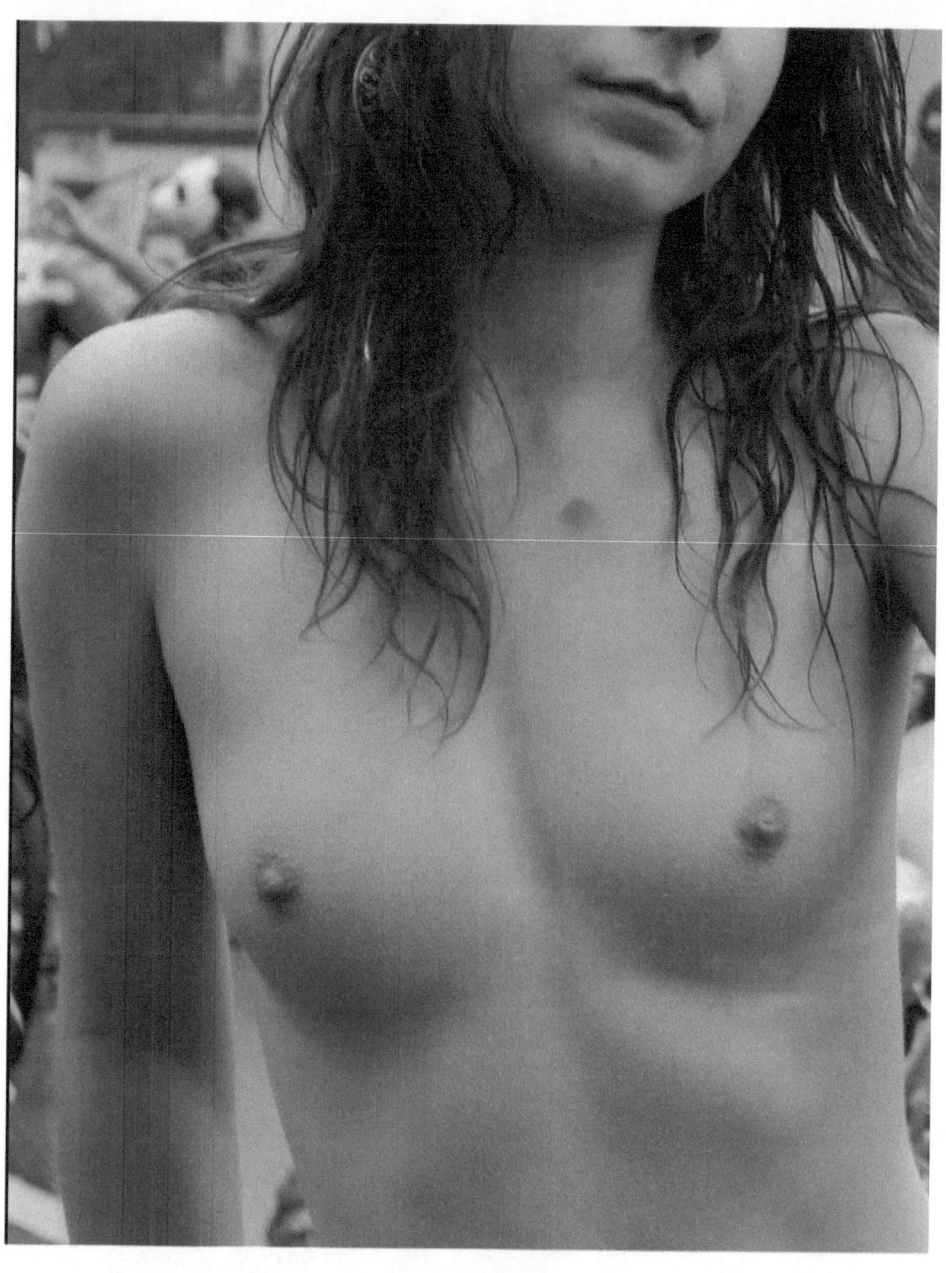

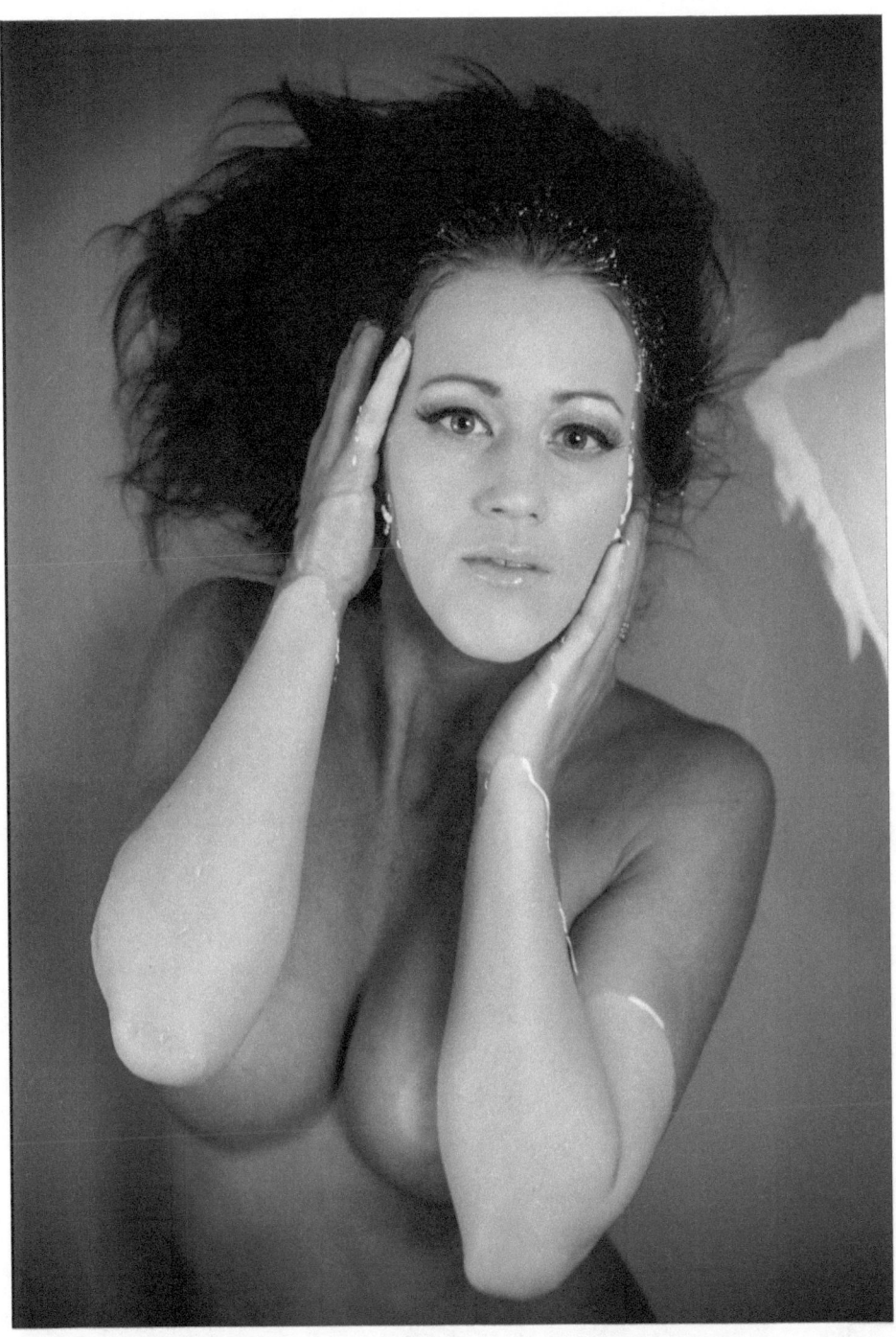

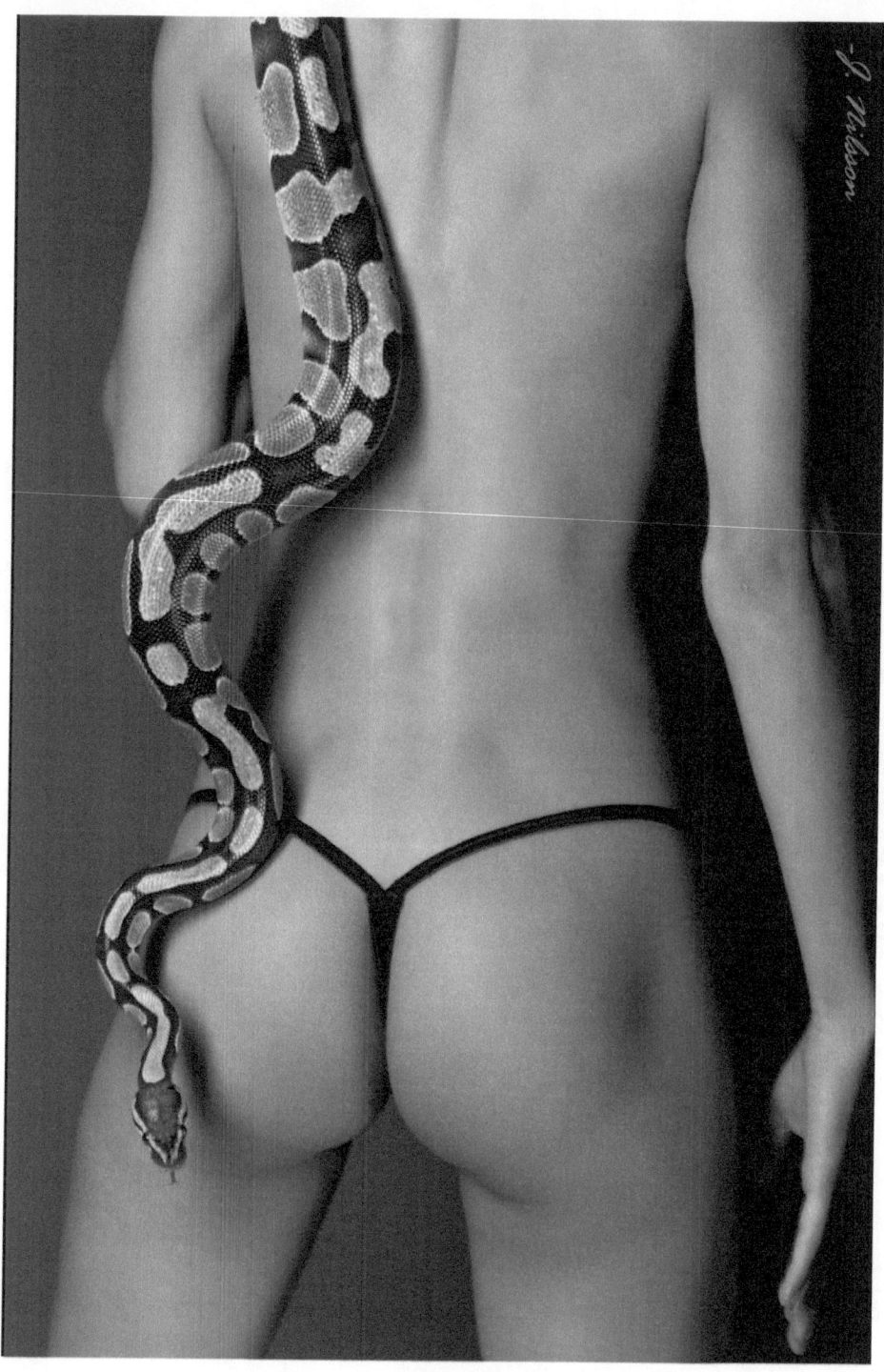

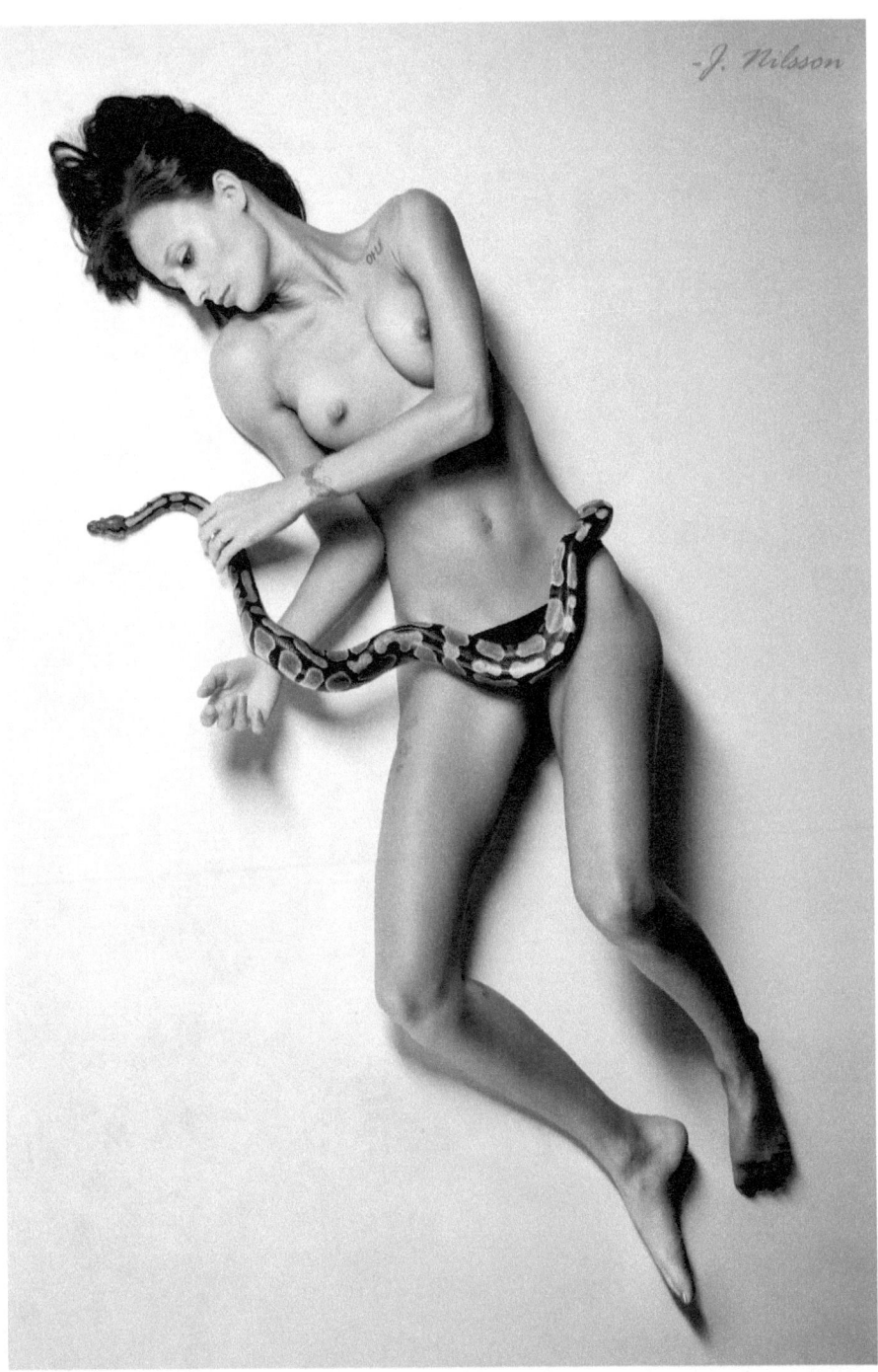

-J. Nilsson

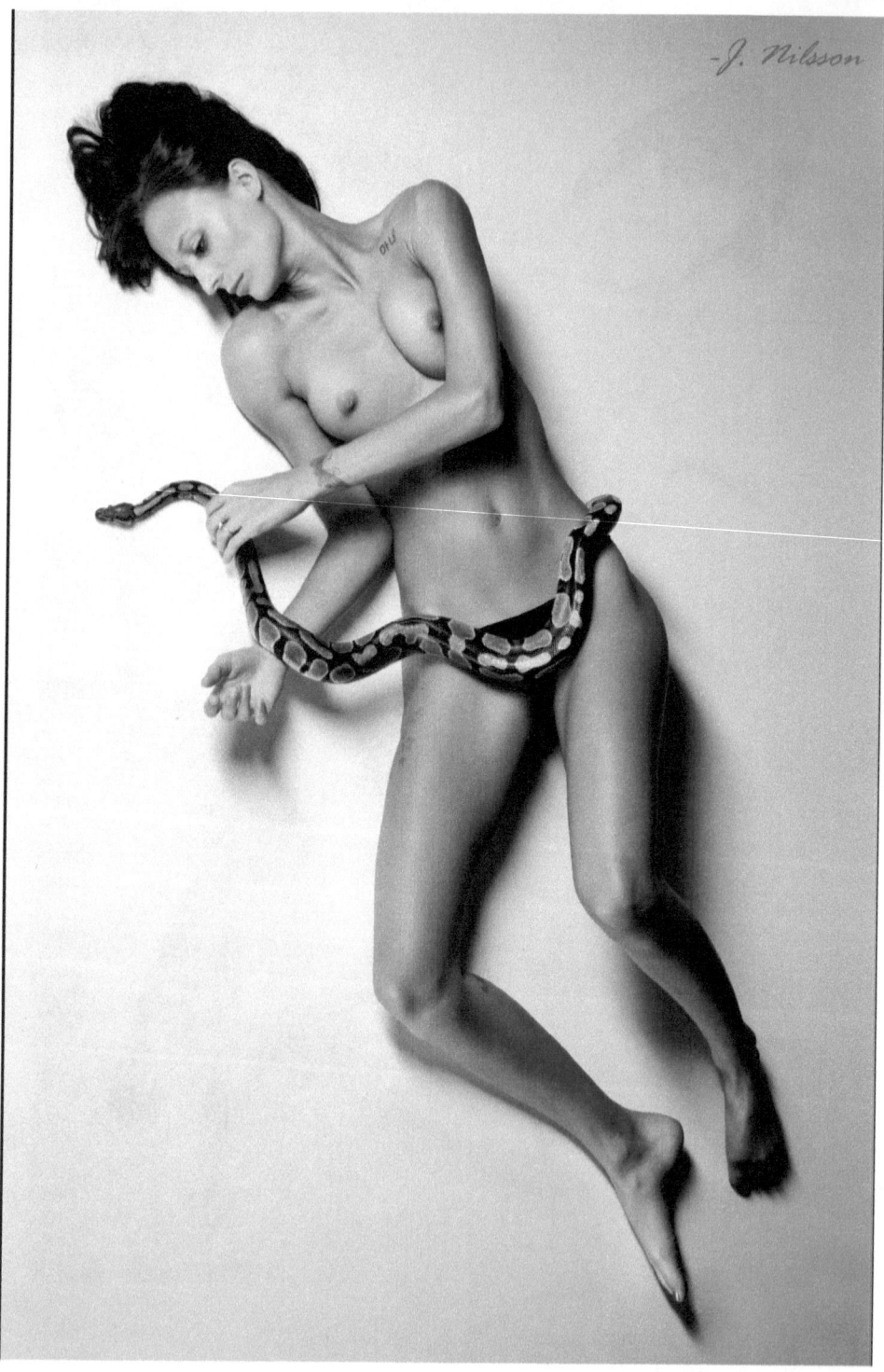

-J. Nilsson

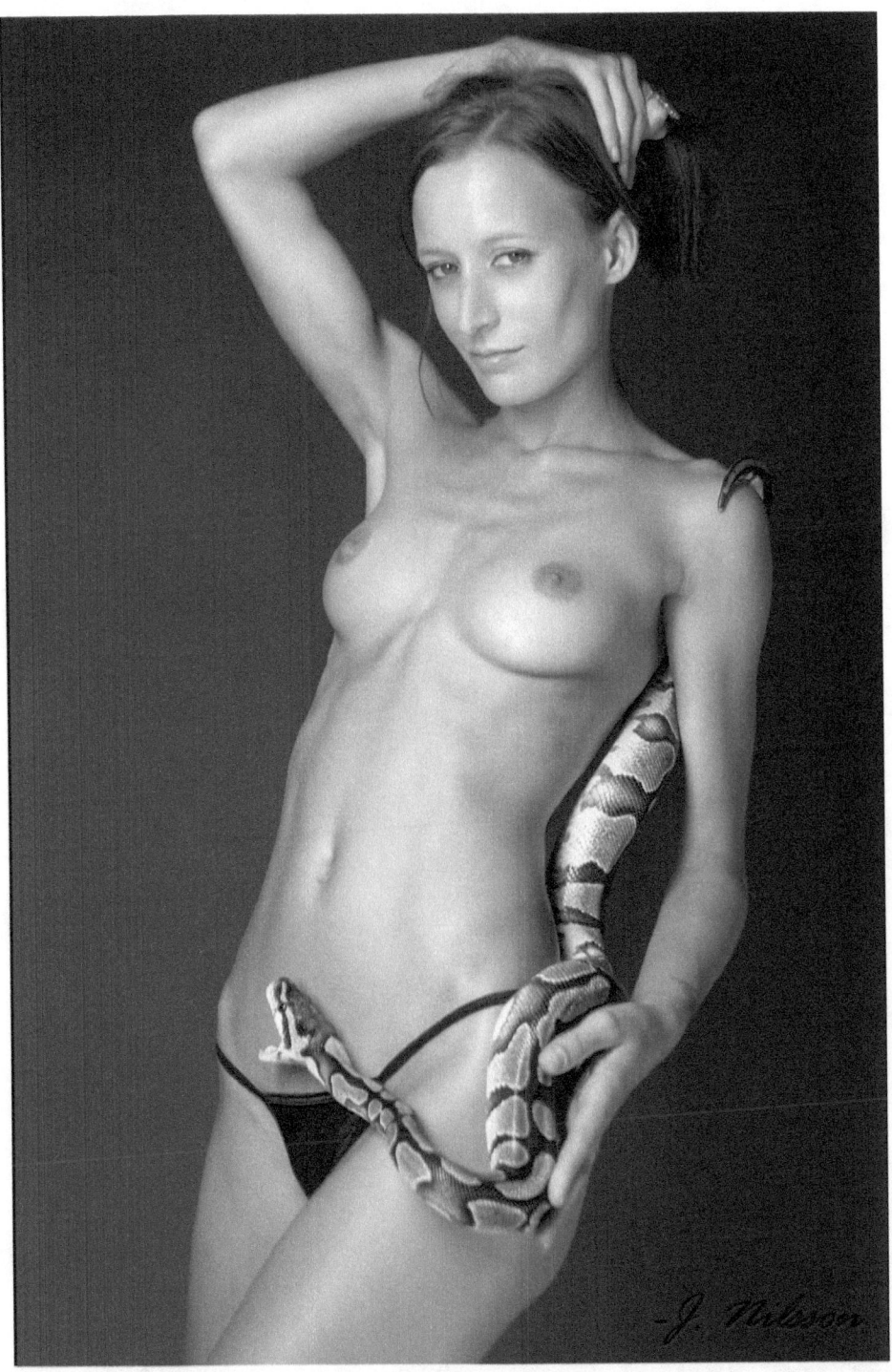

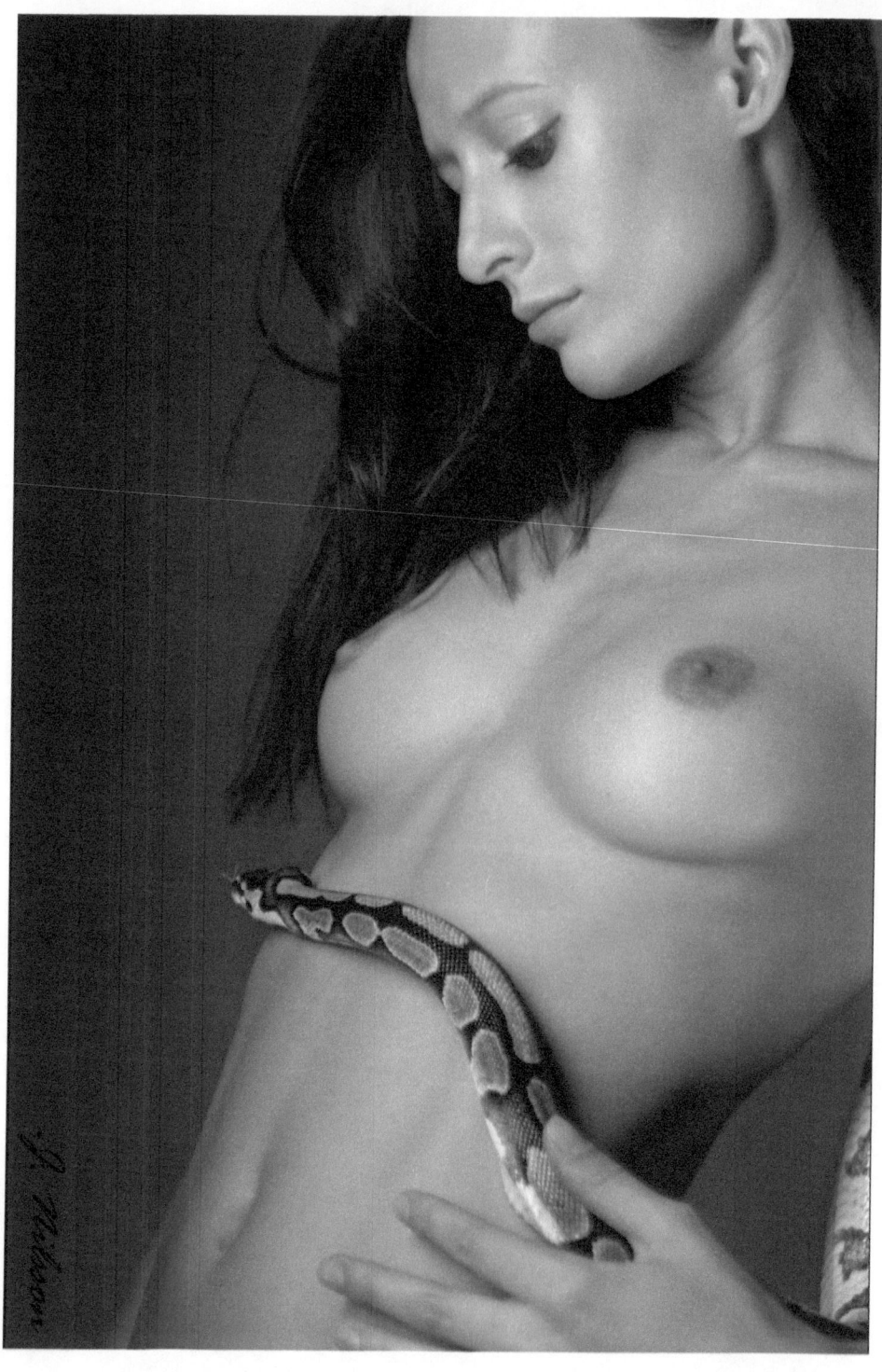

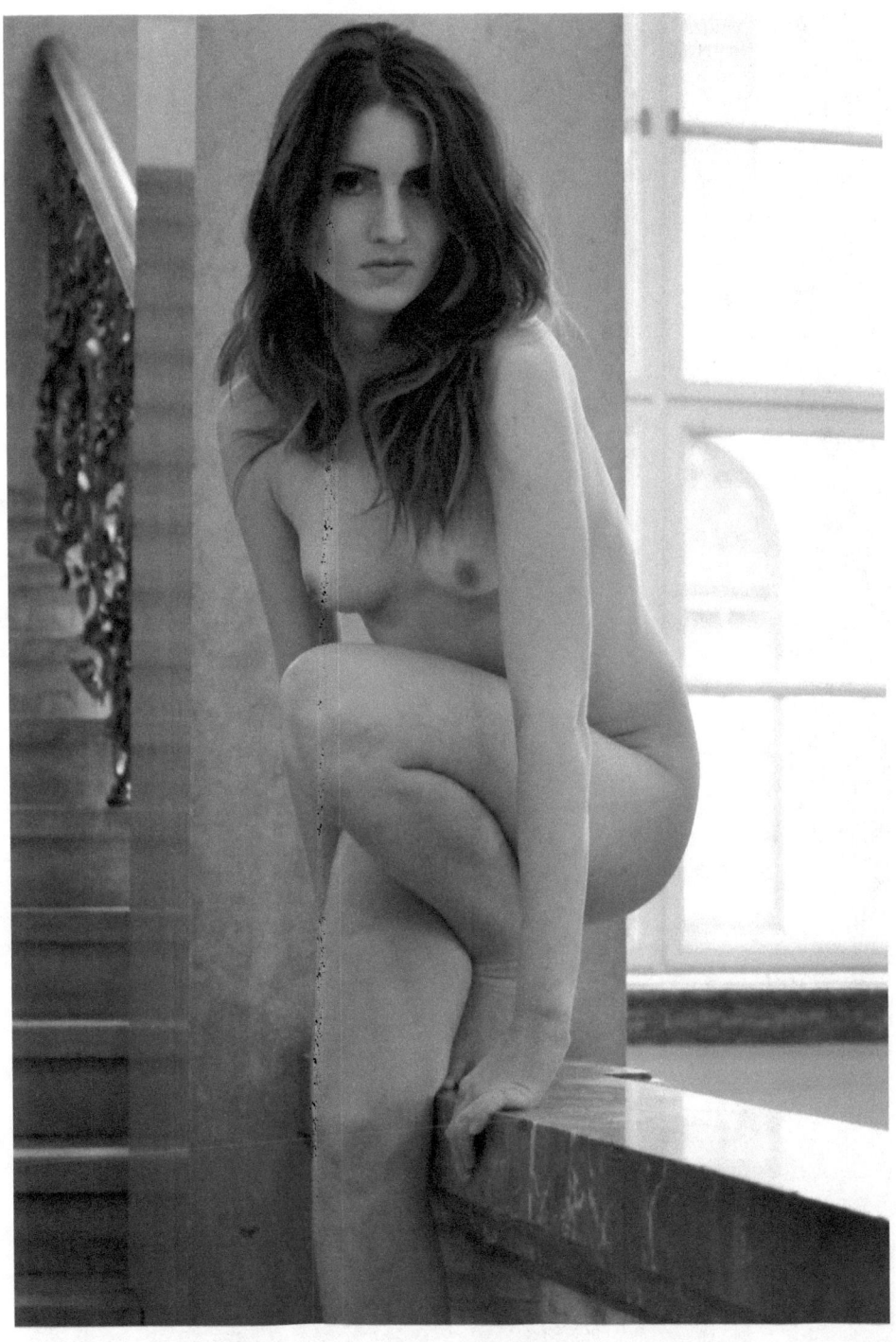

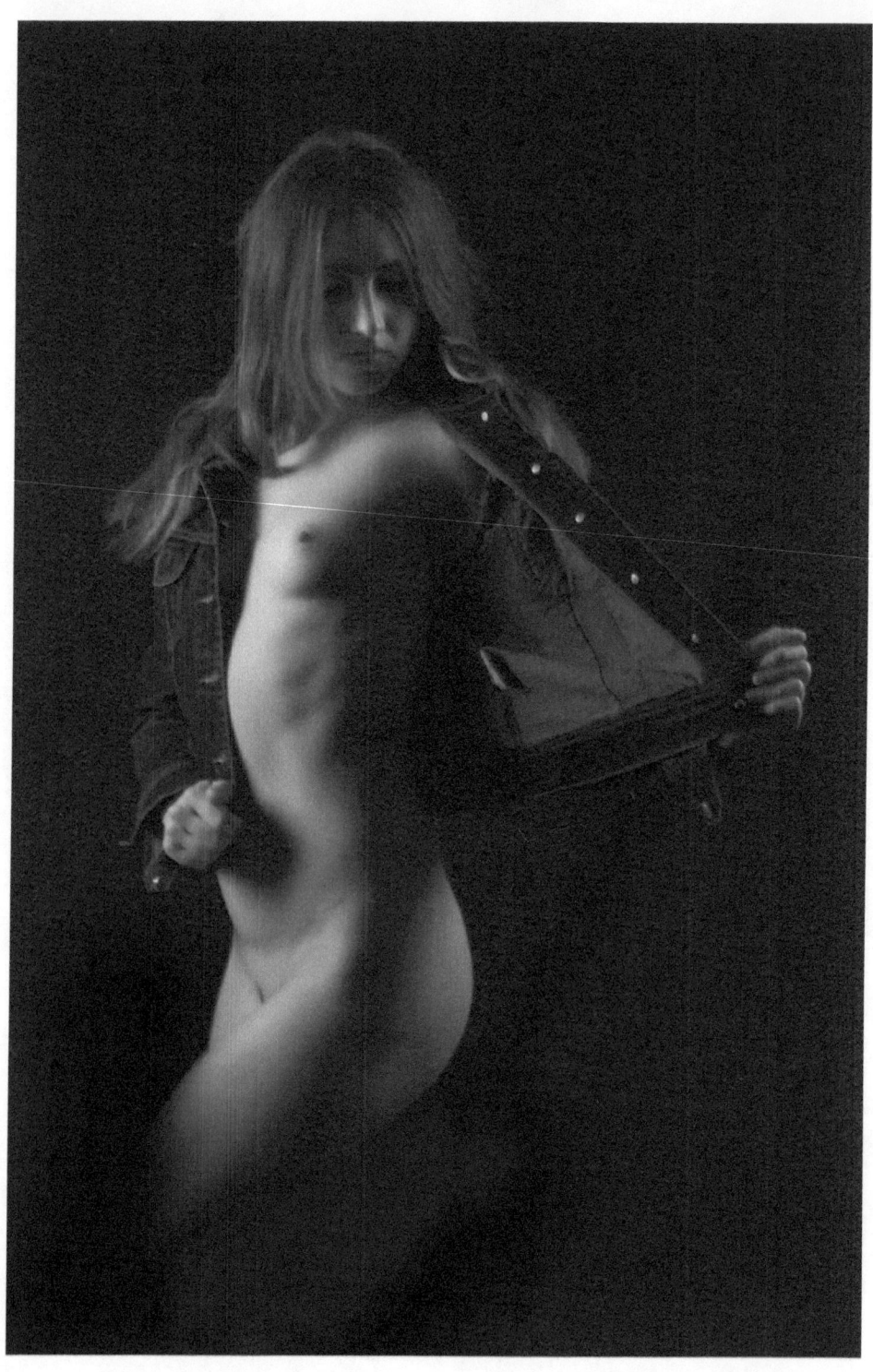

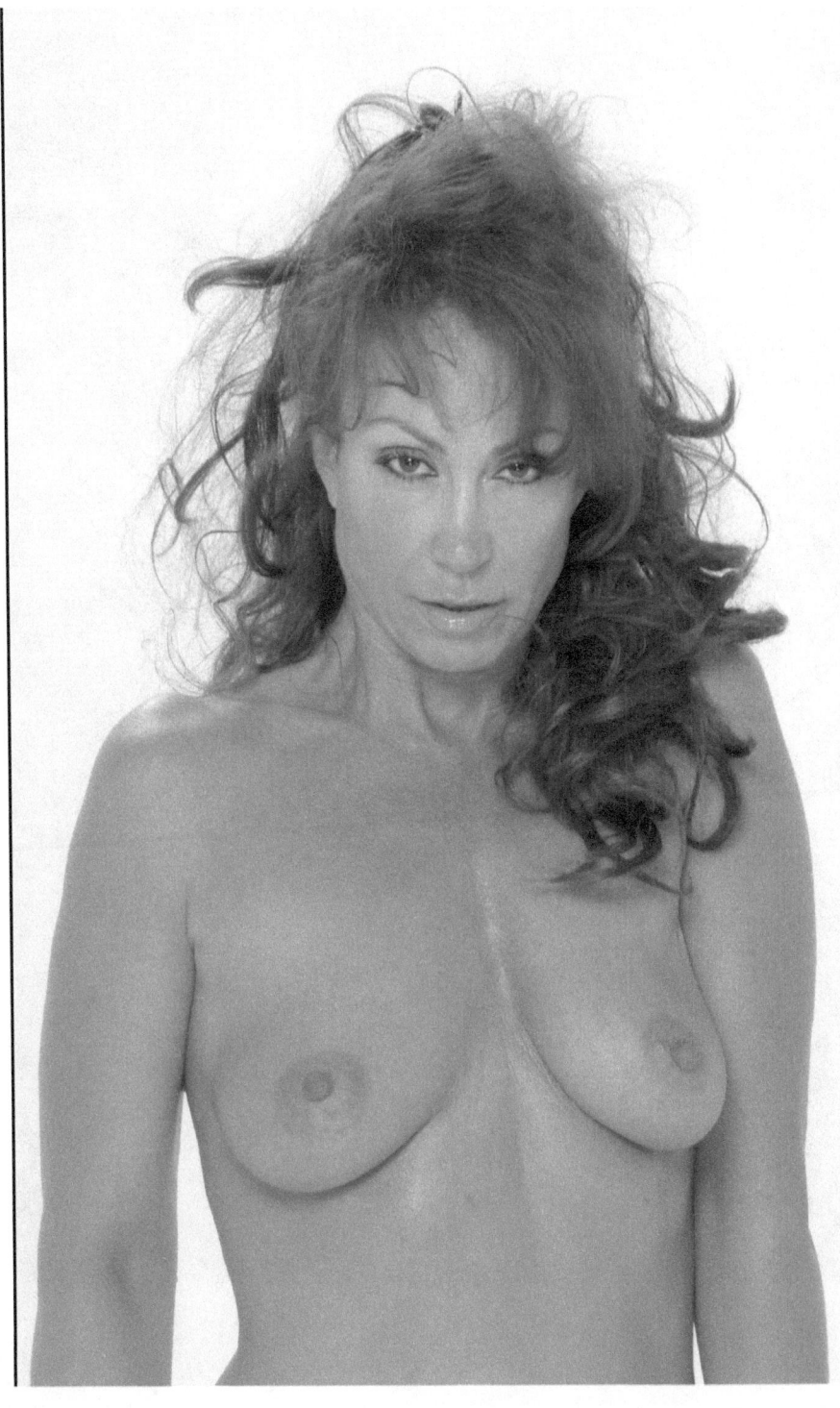

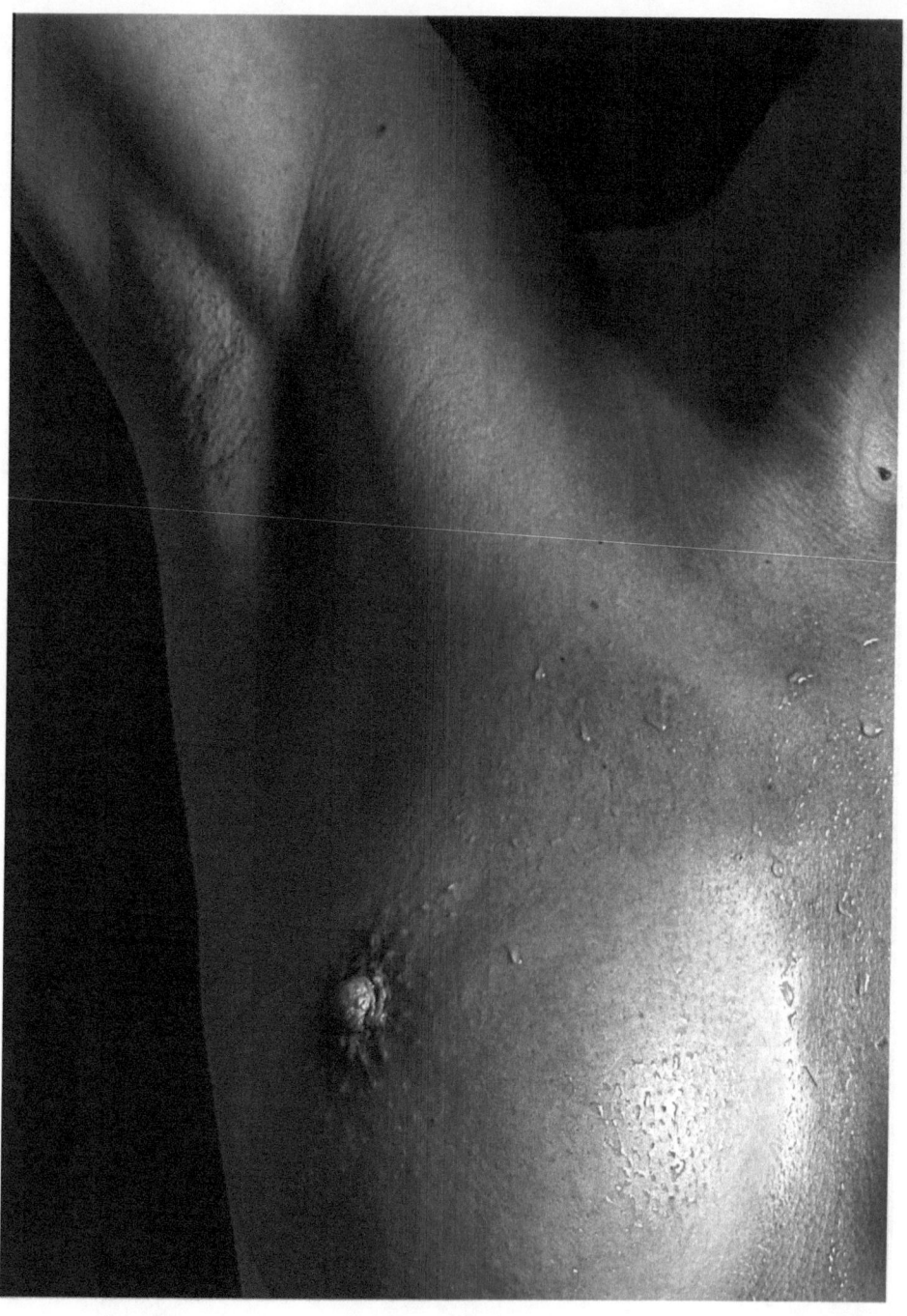

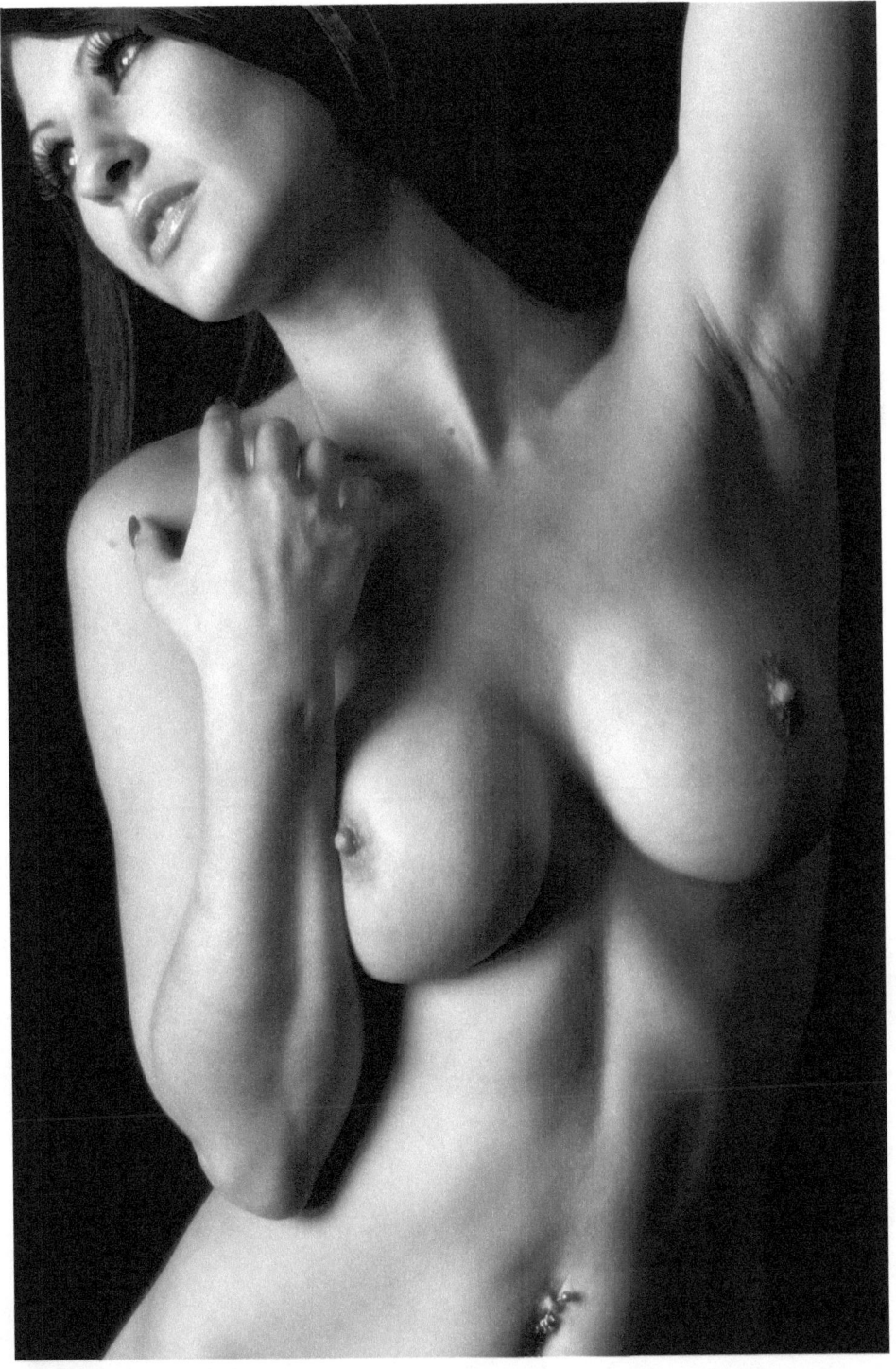

95

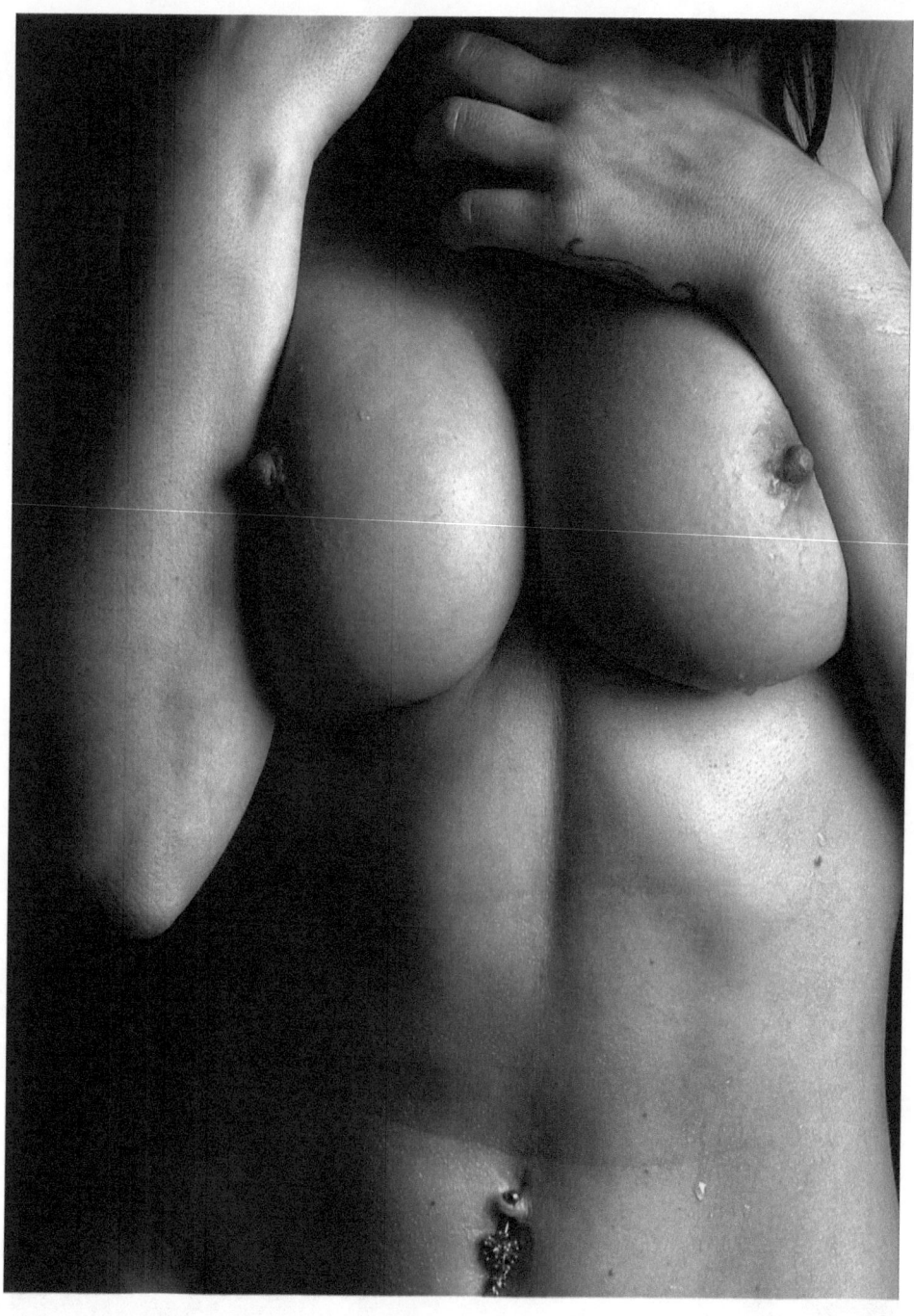

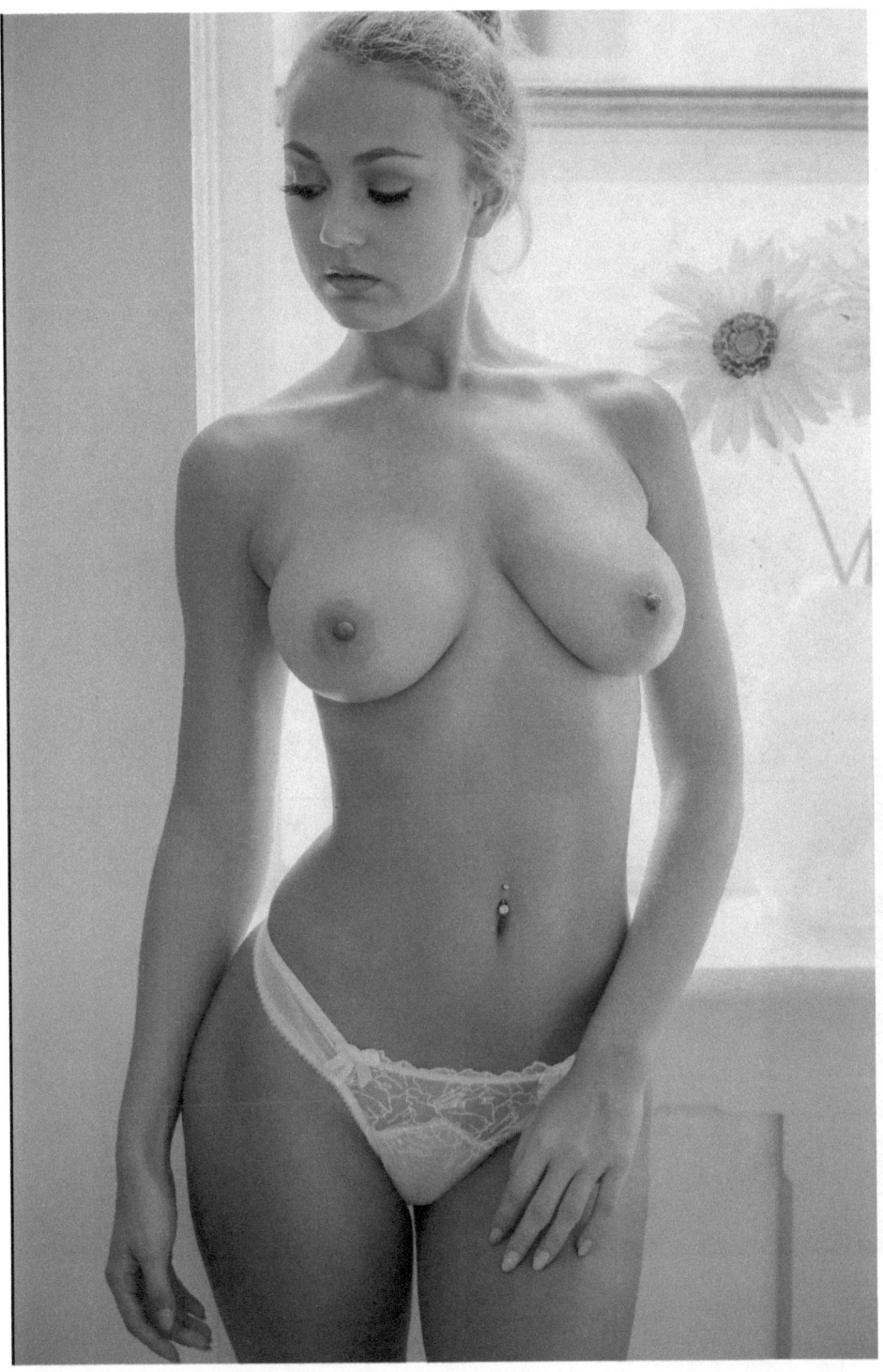

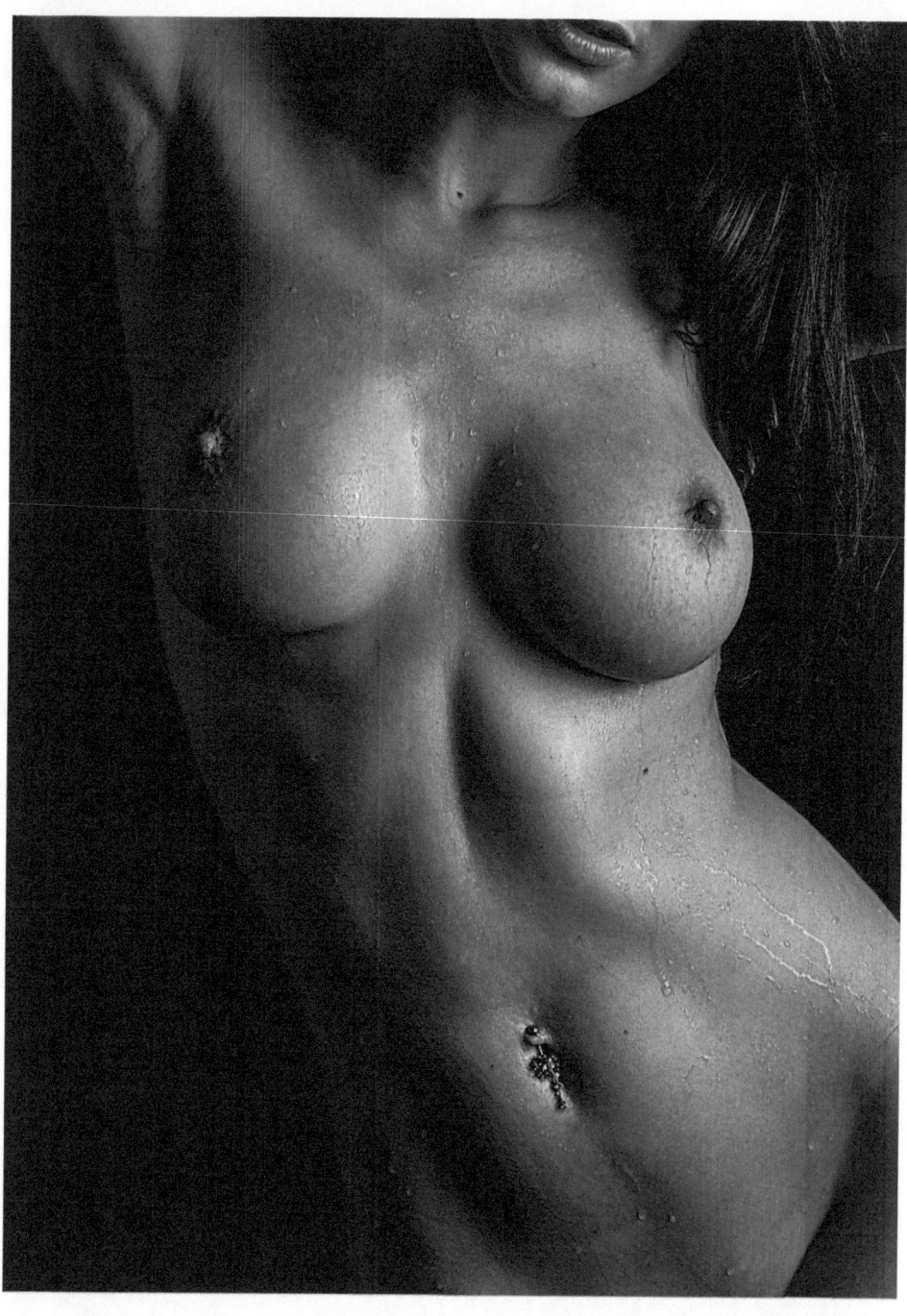

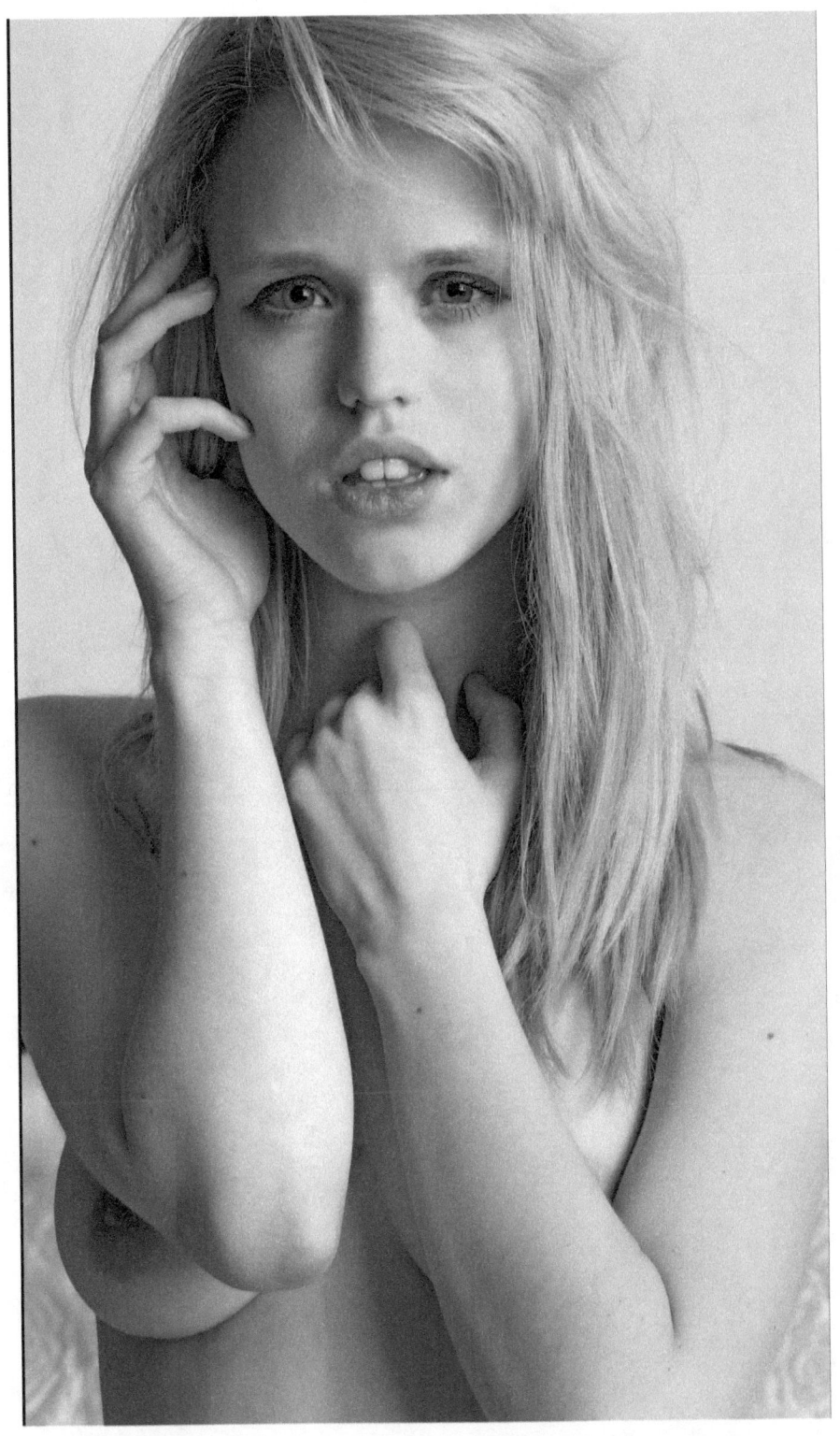

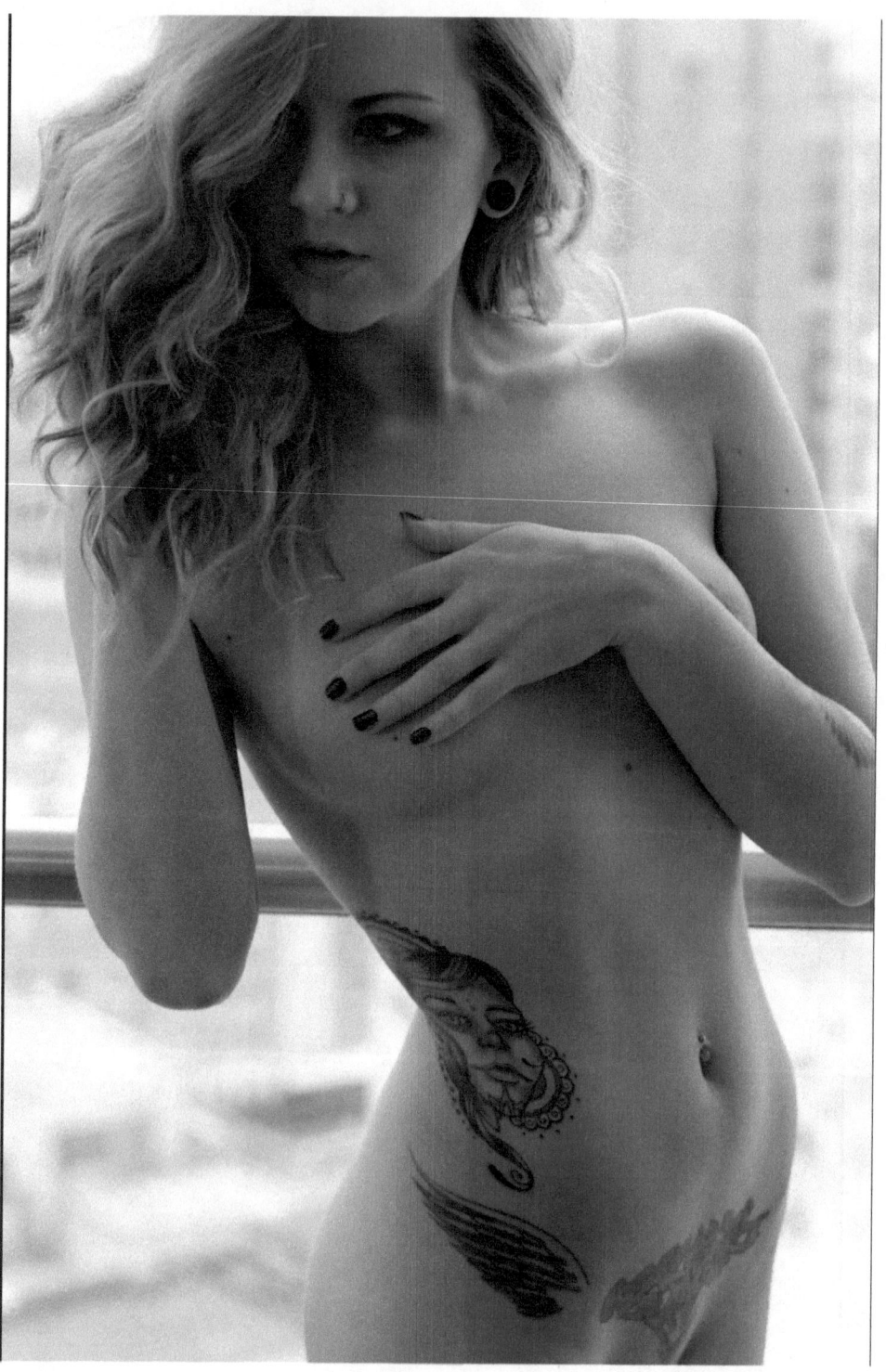

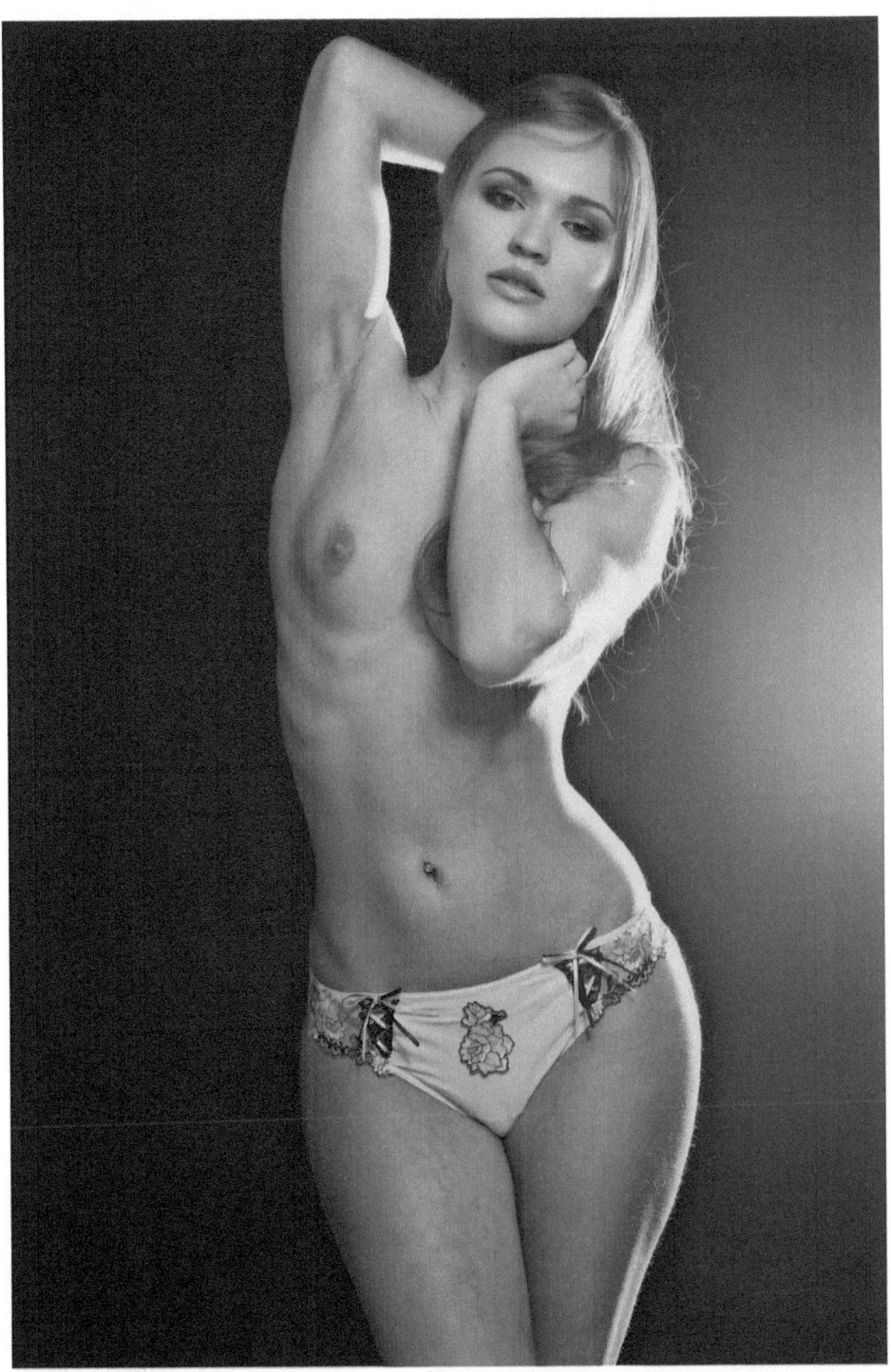

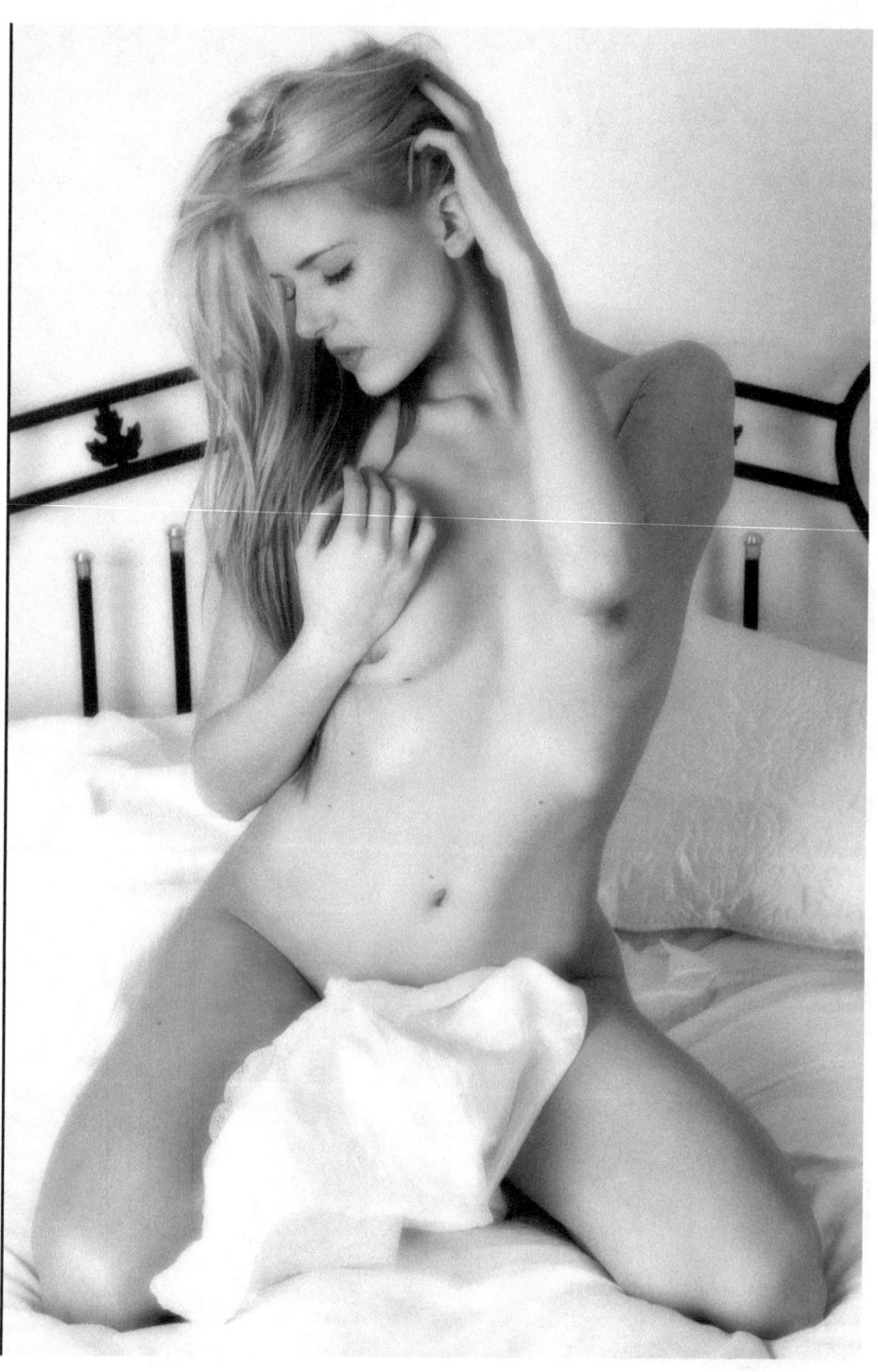

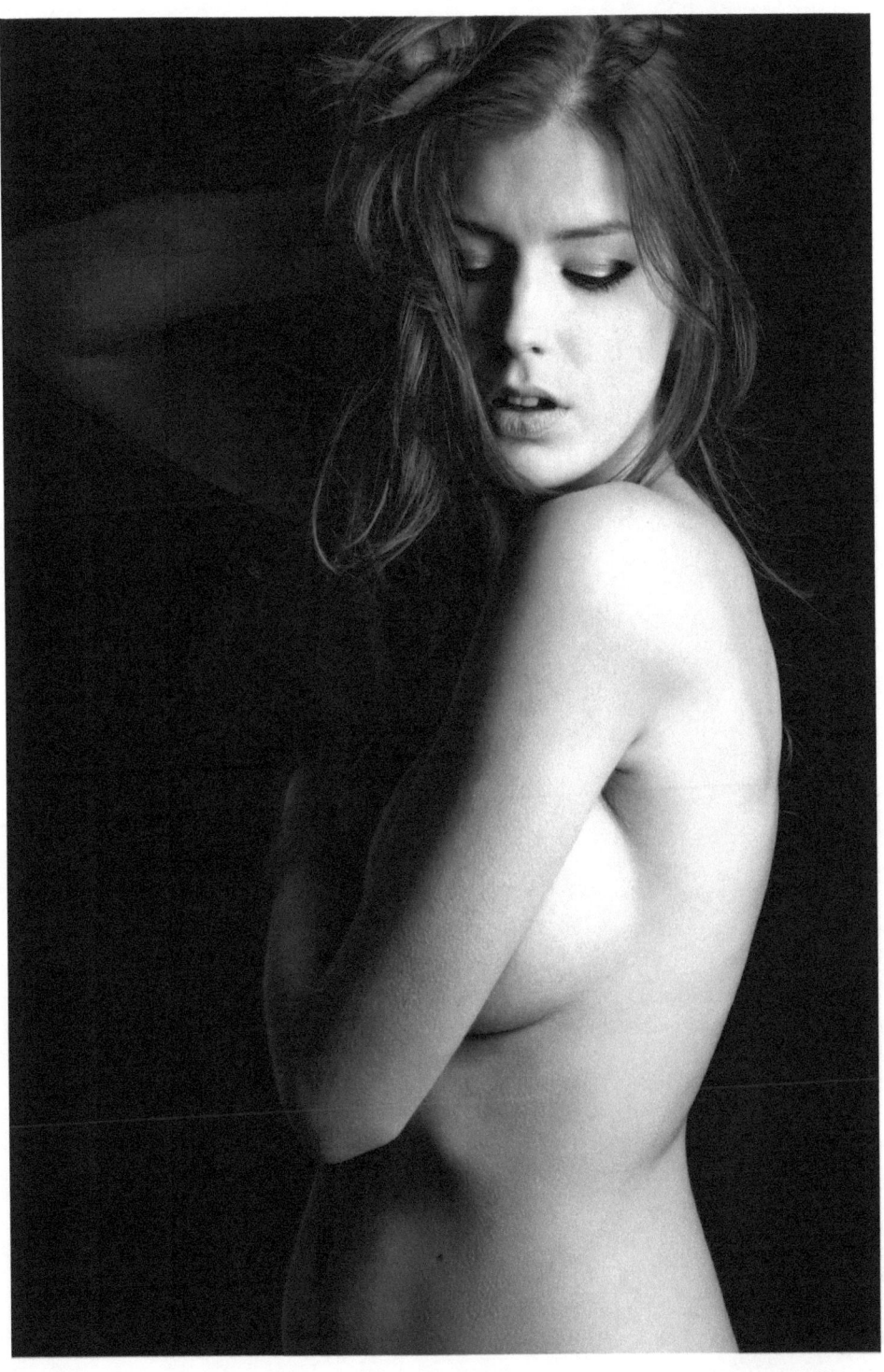

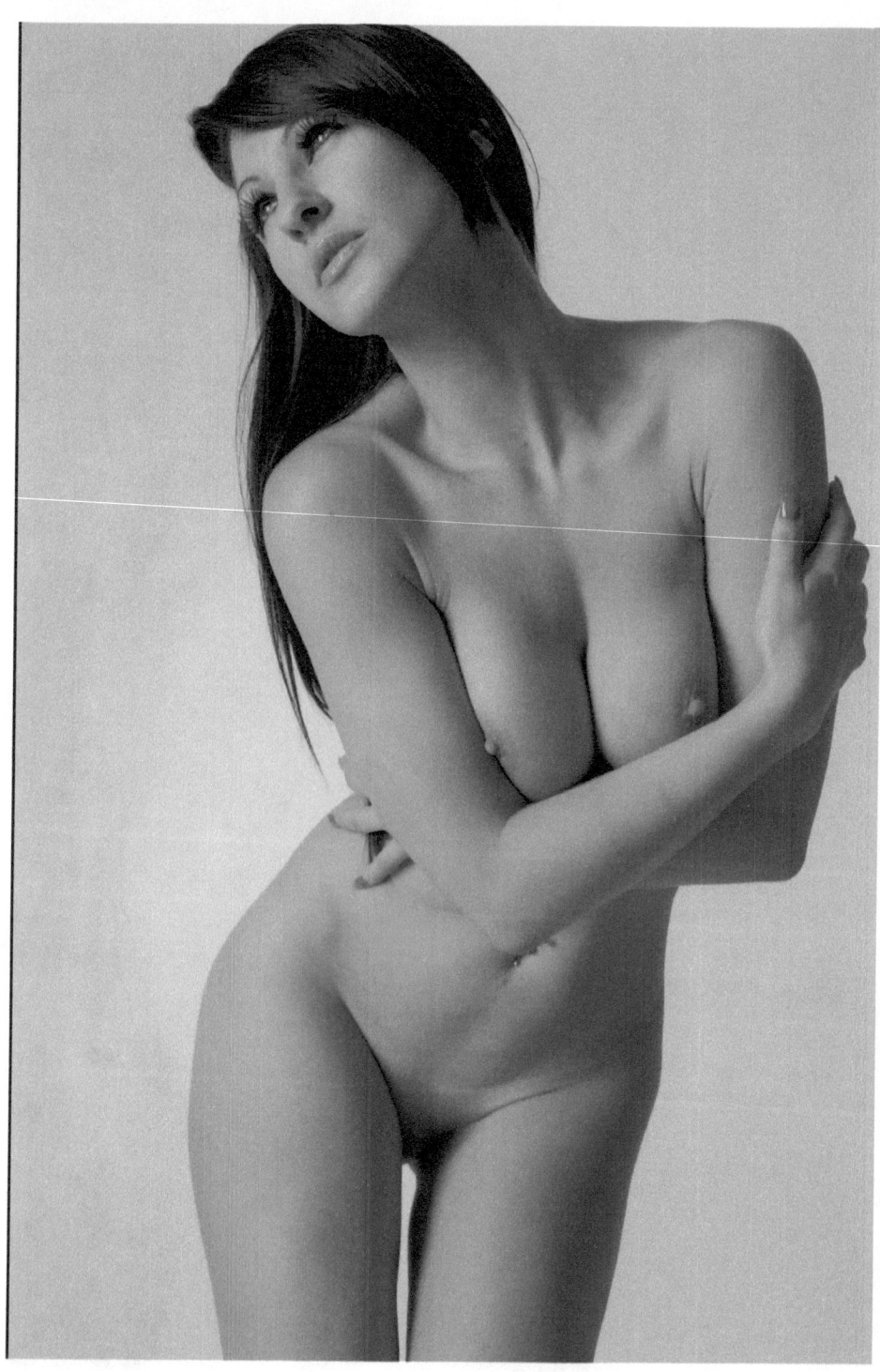

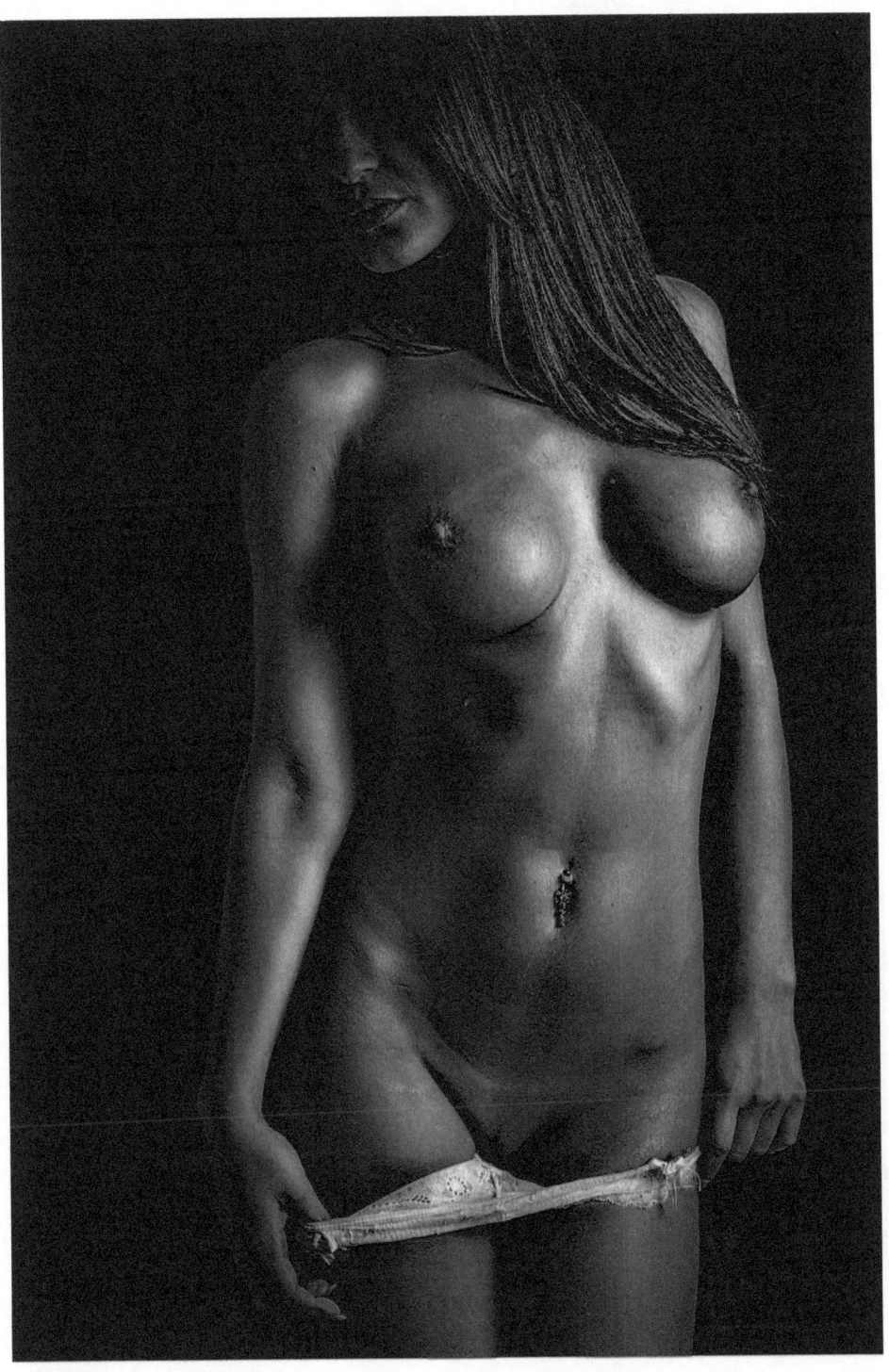

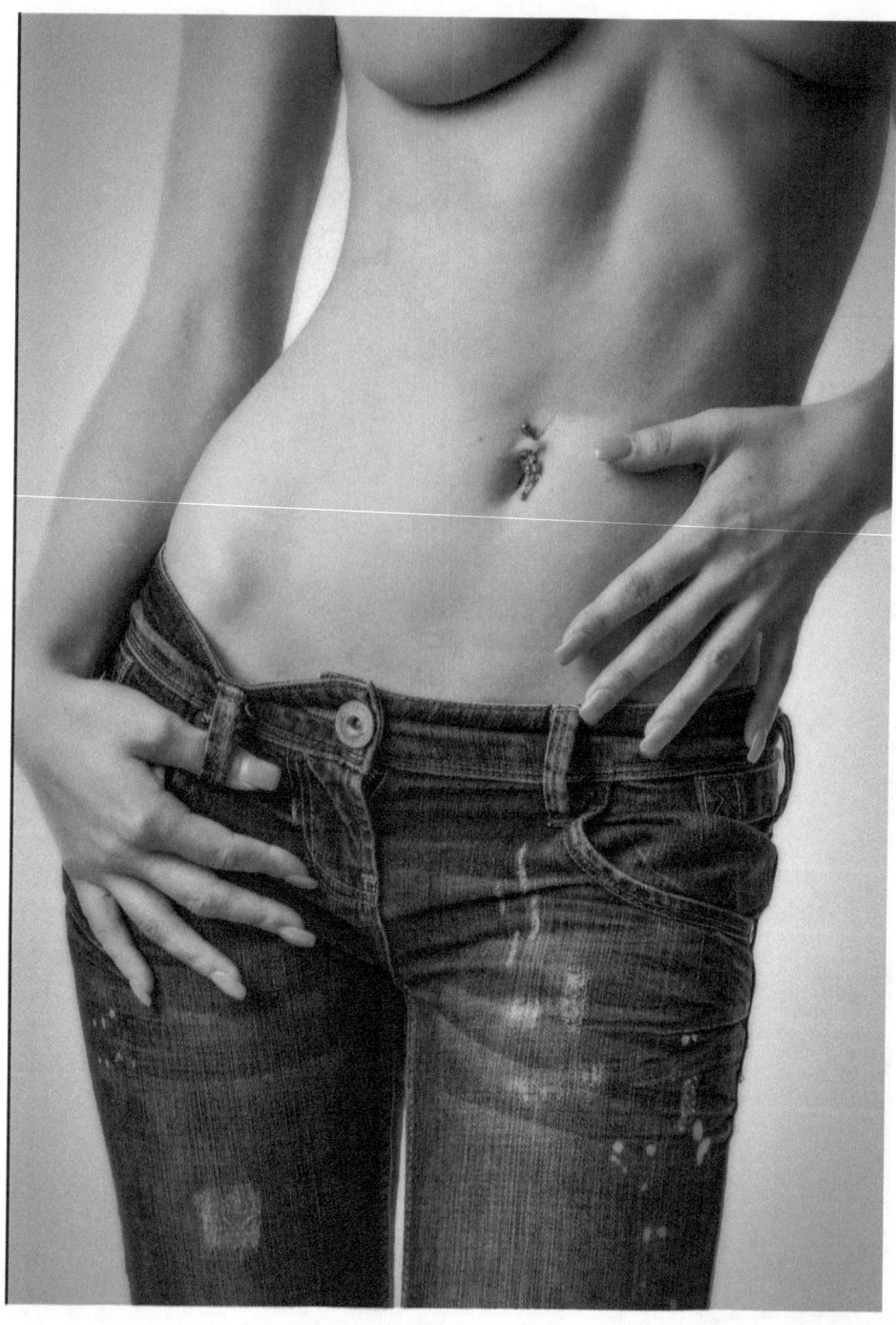

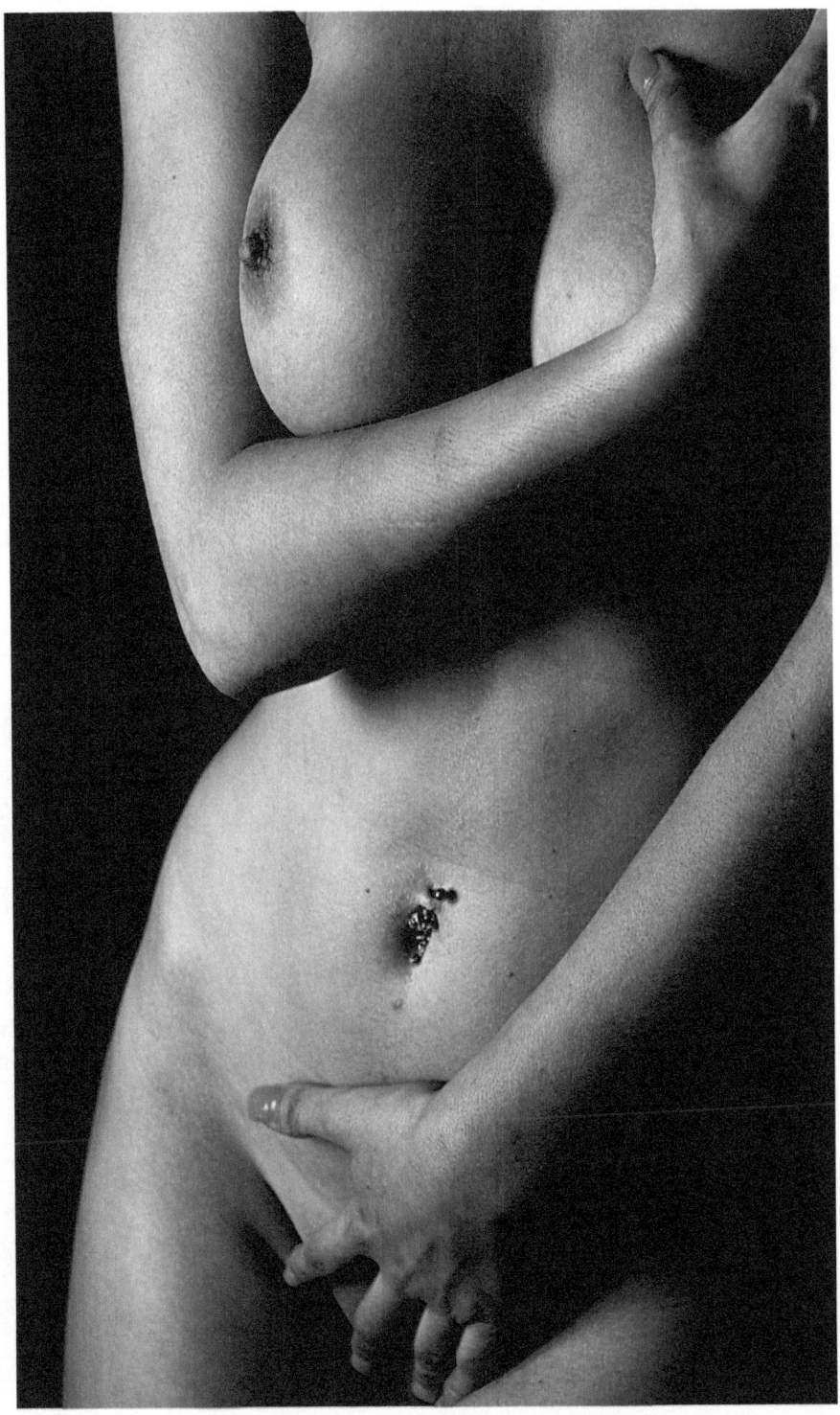

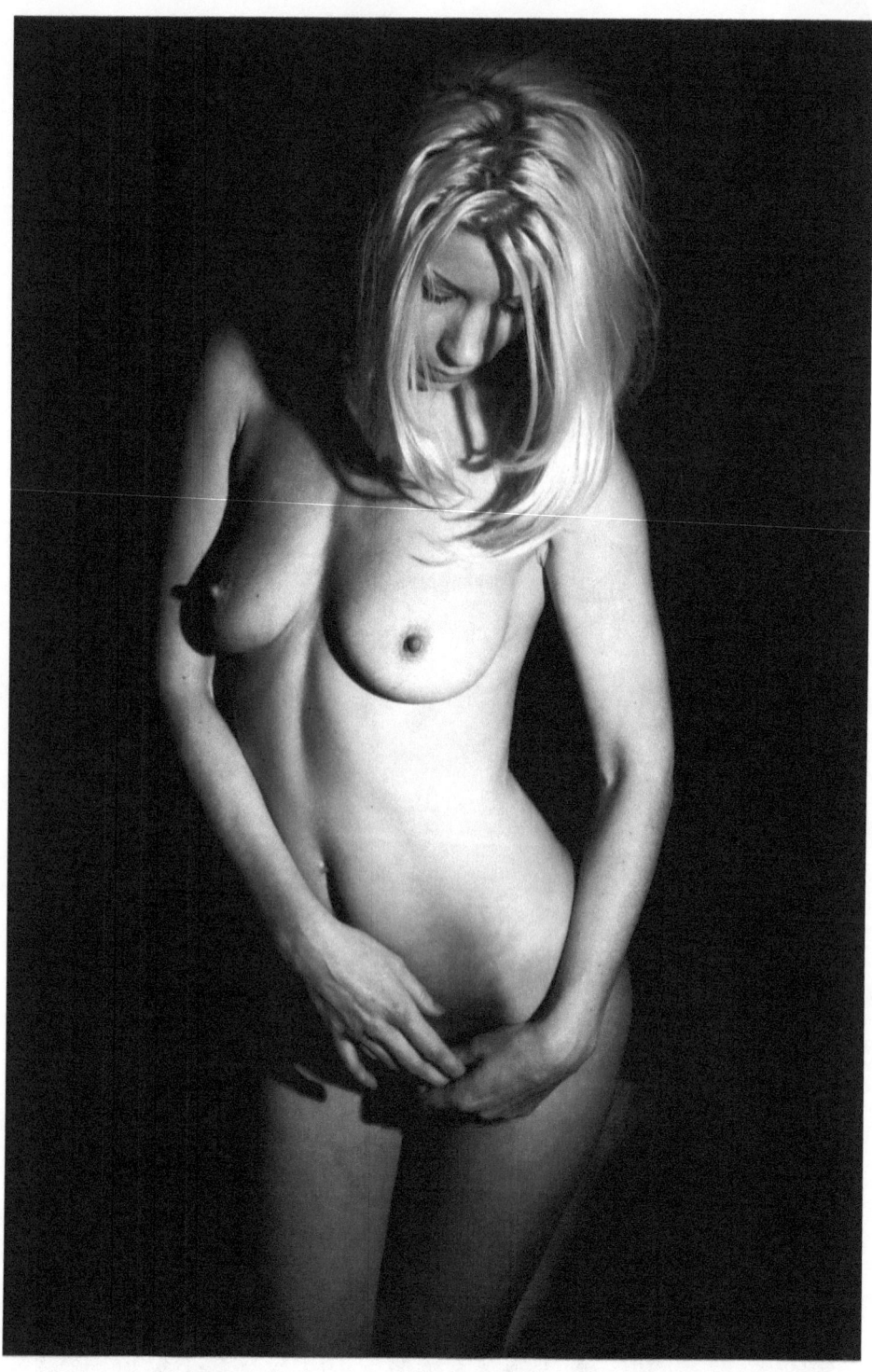

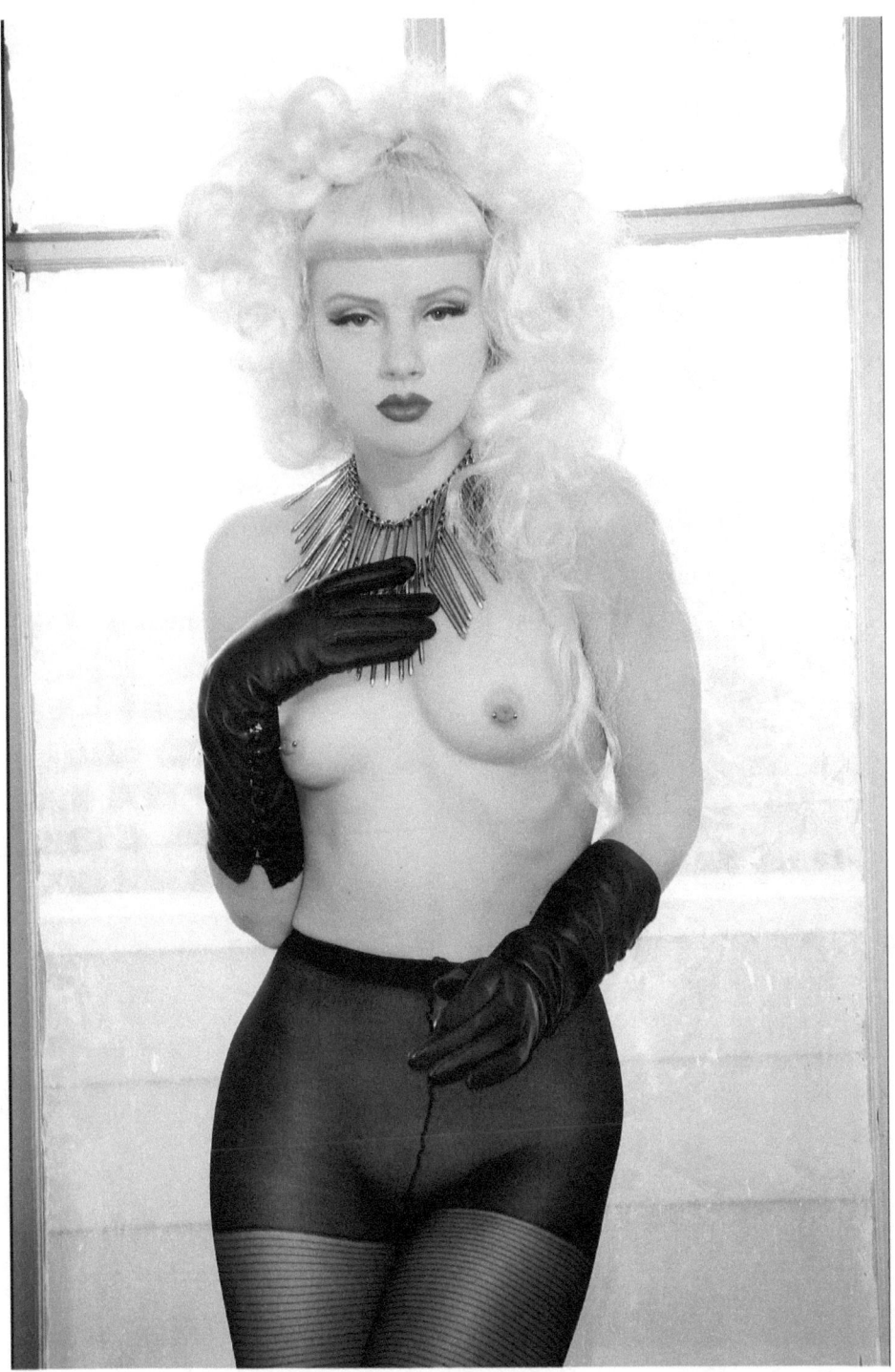

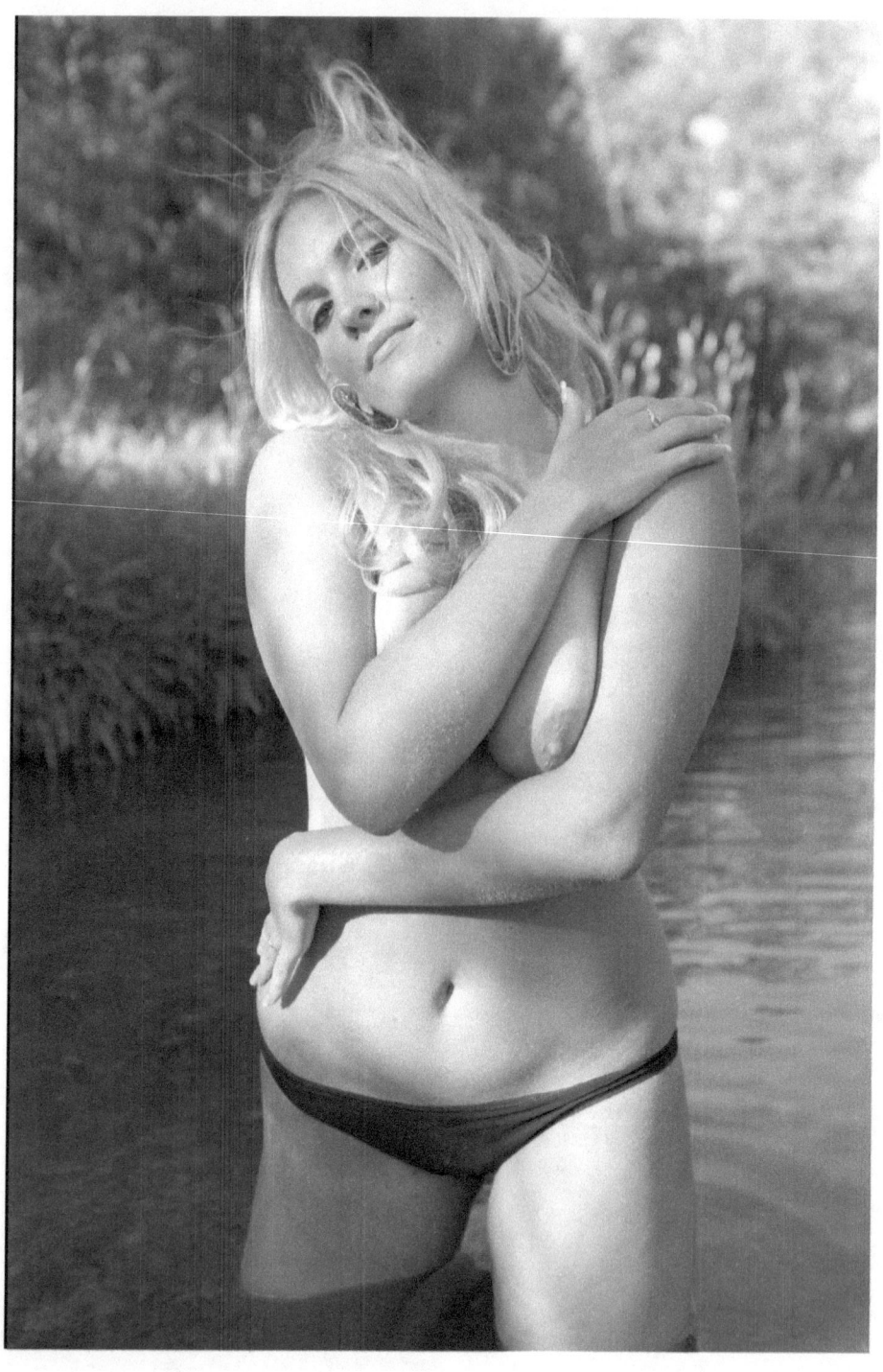

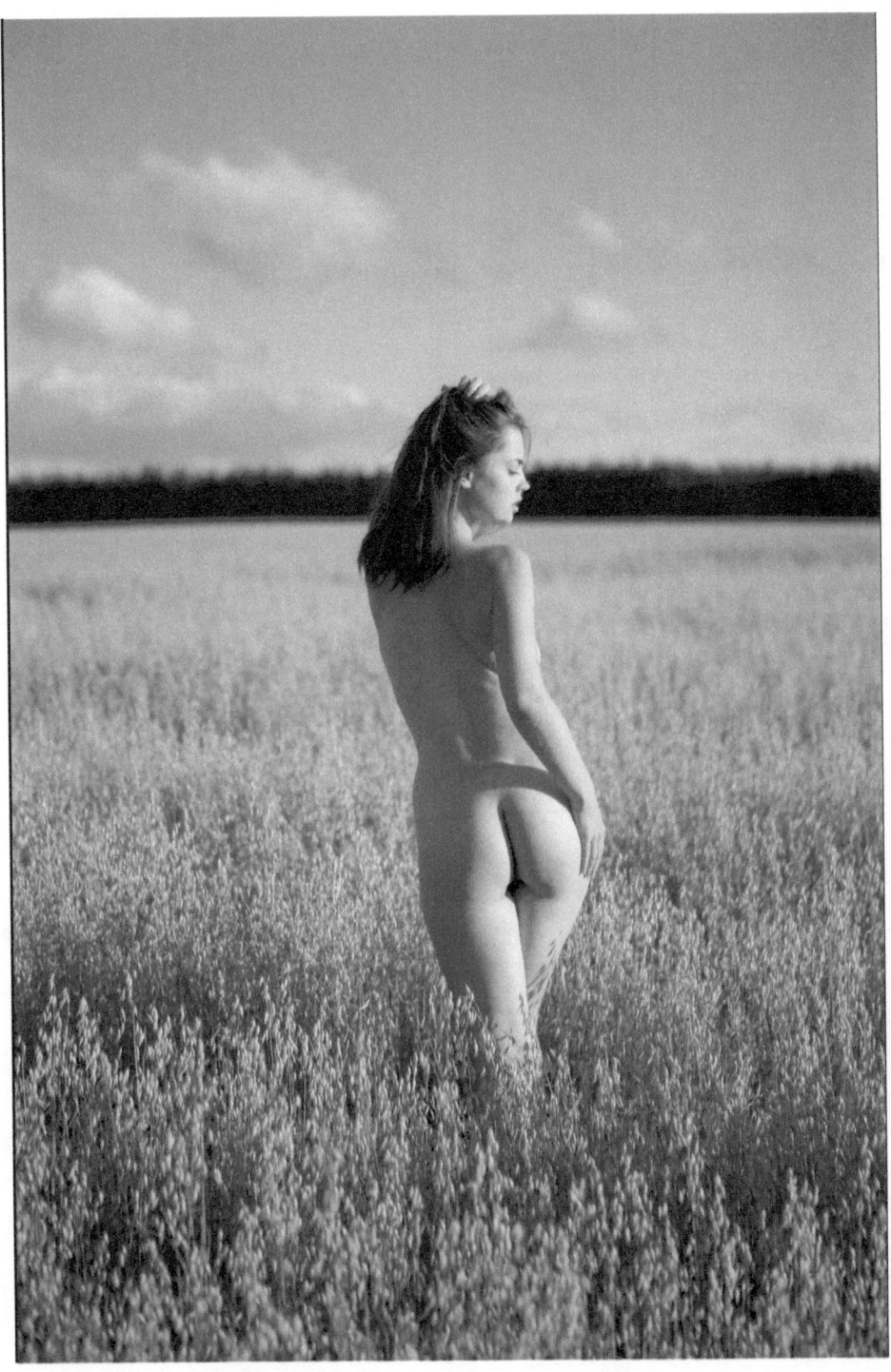

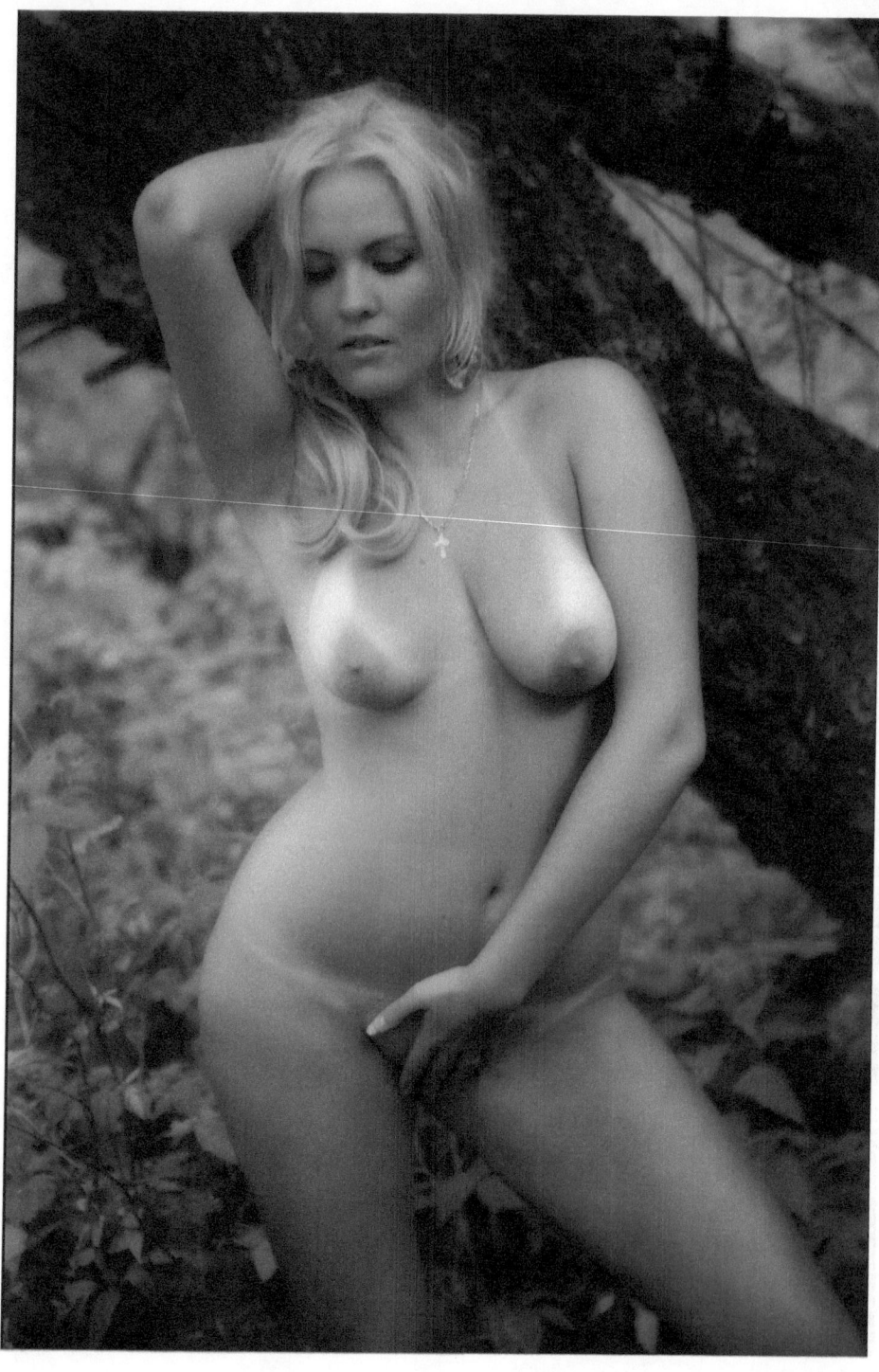

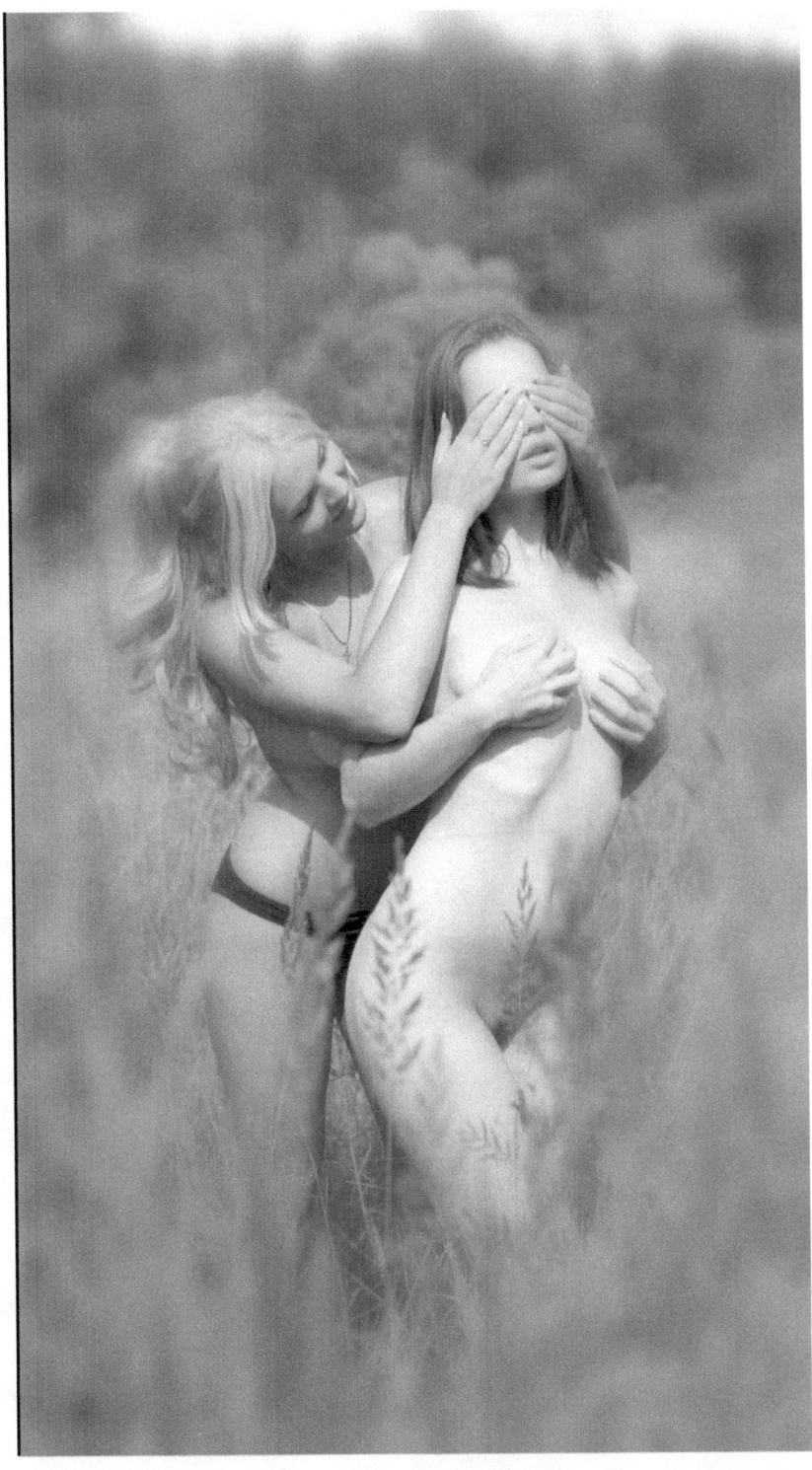

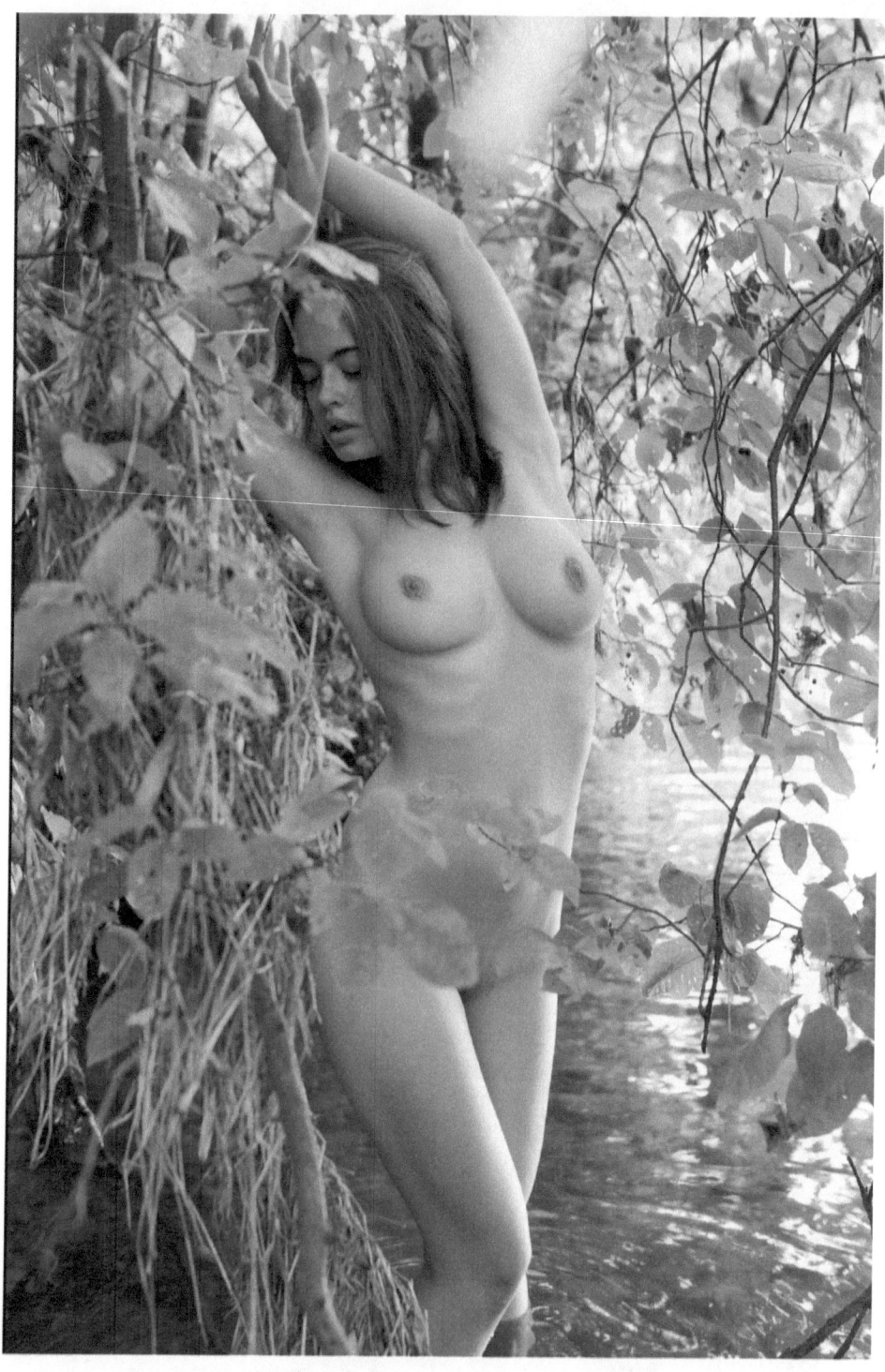

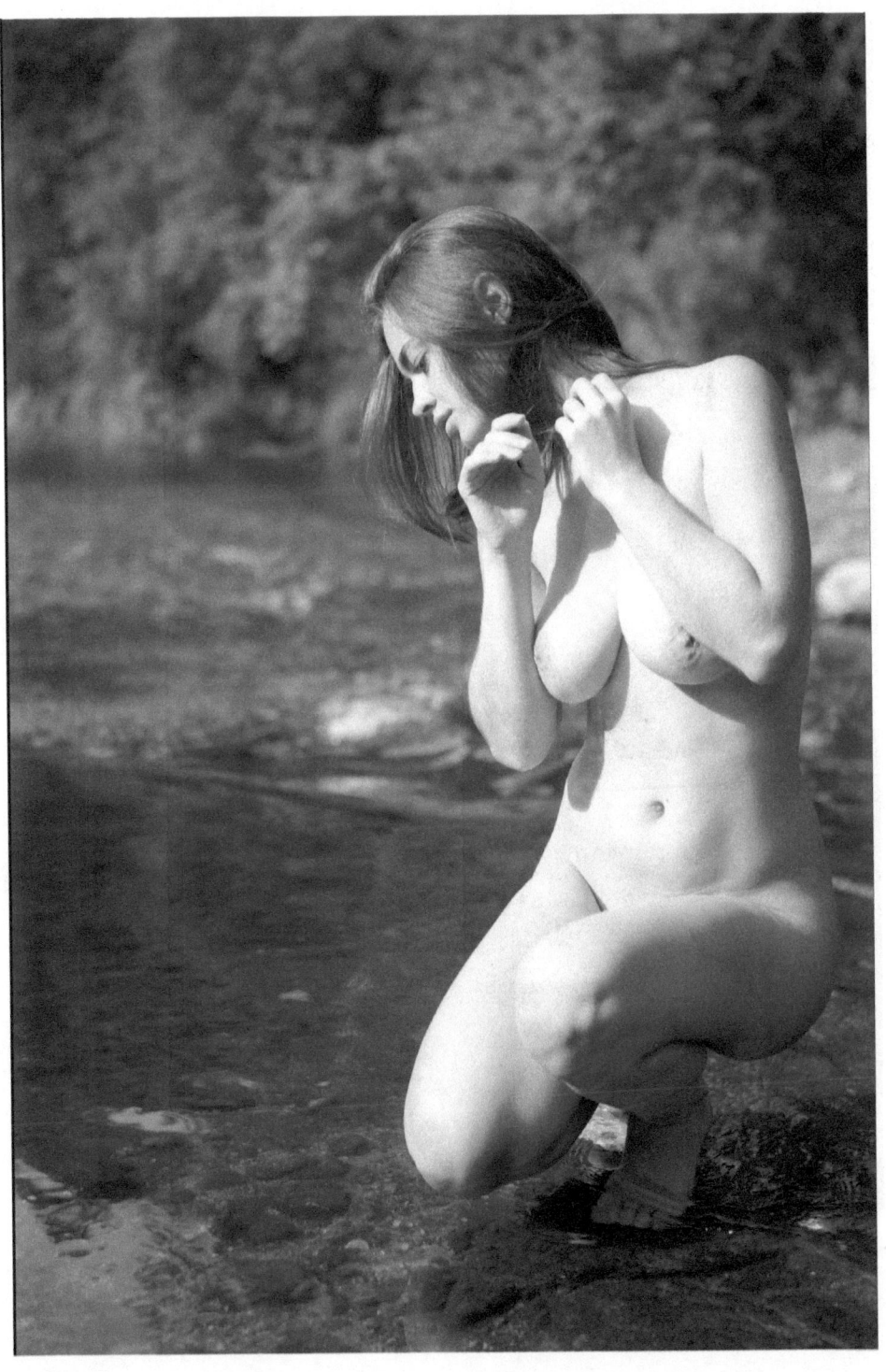

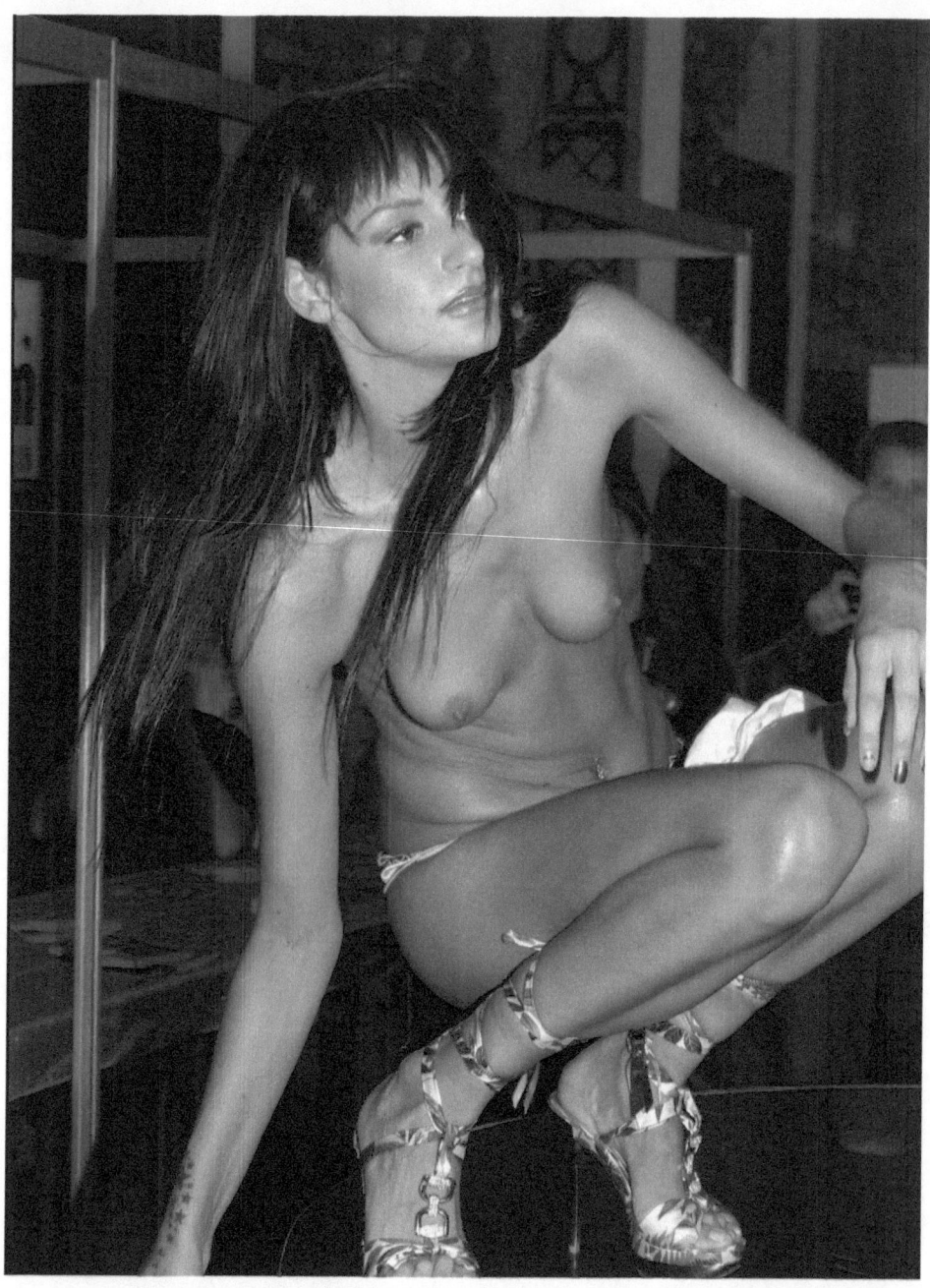

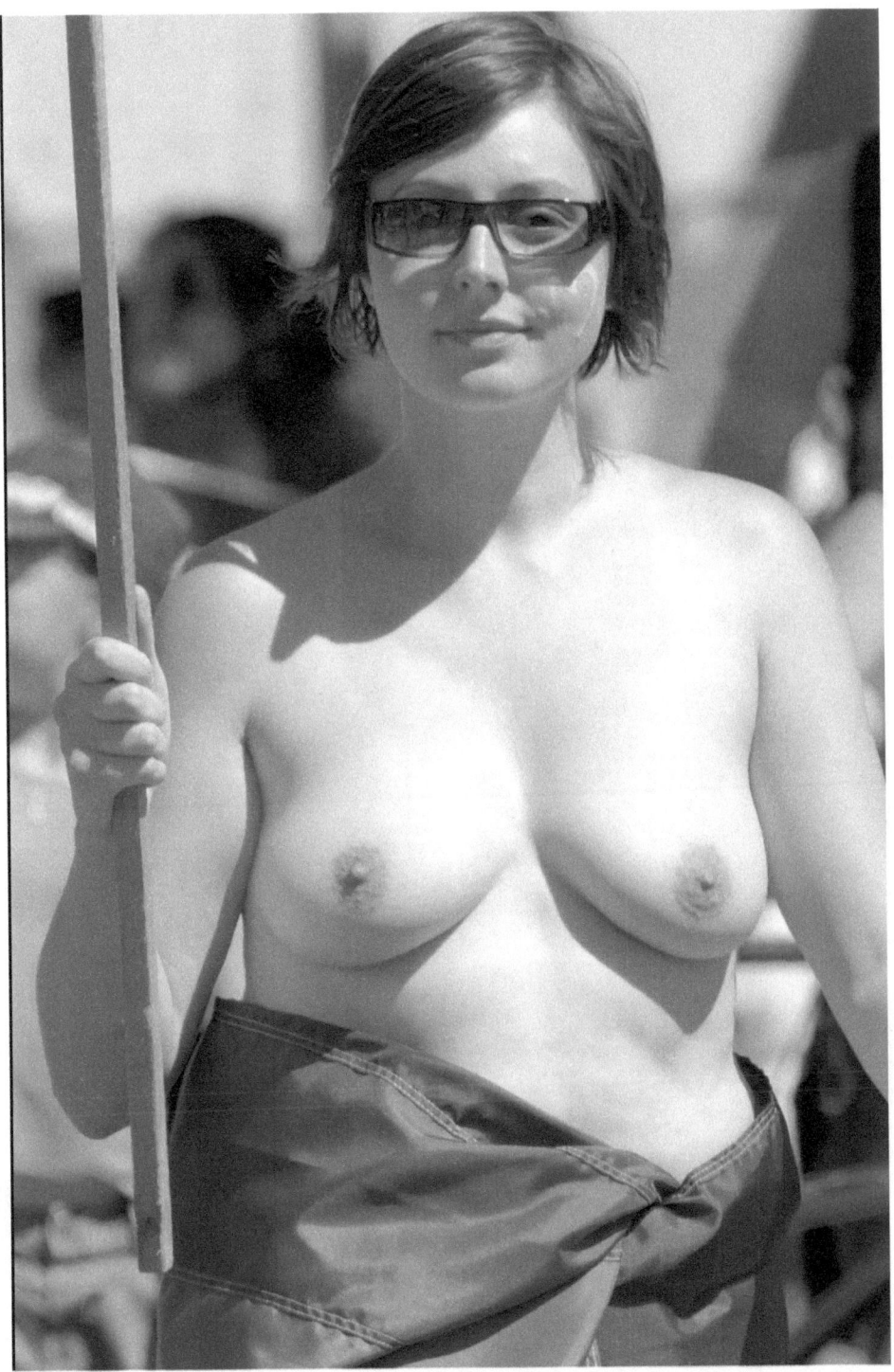

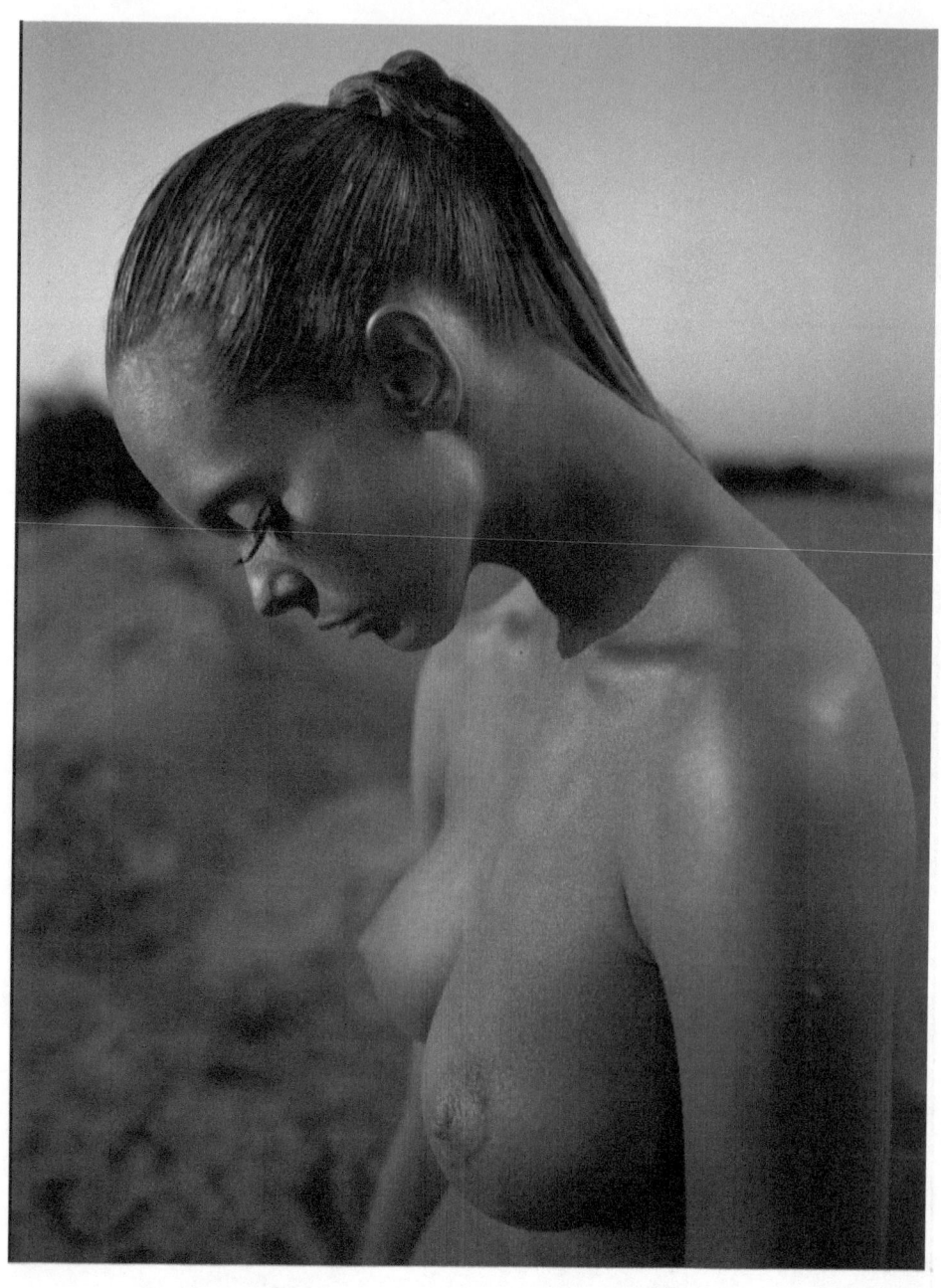

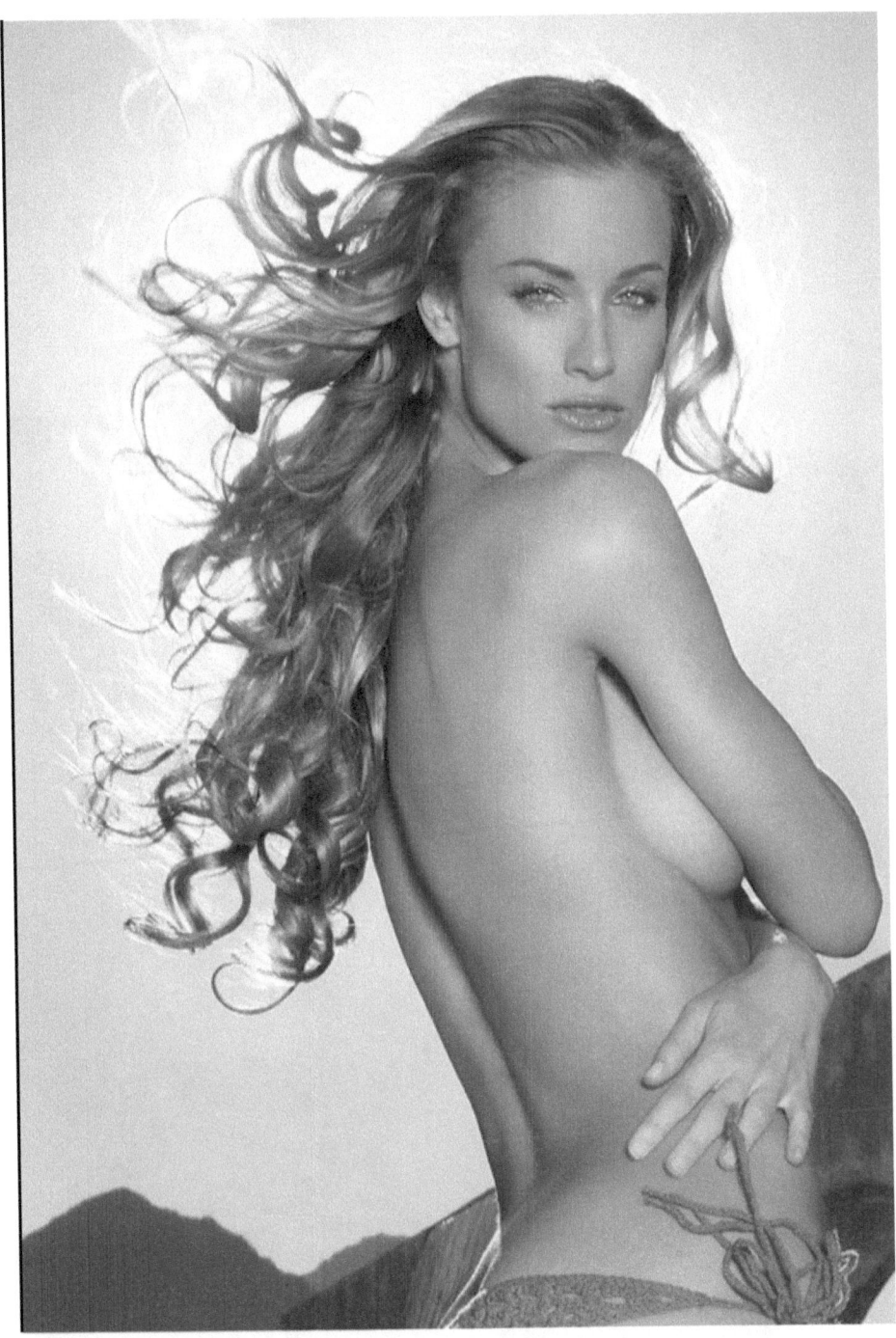

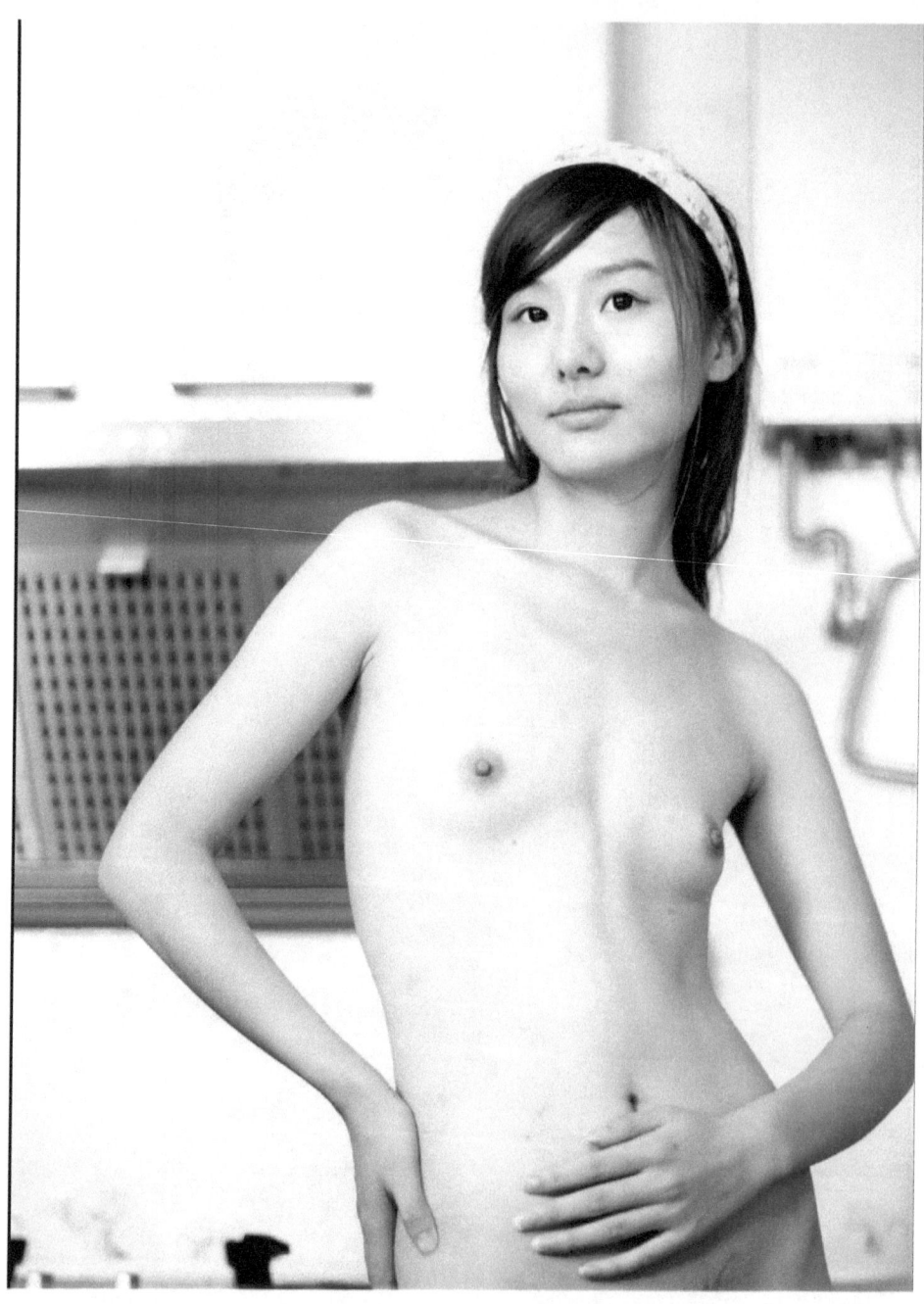

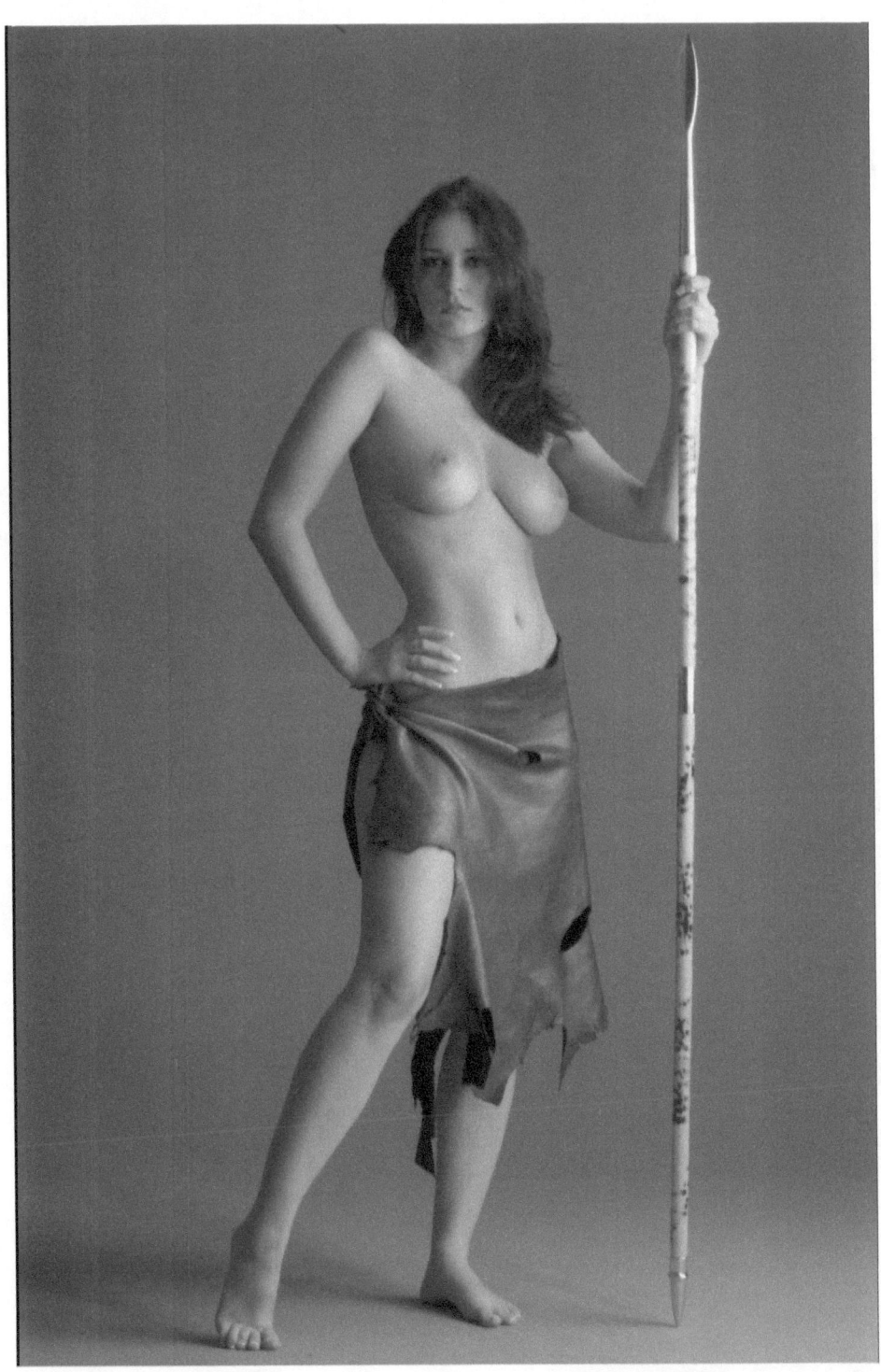

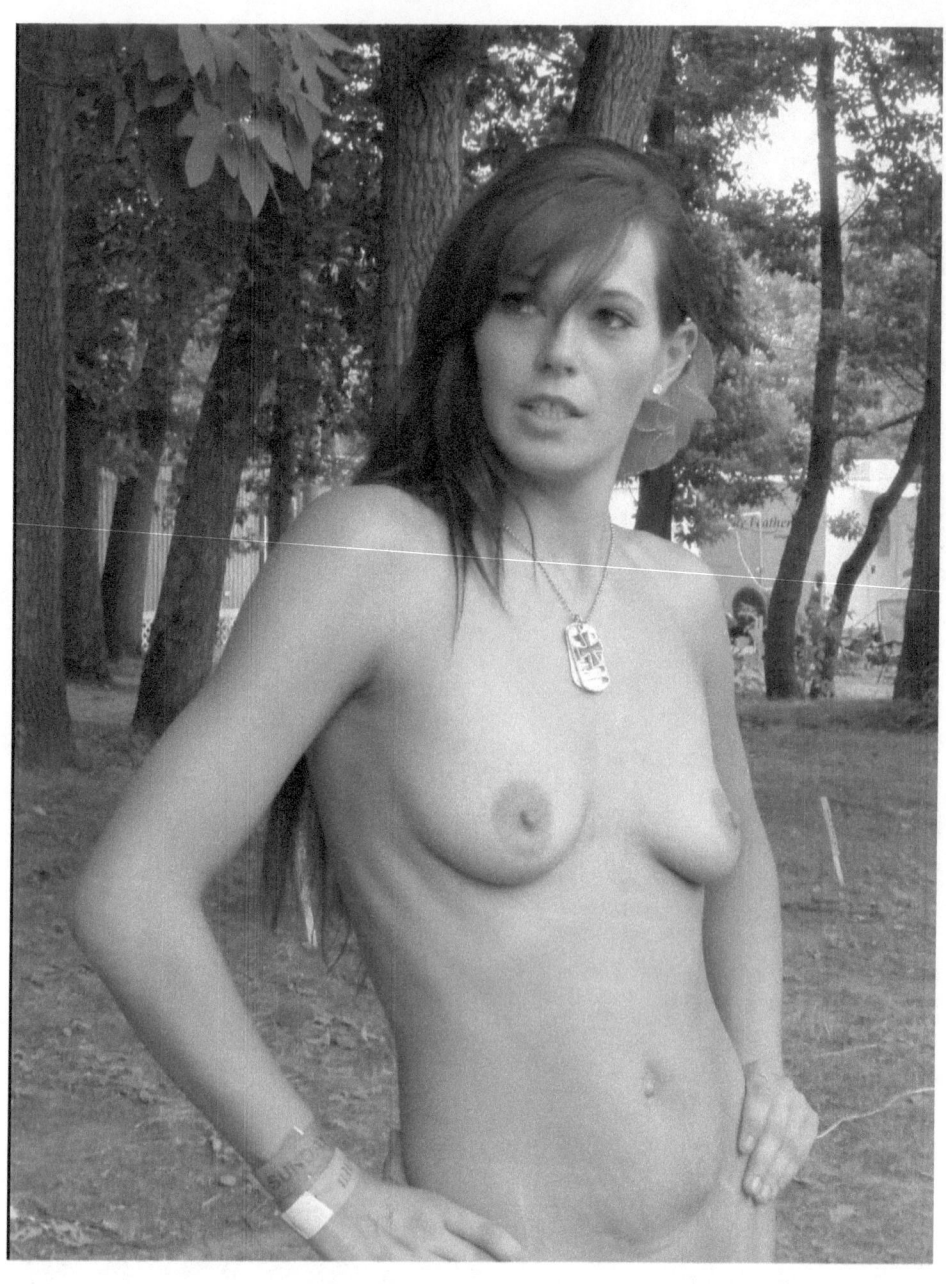

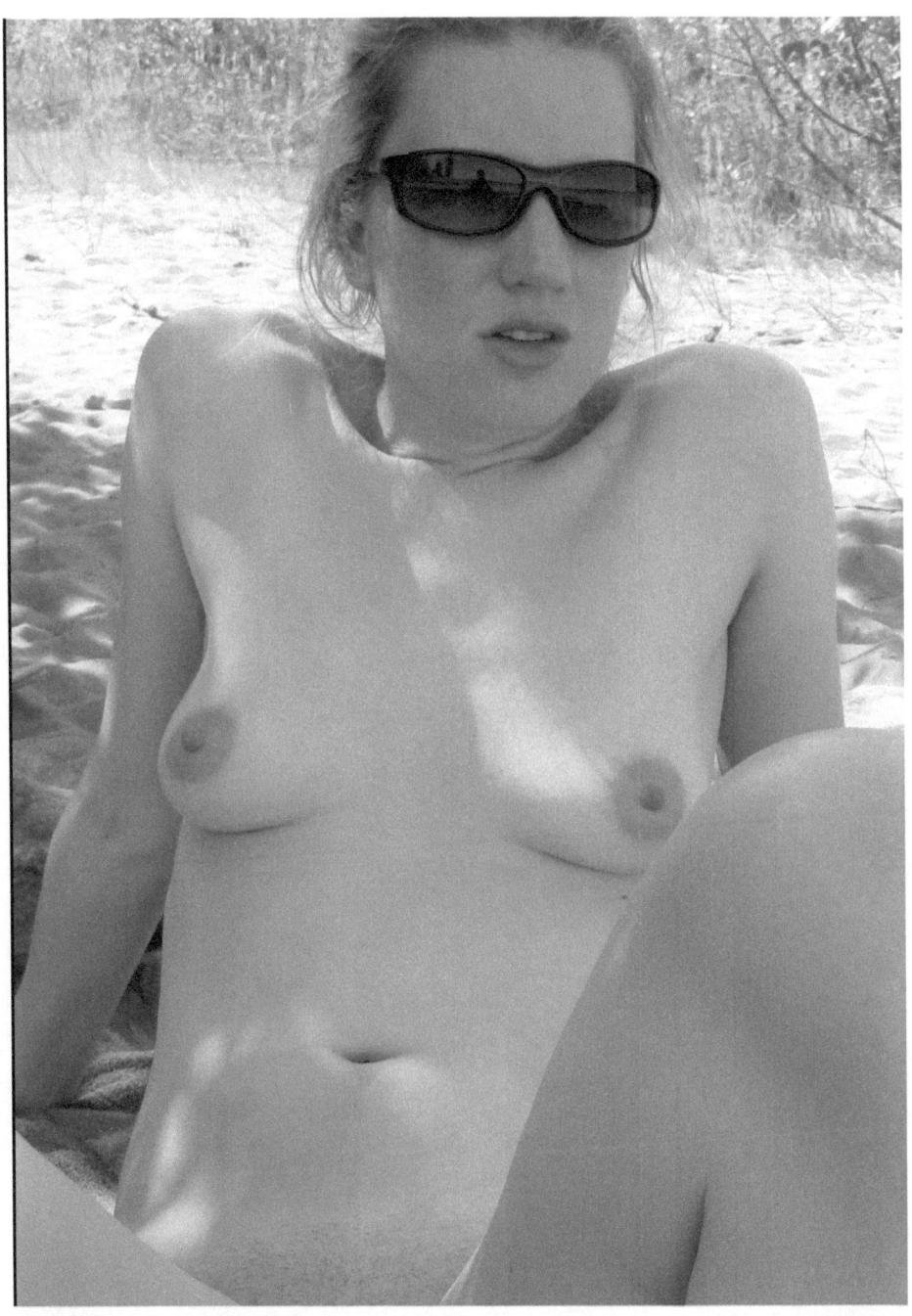

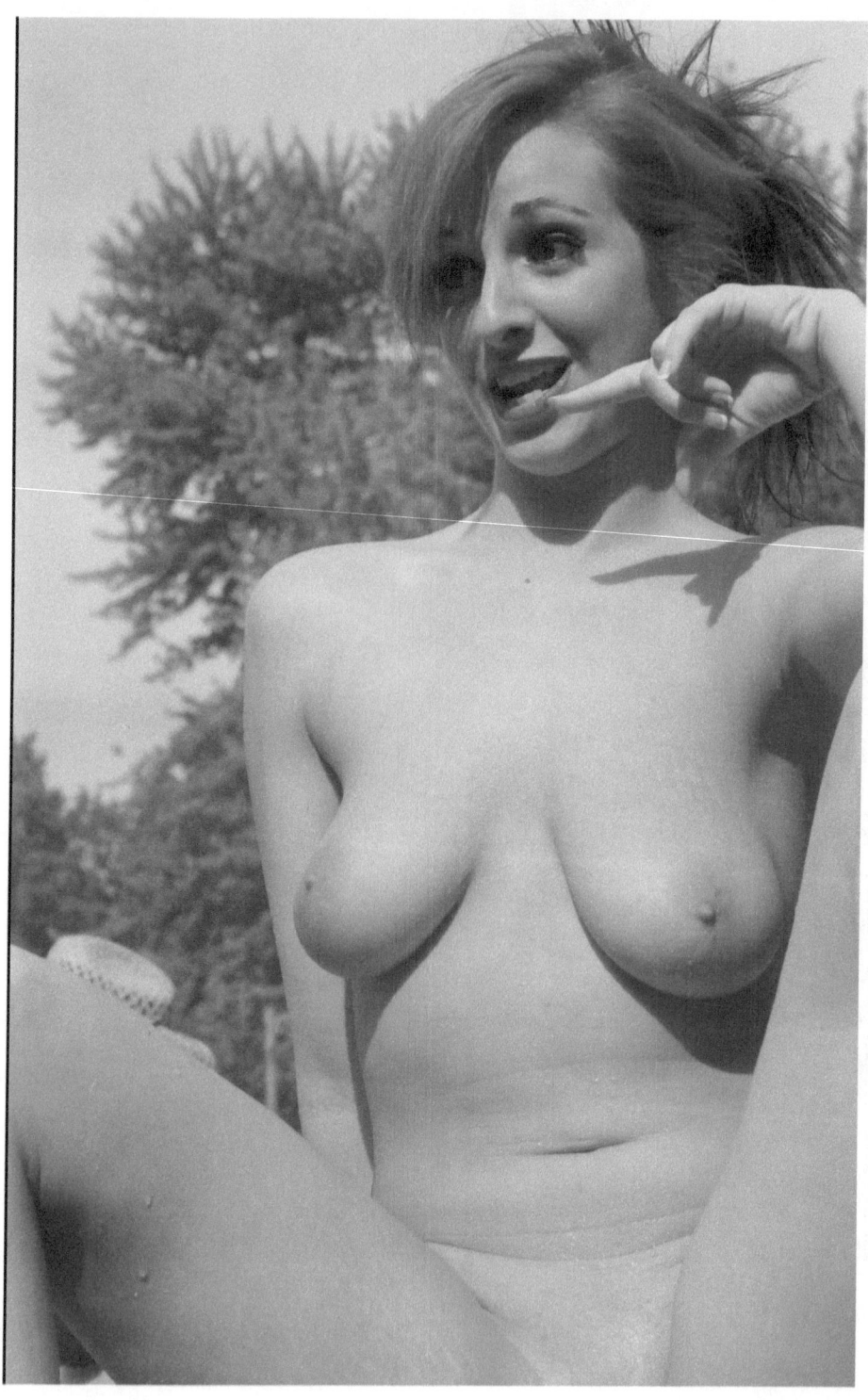

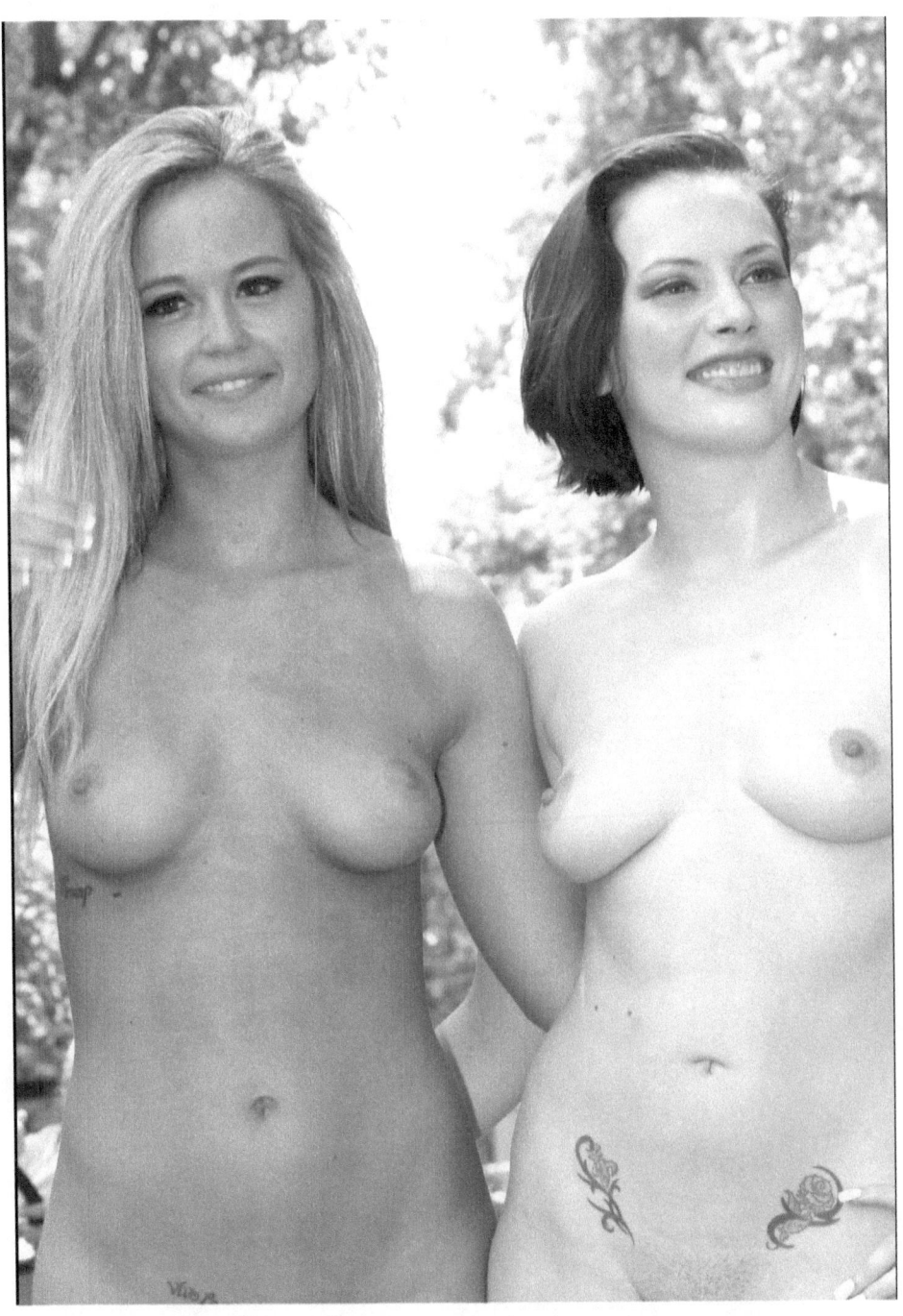

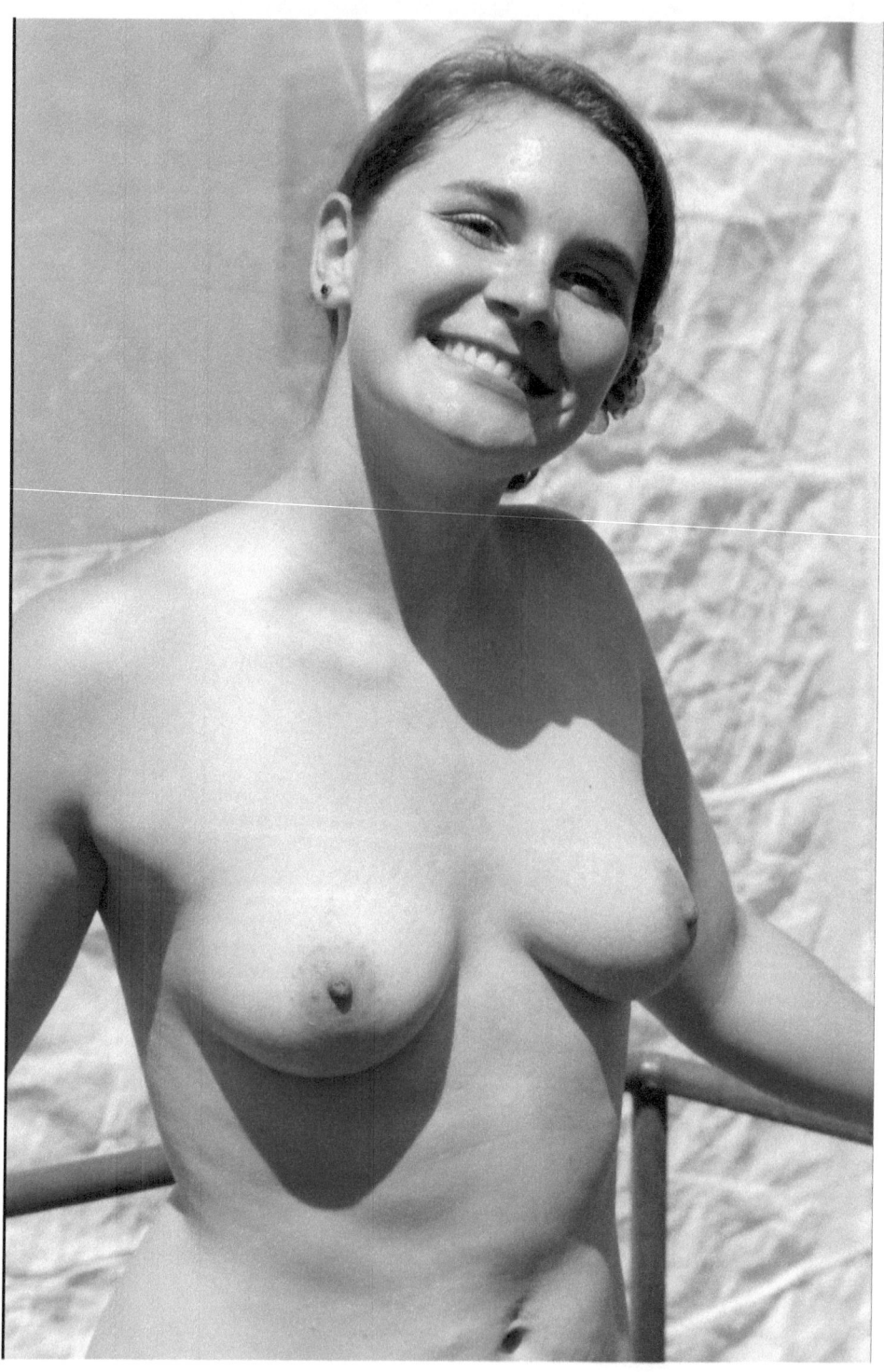

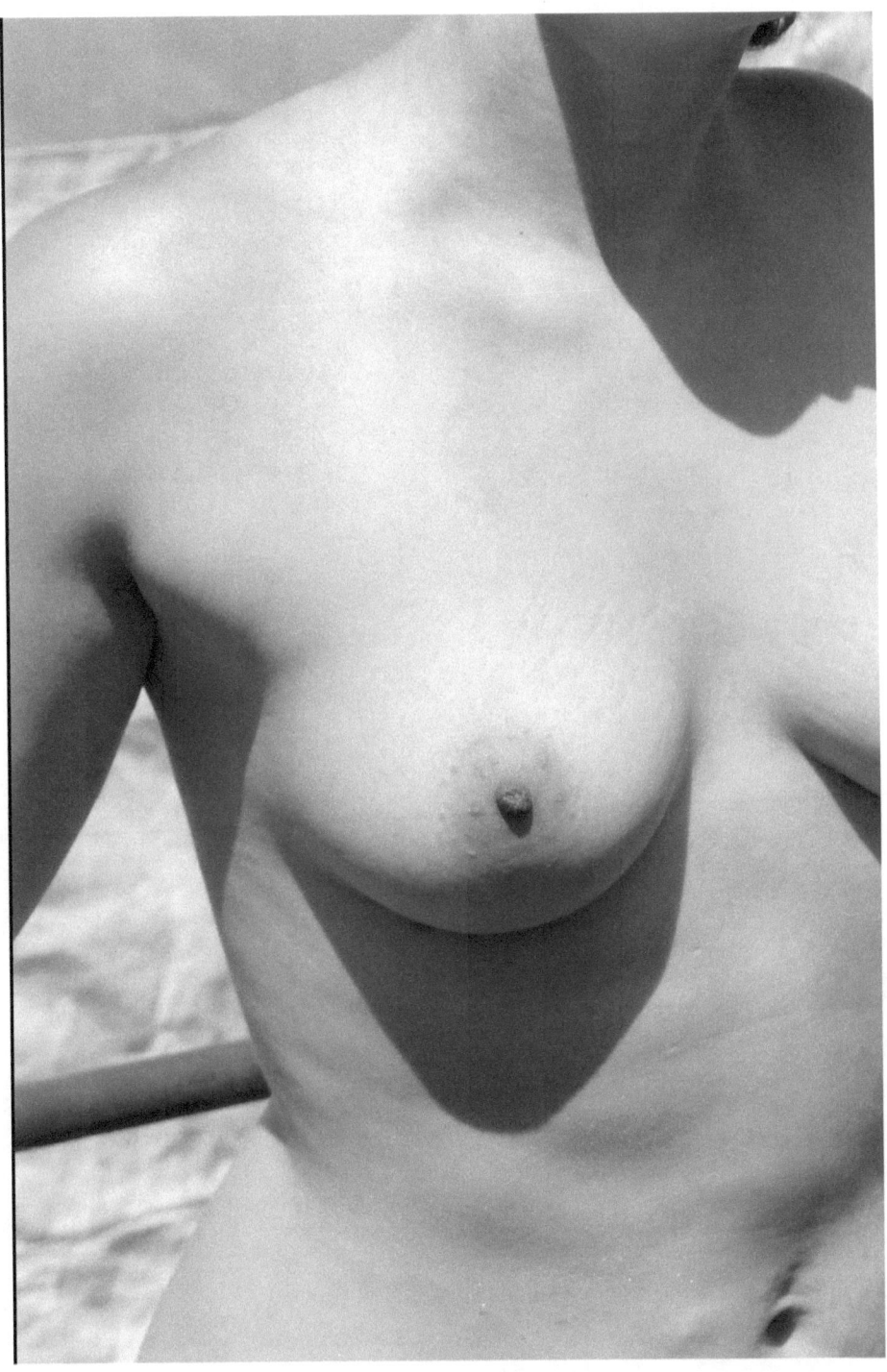

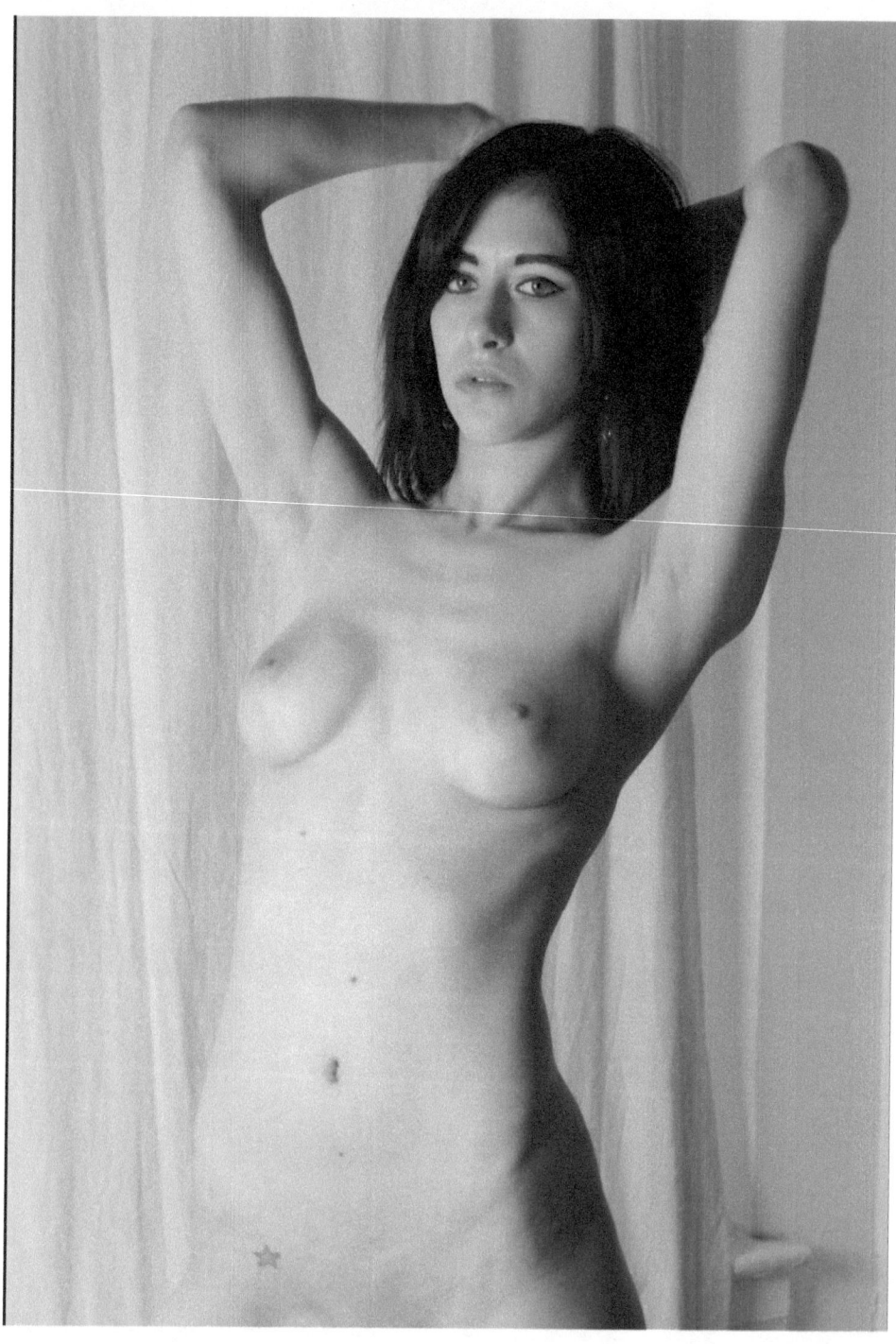

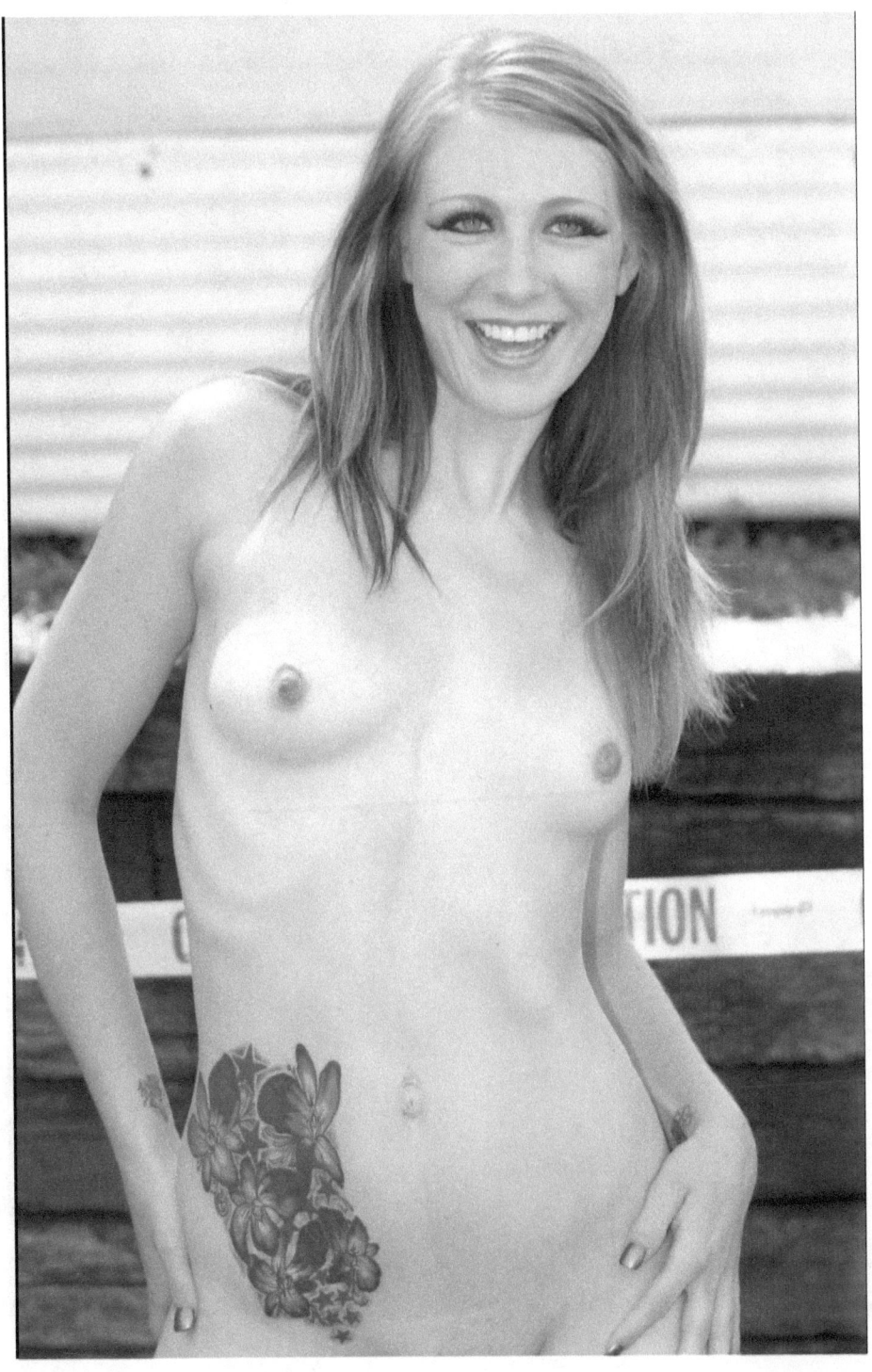

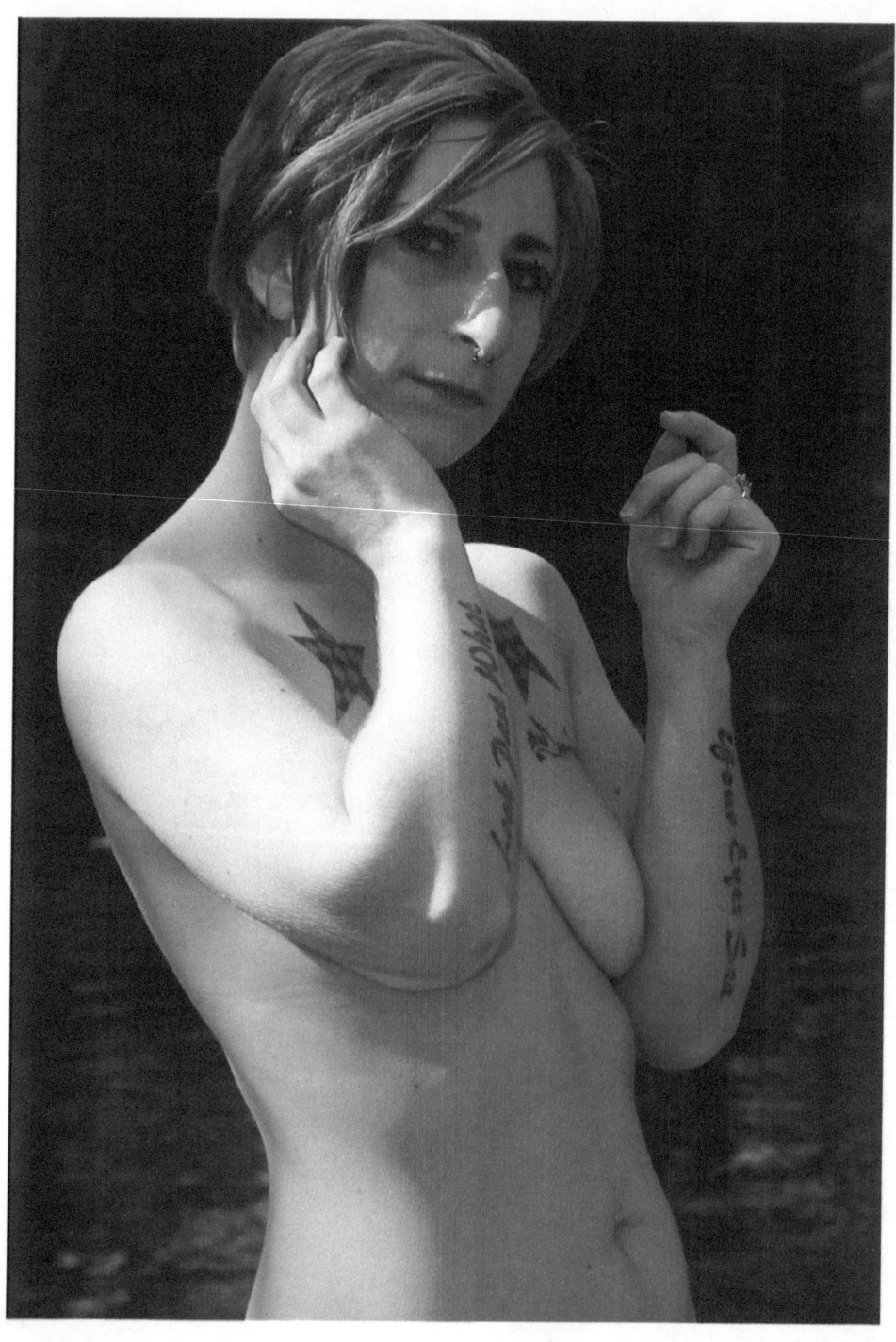

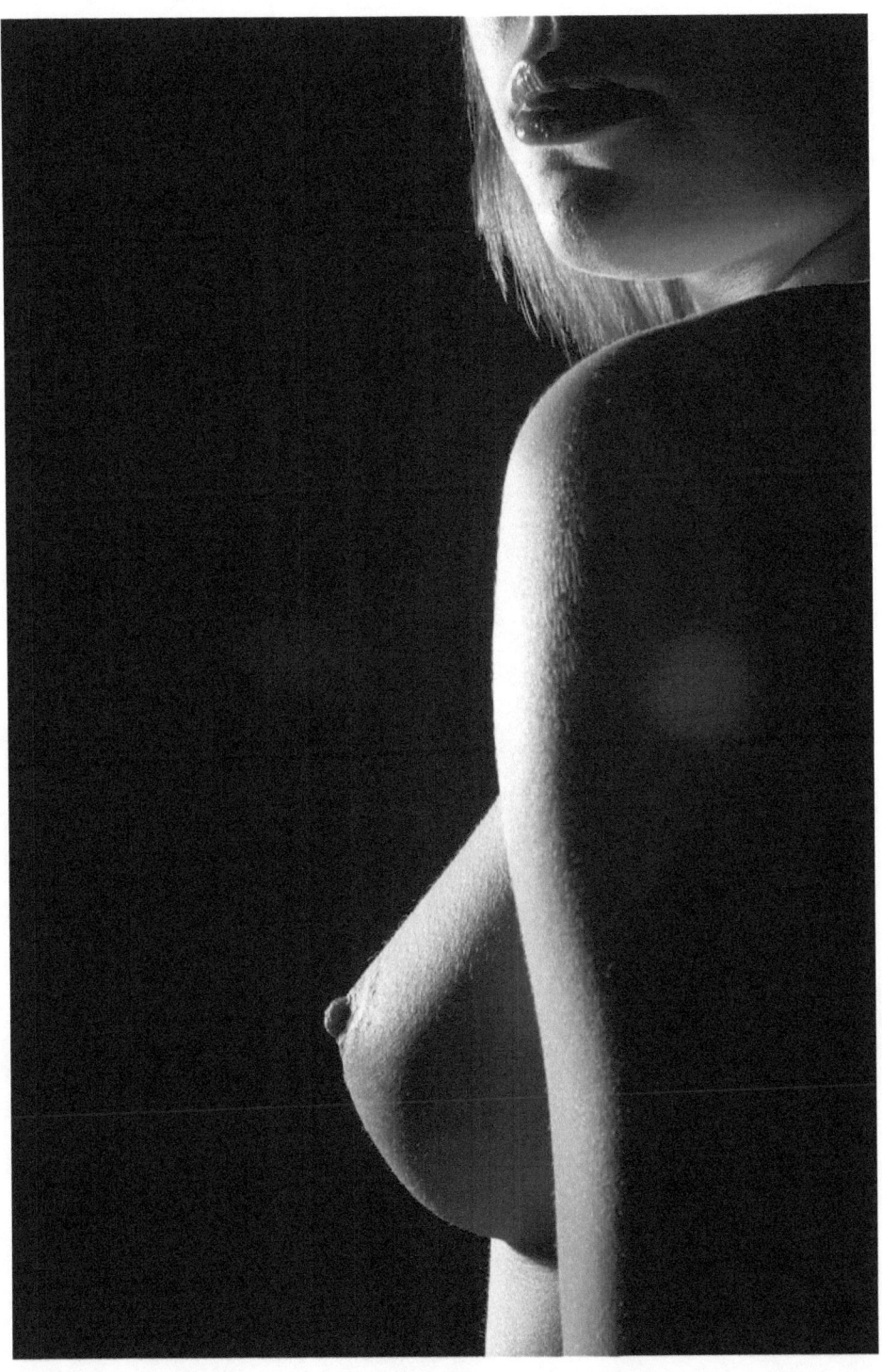

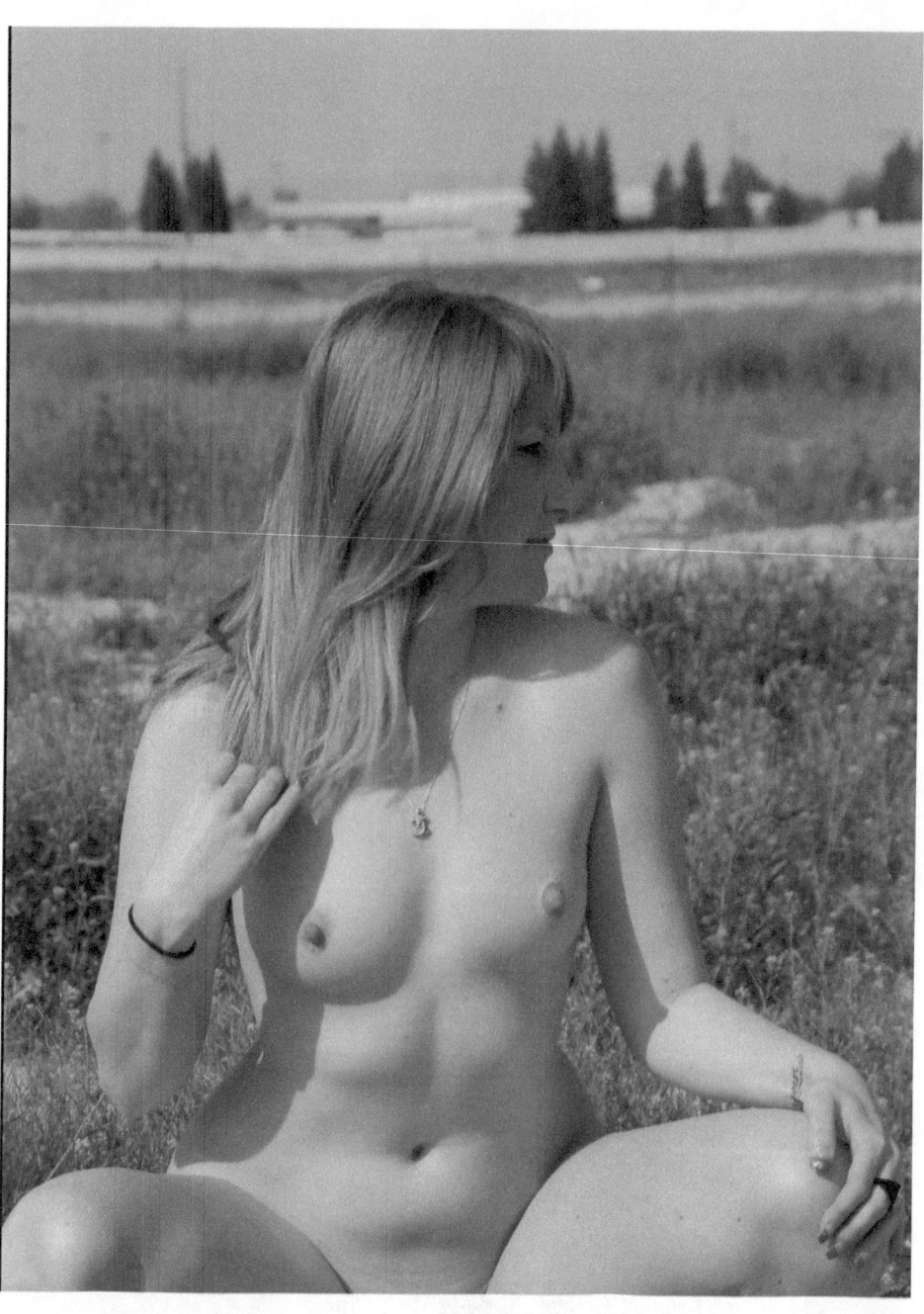

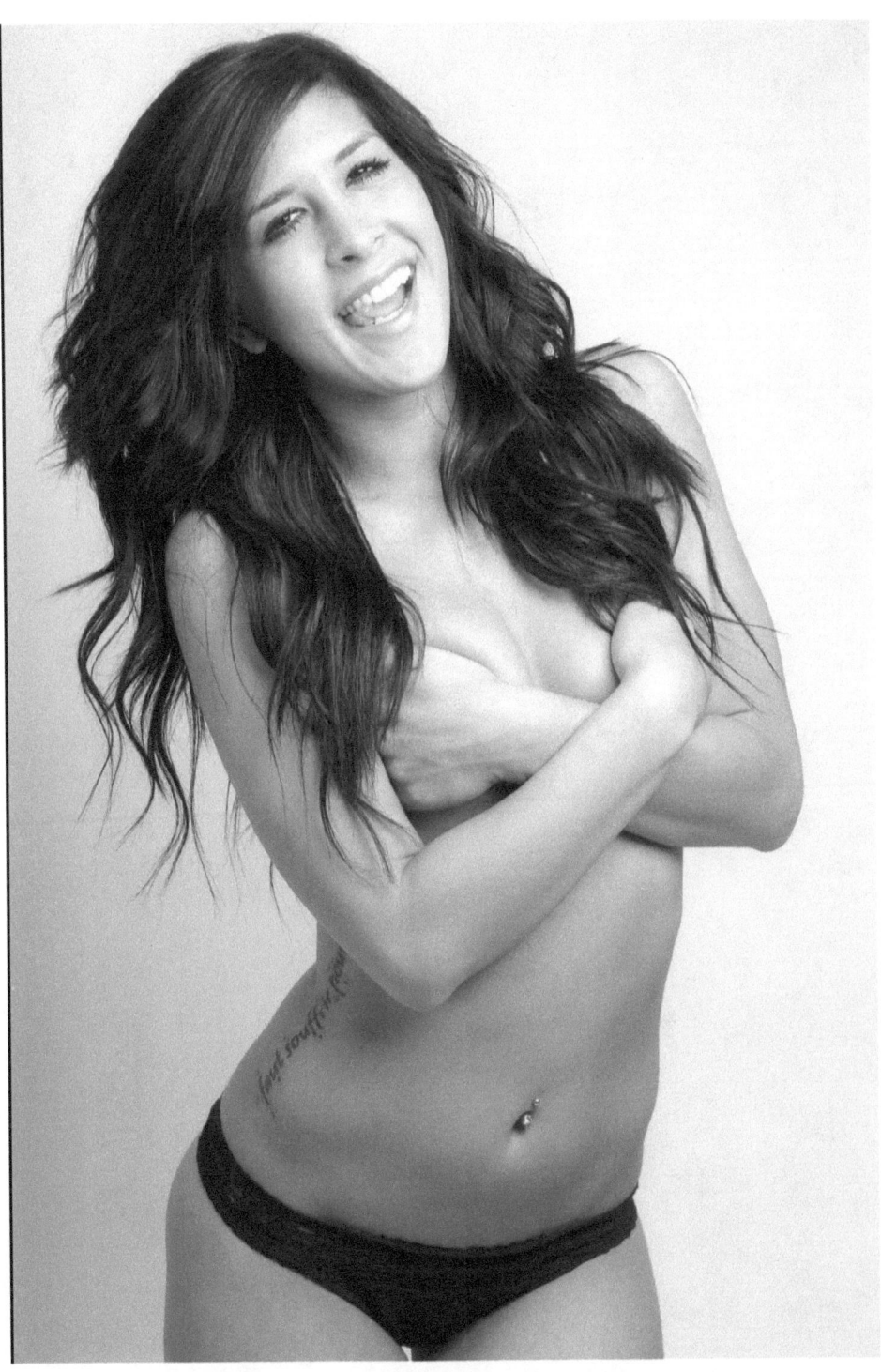

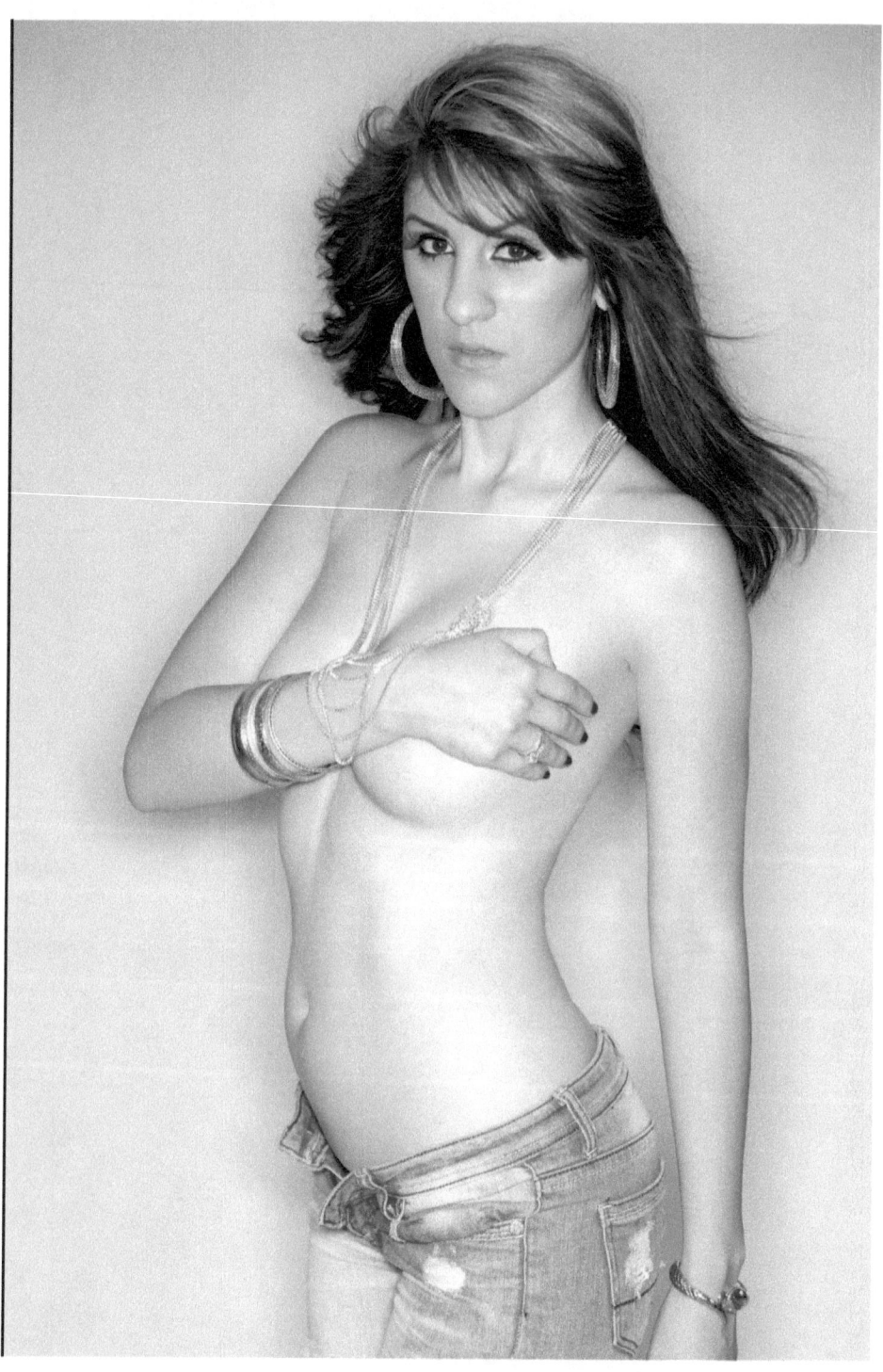

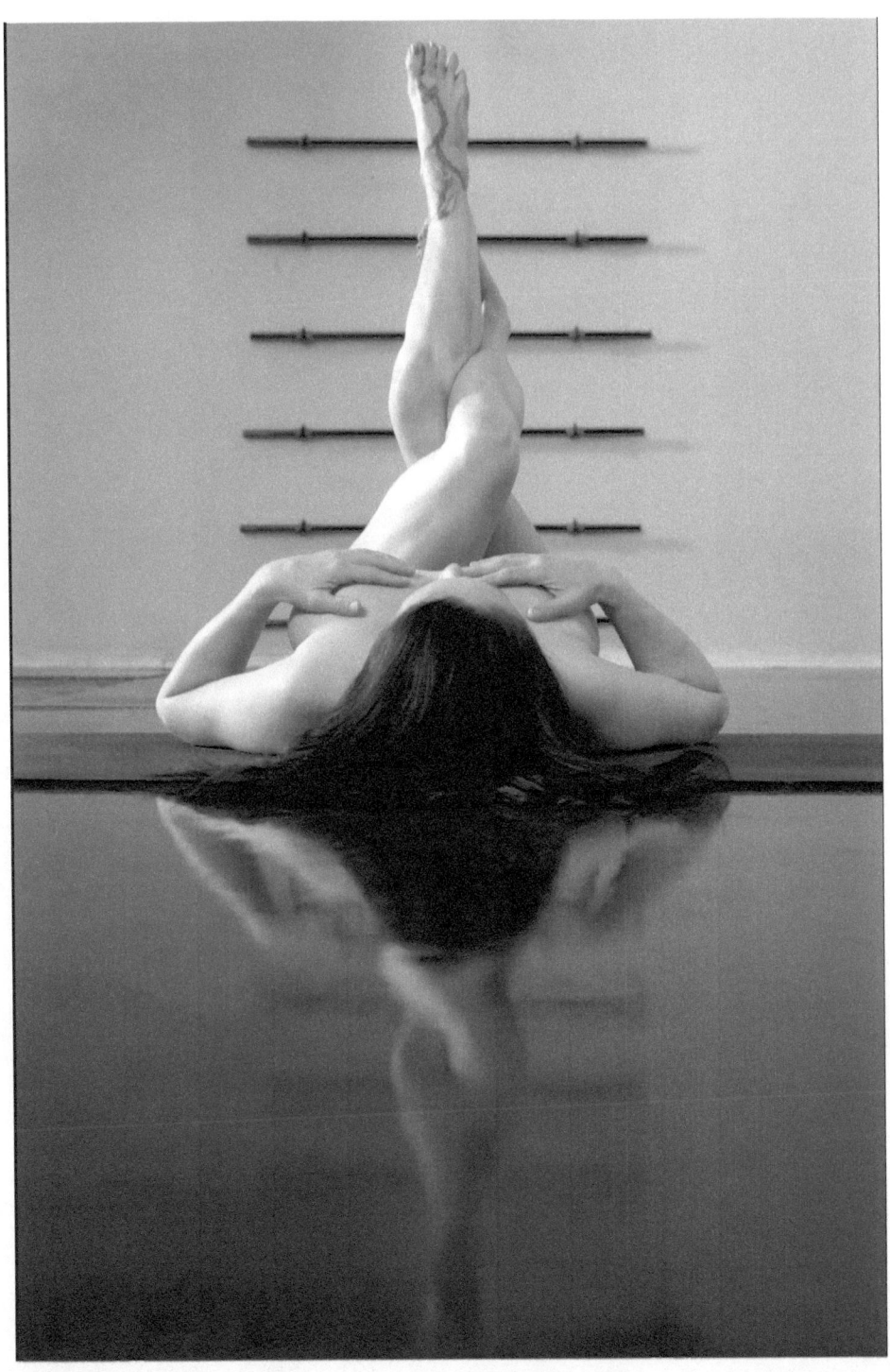

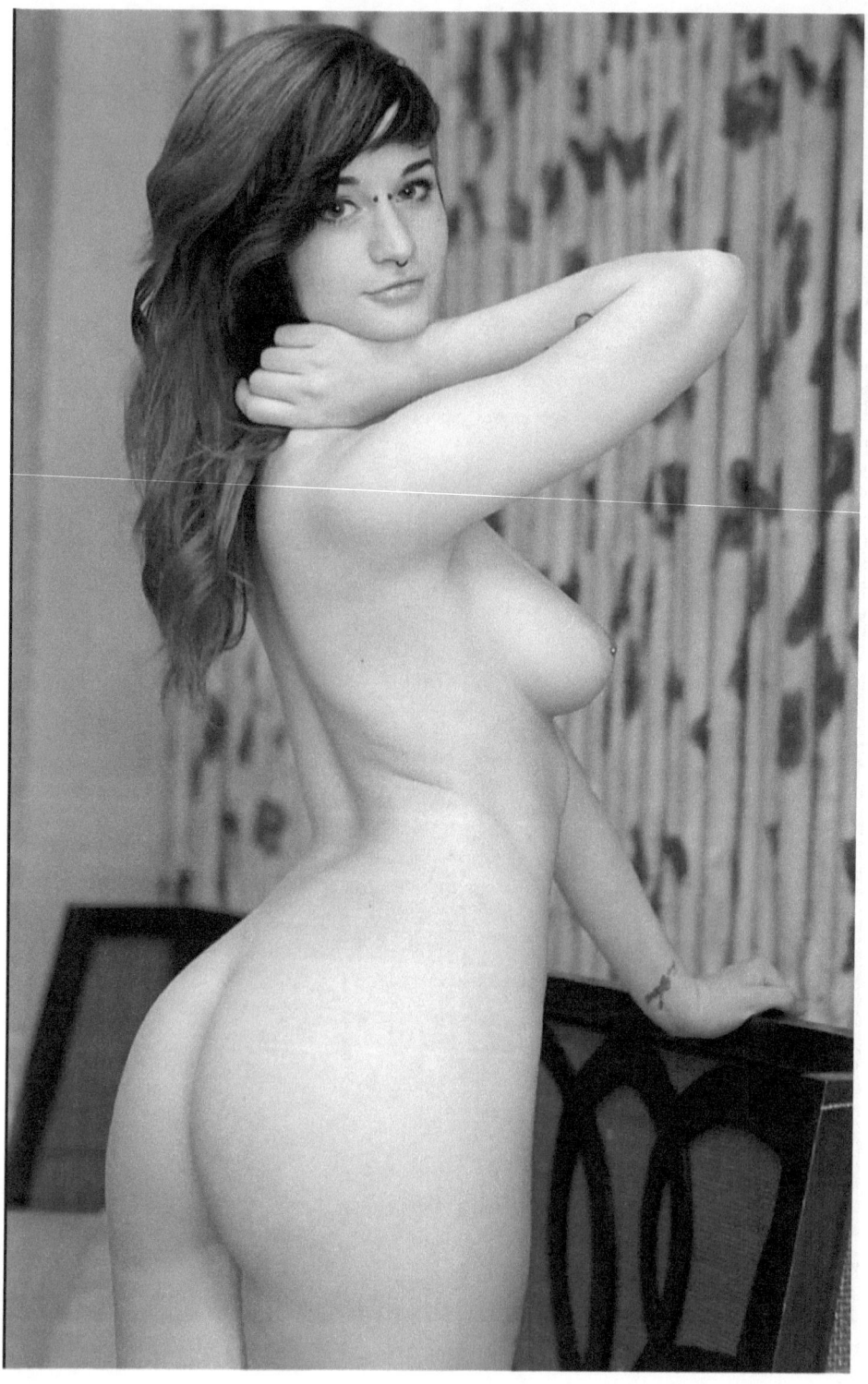

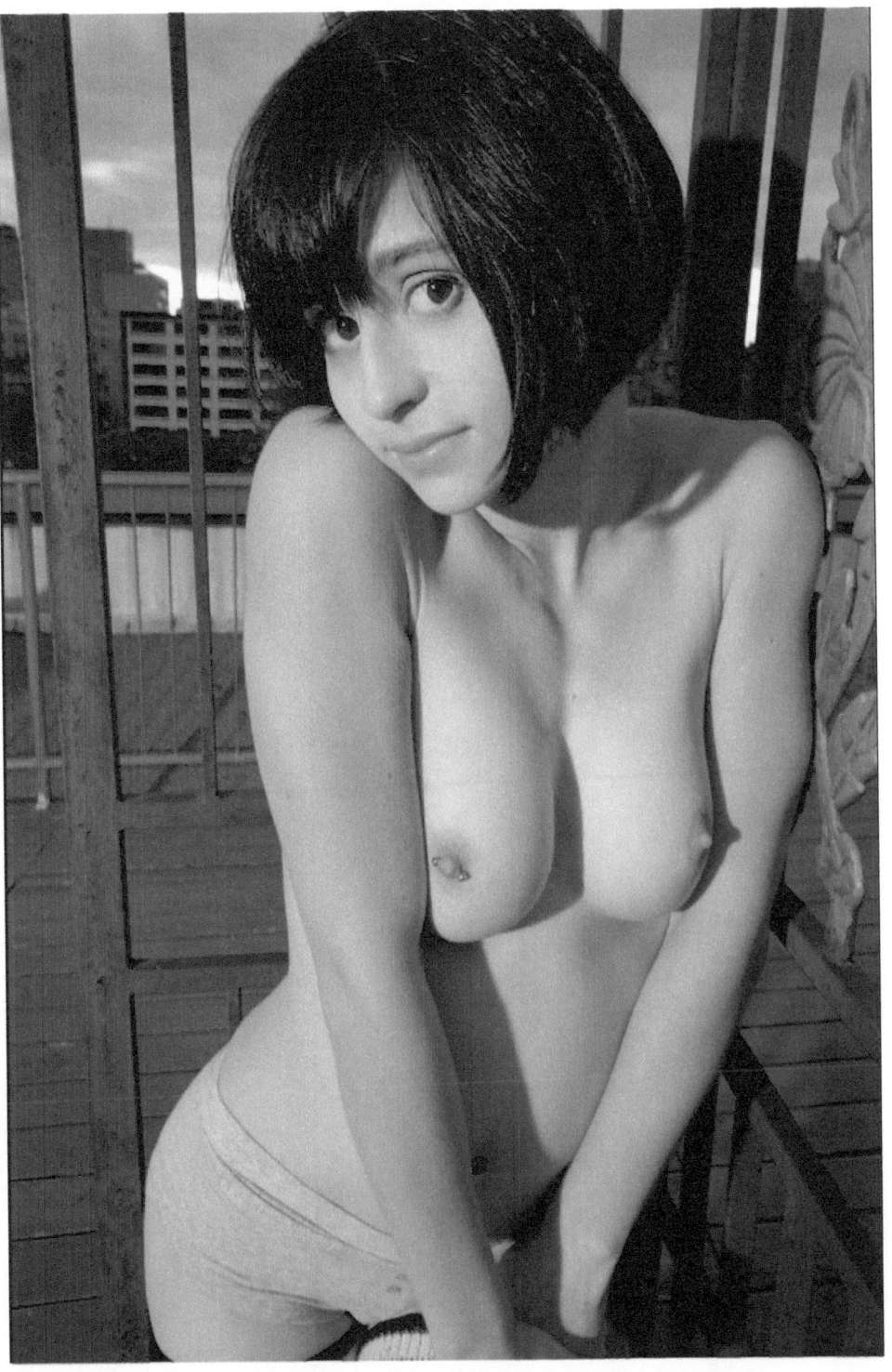

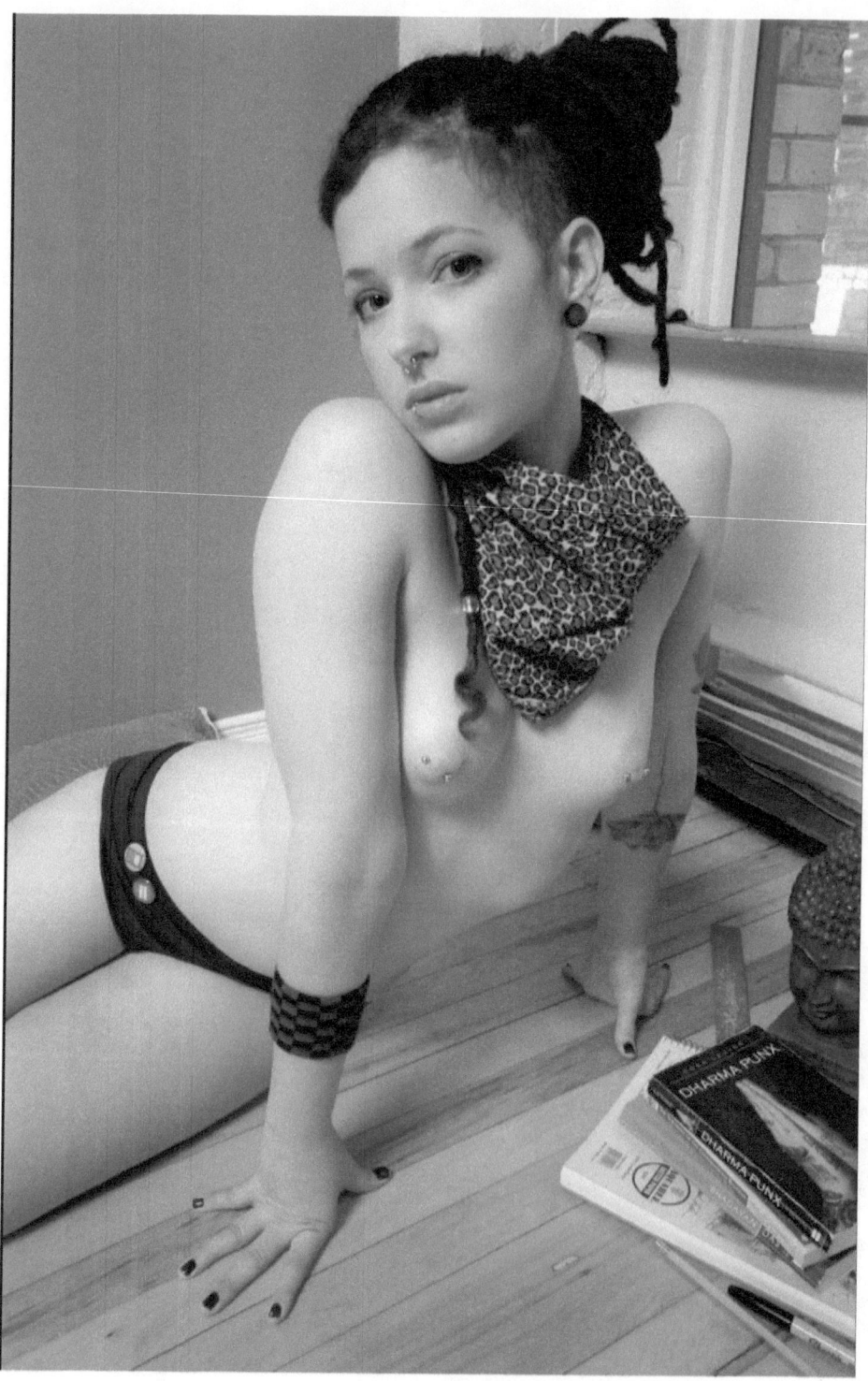

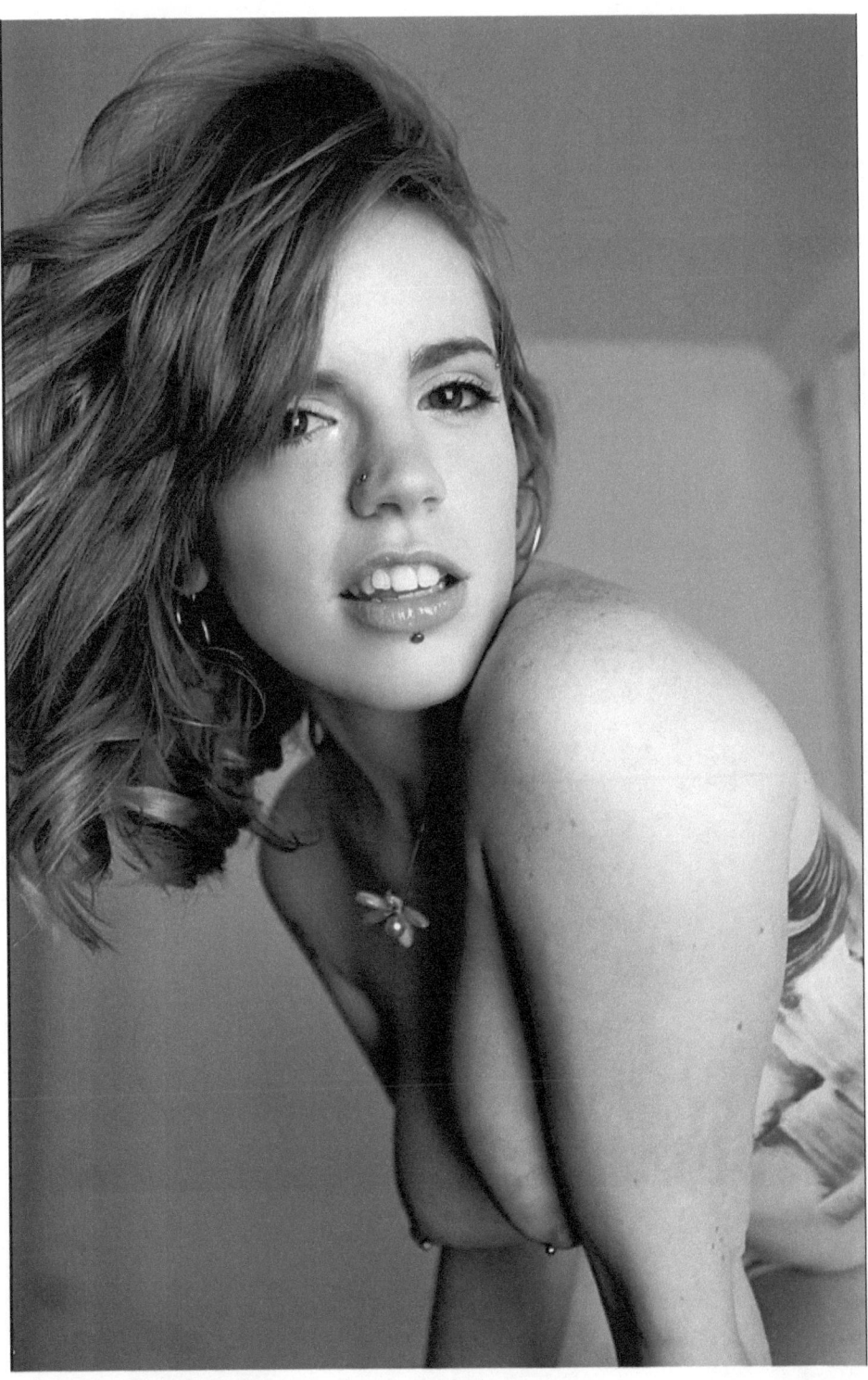

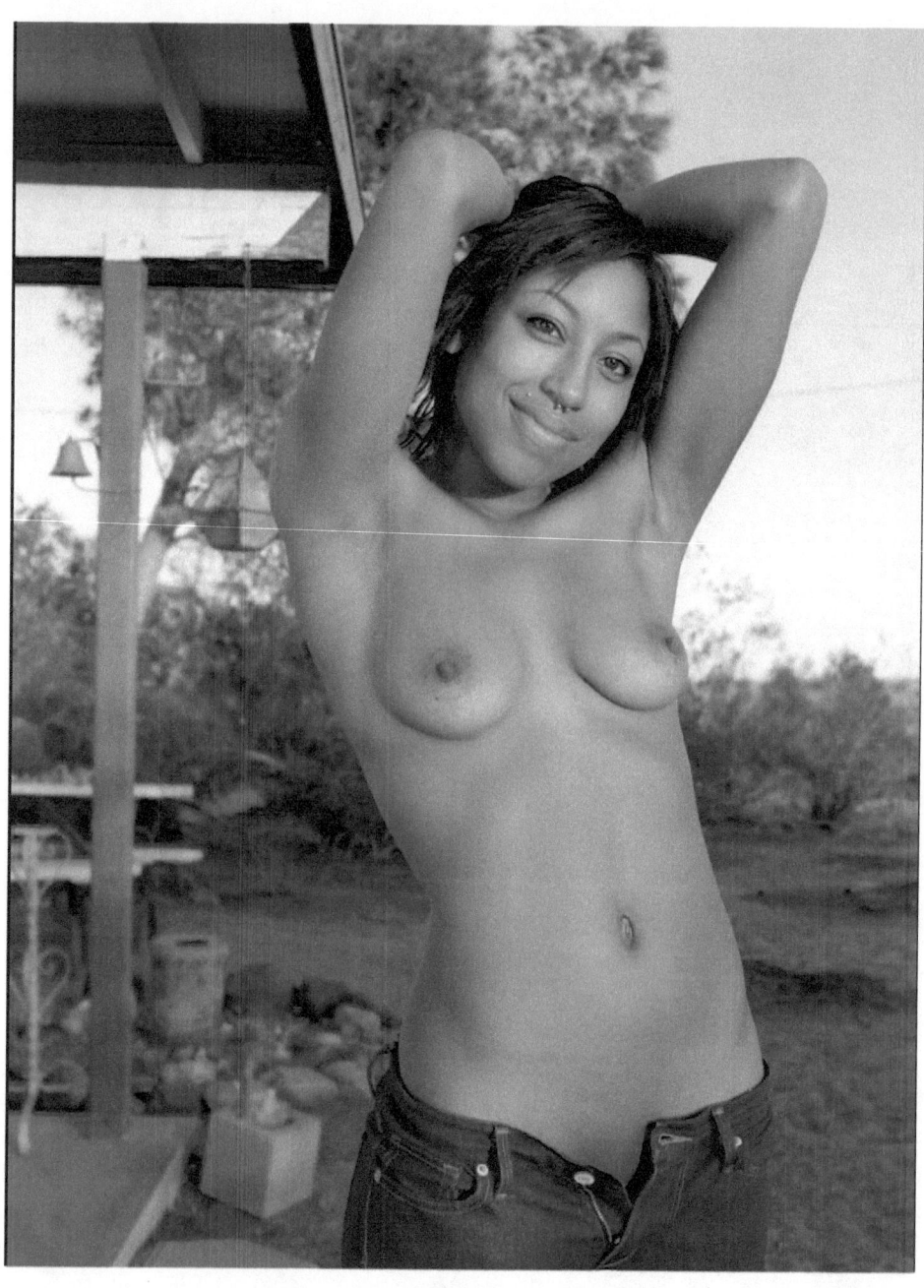

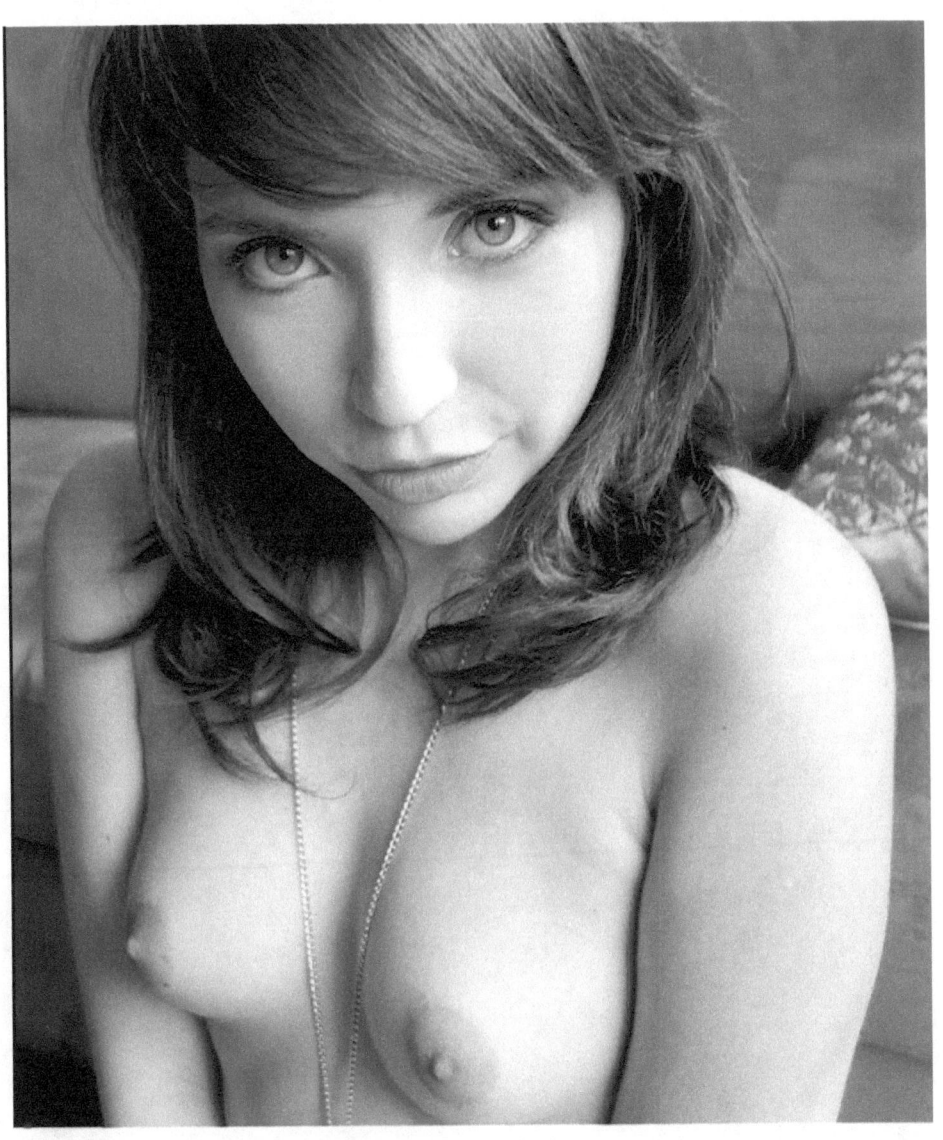

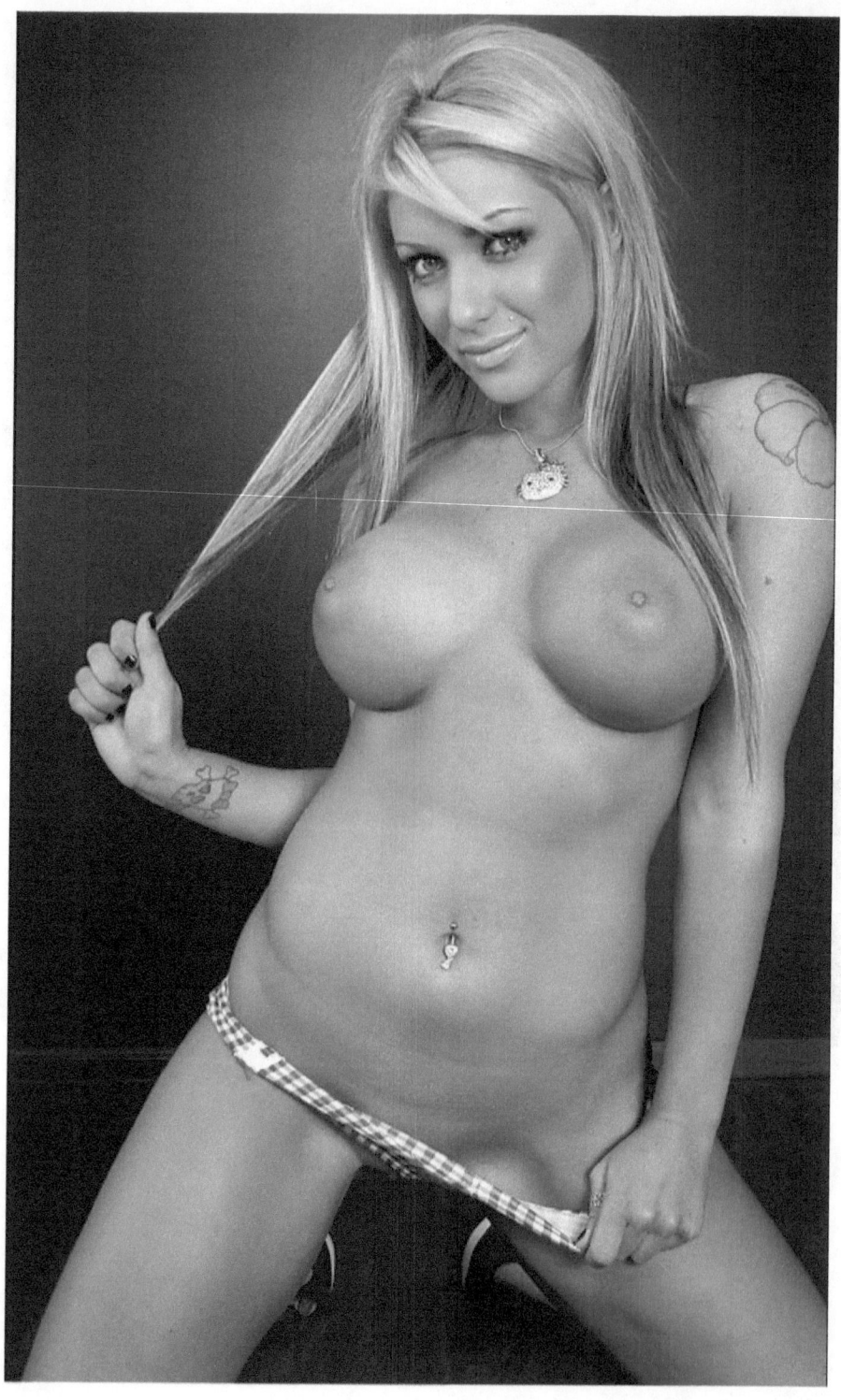

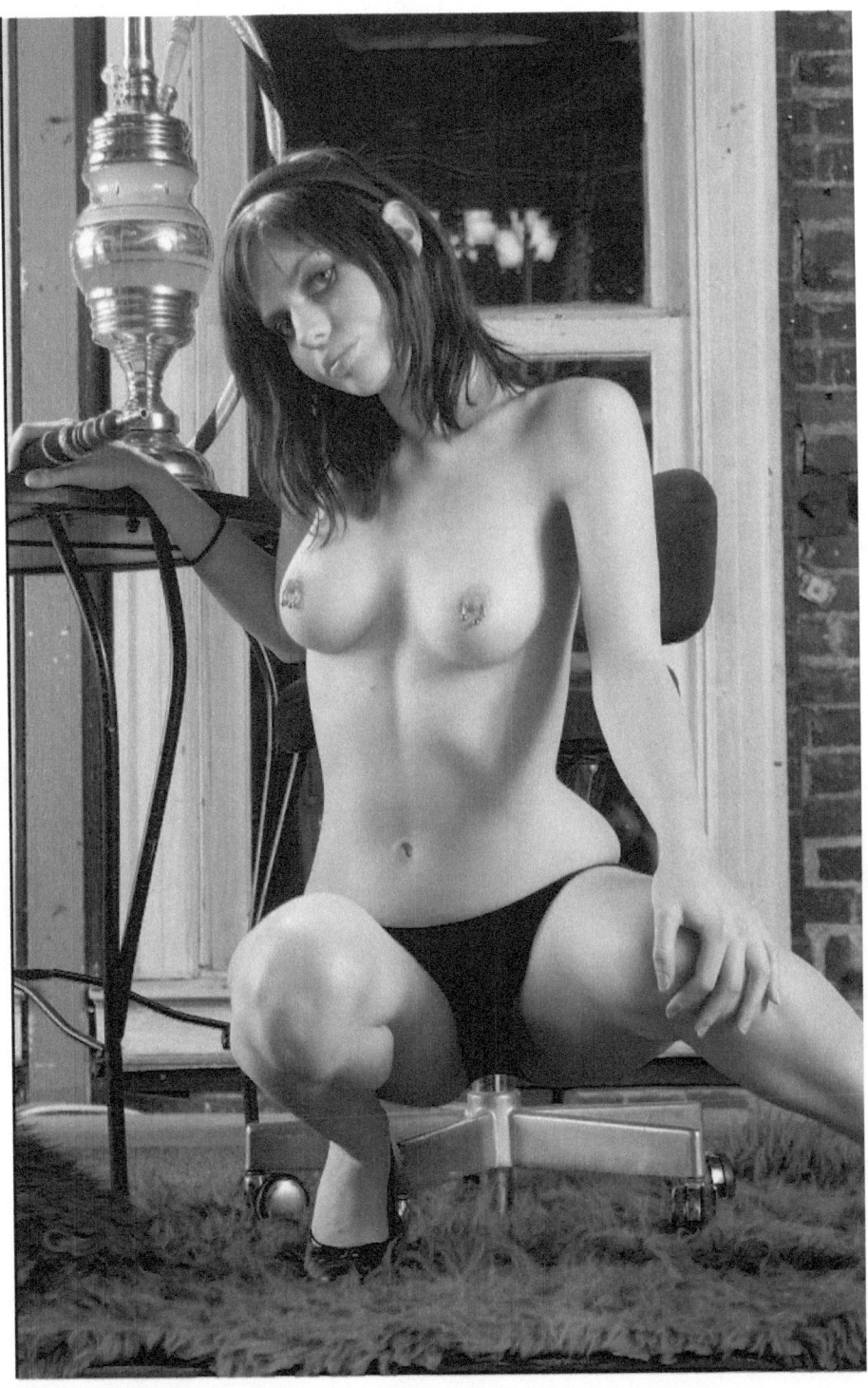

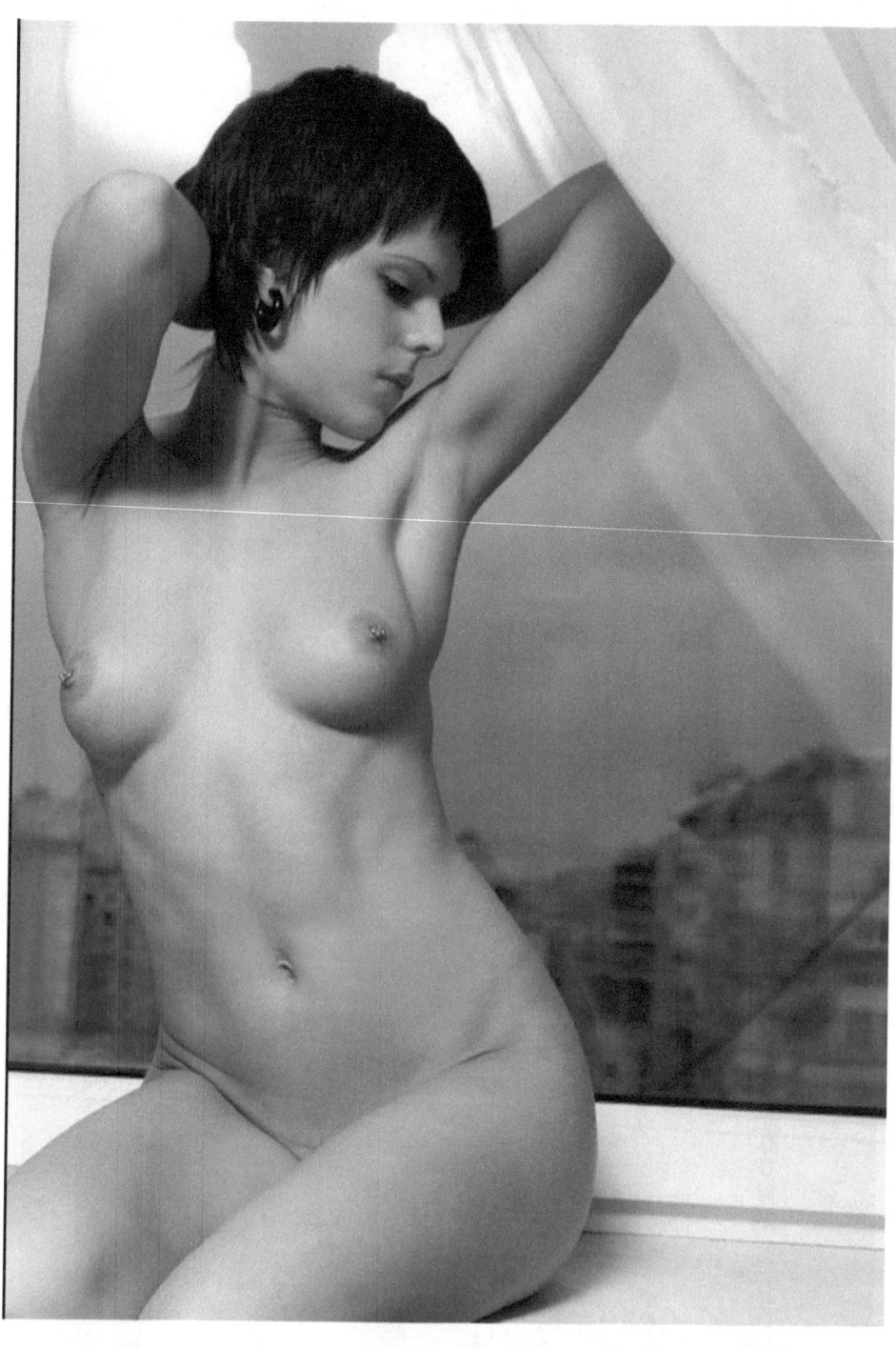

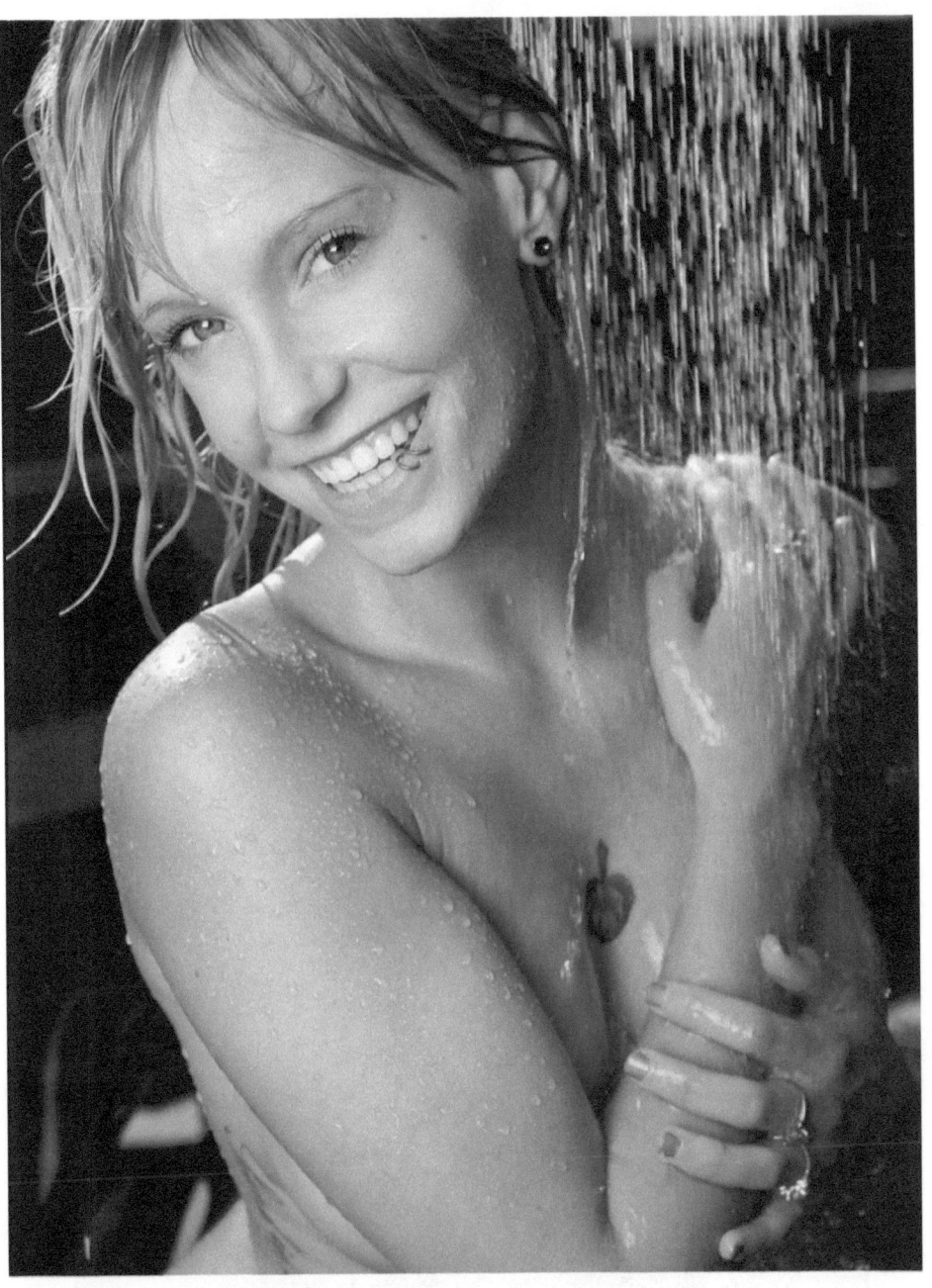

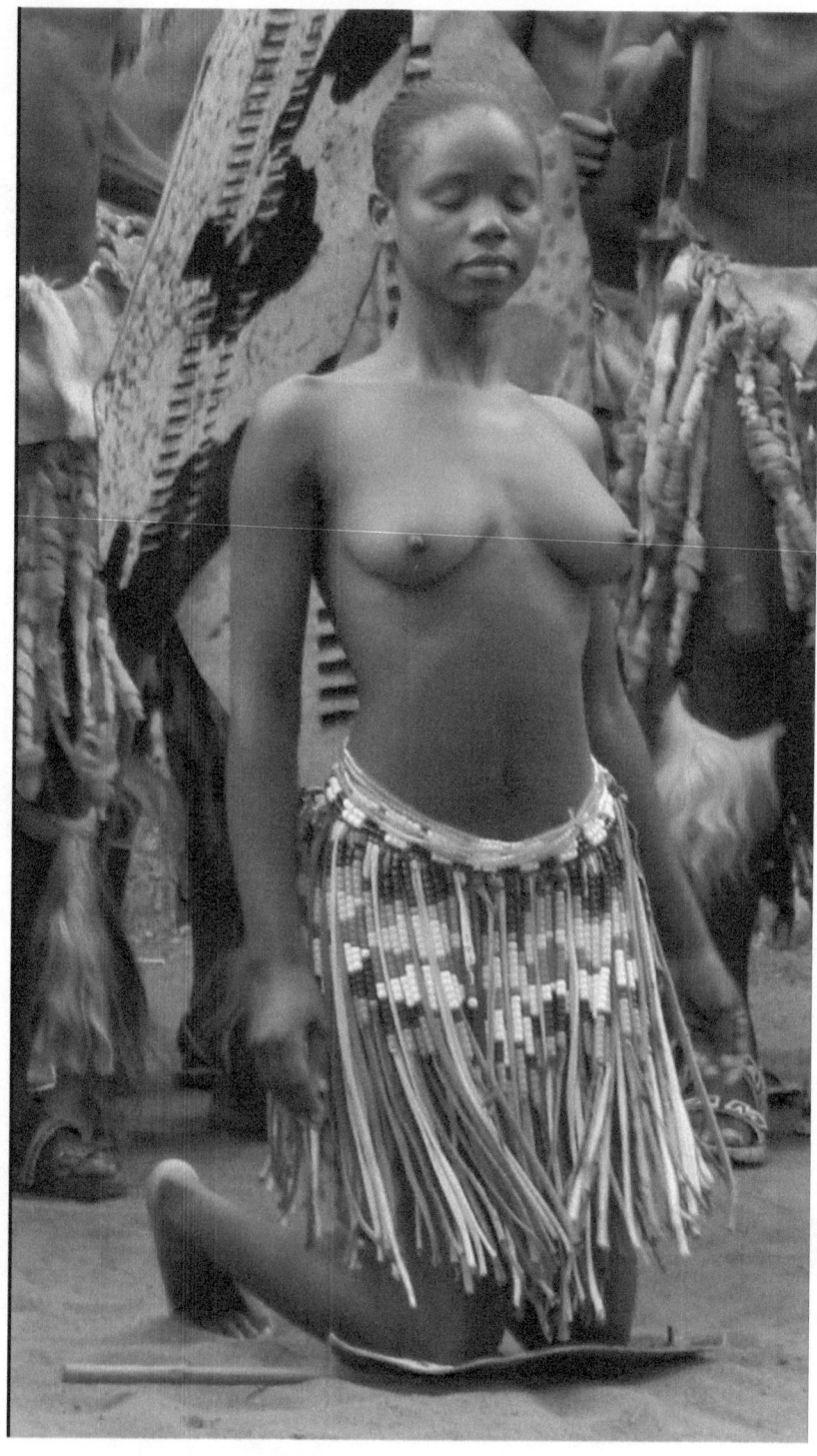

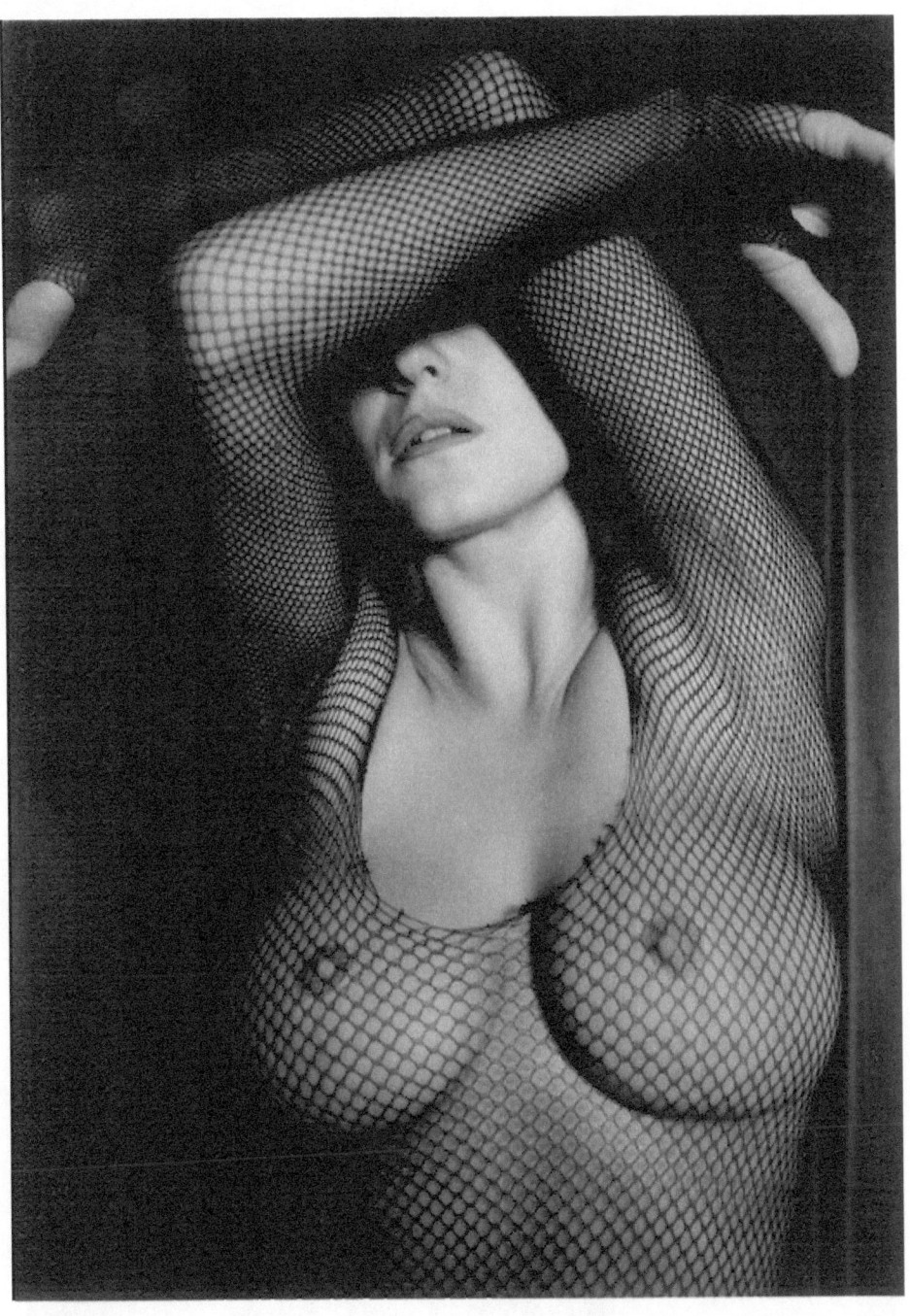

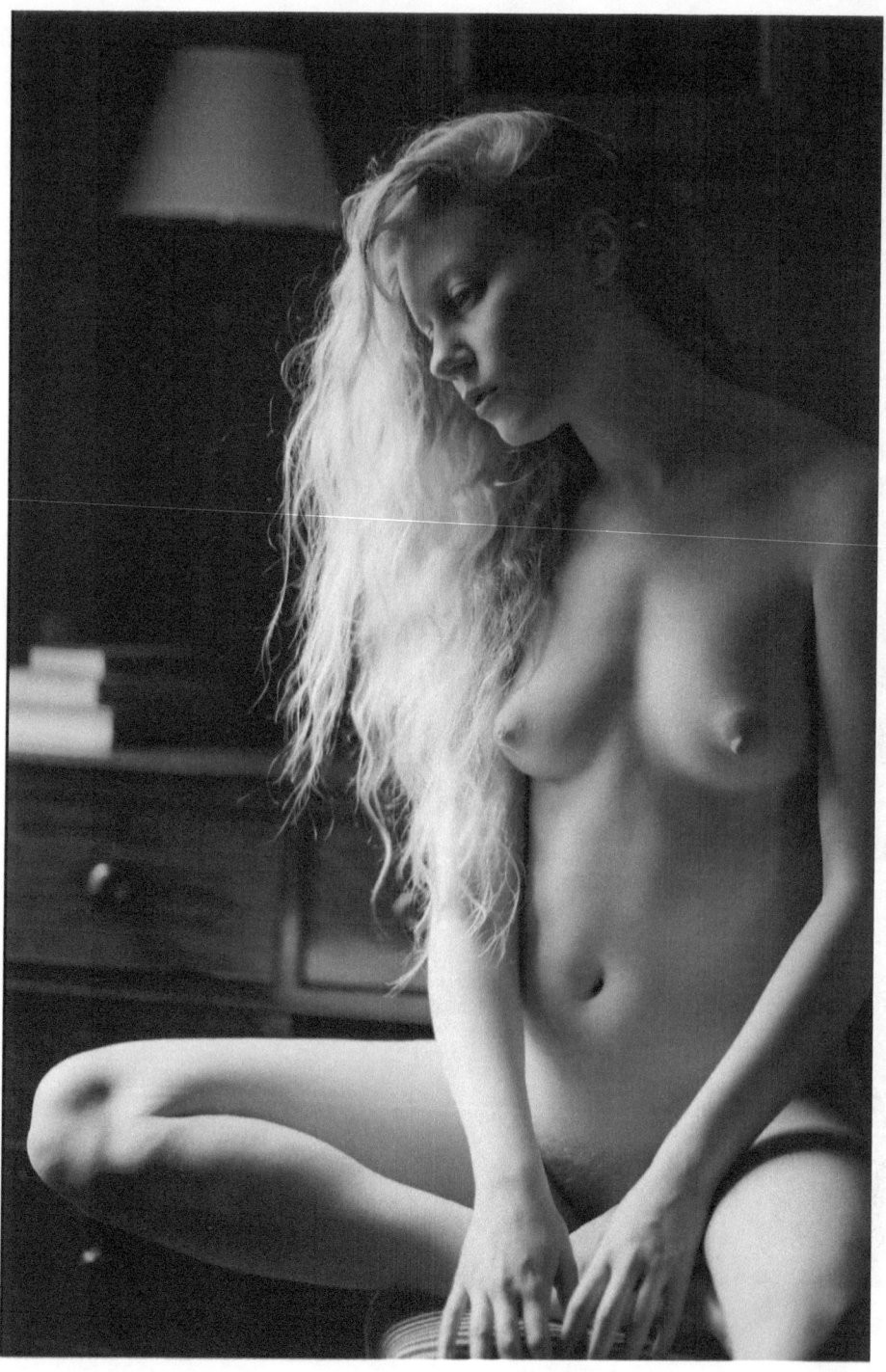

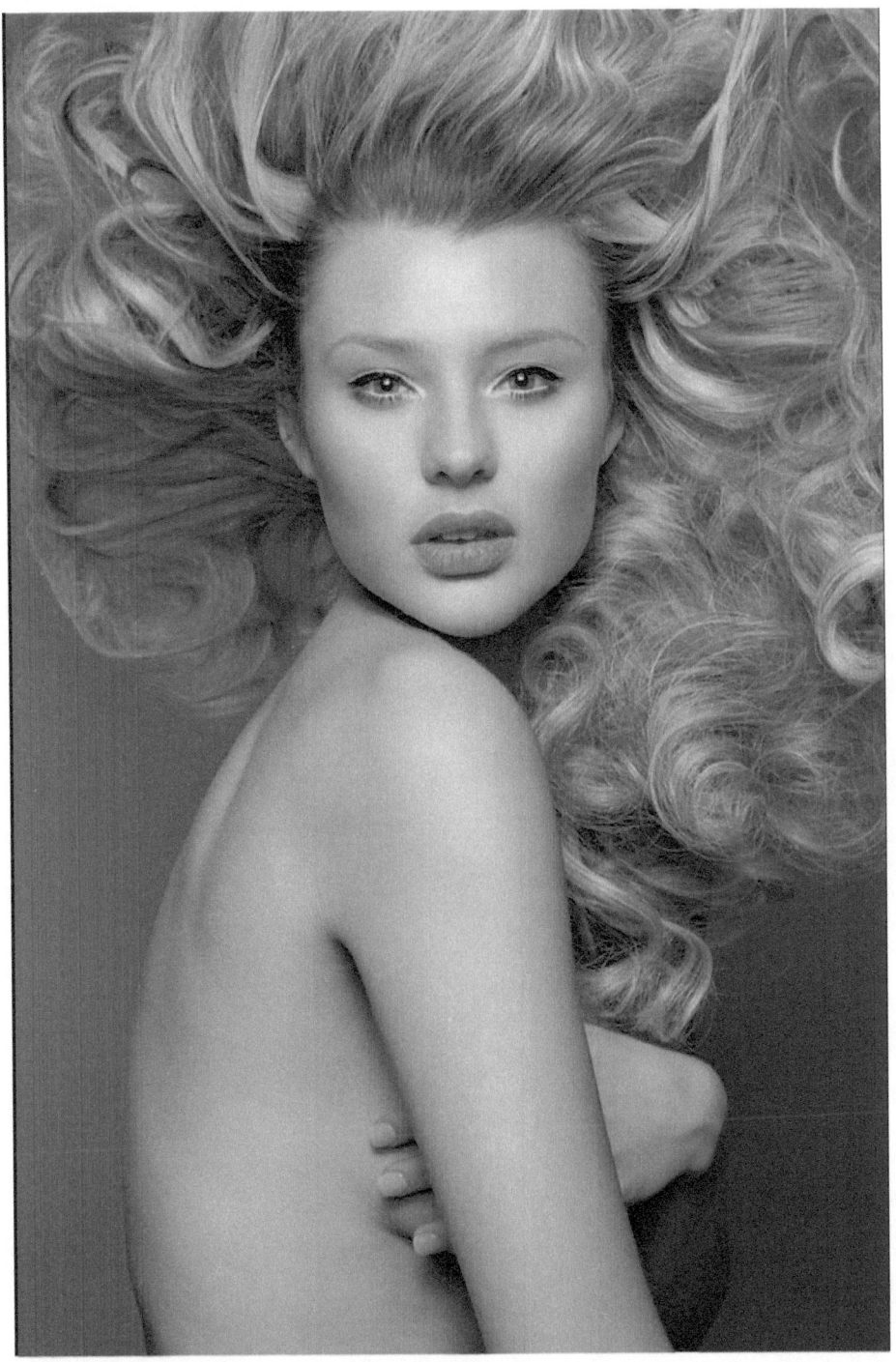

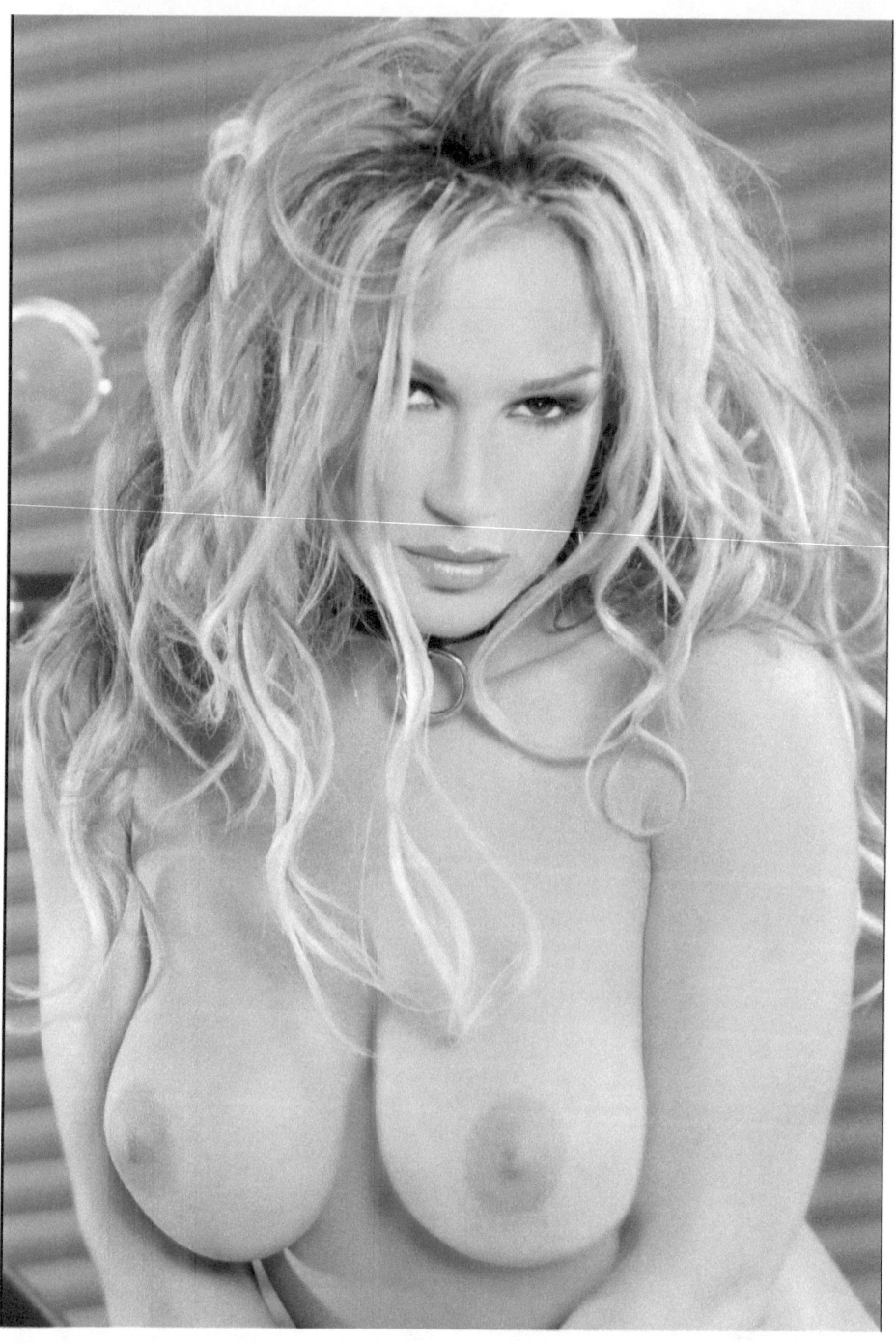

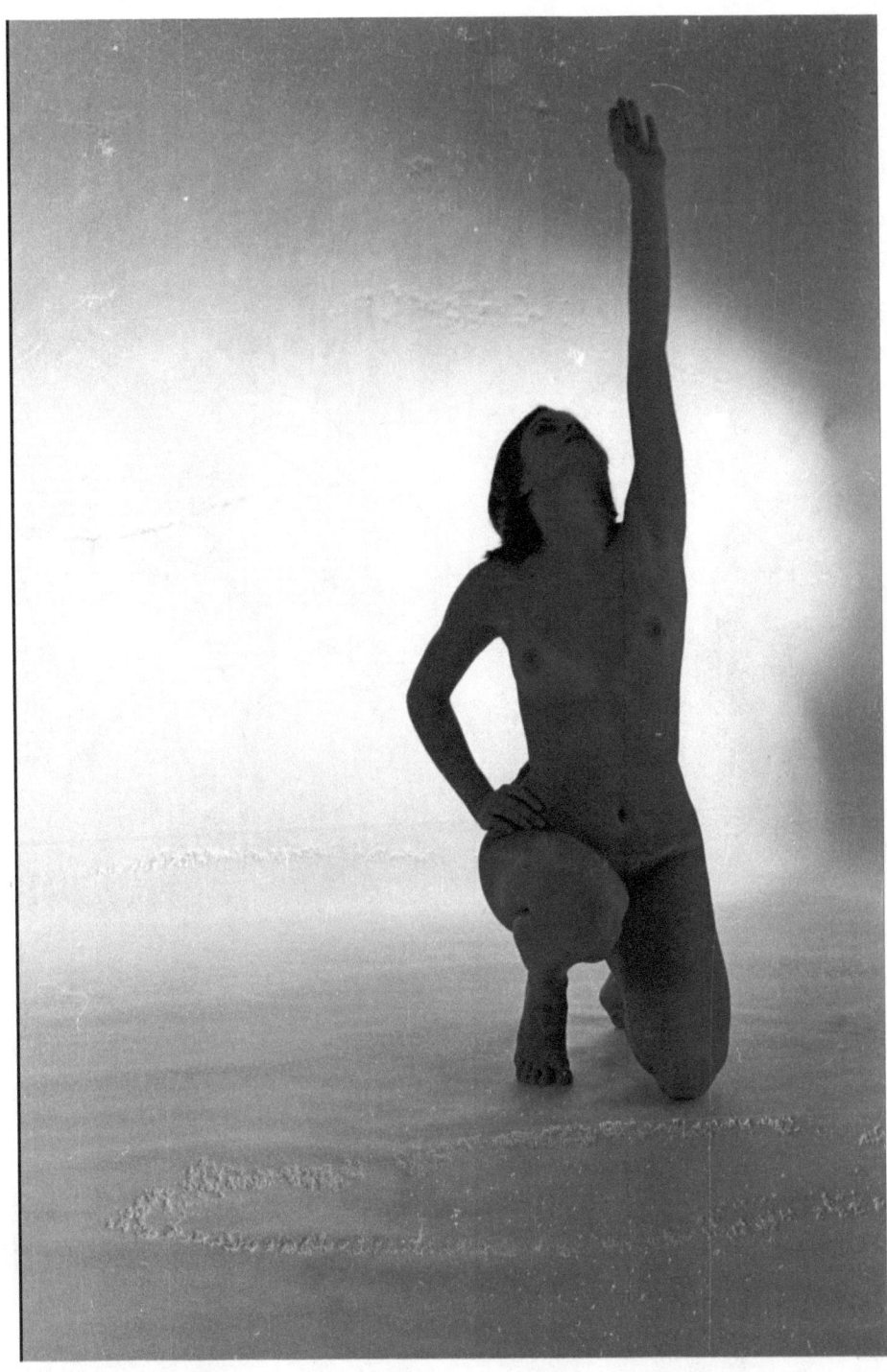

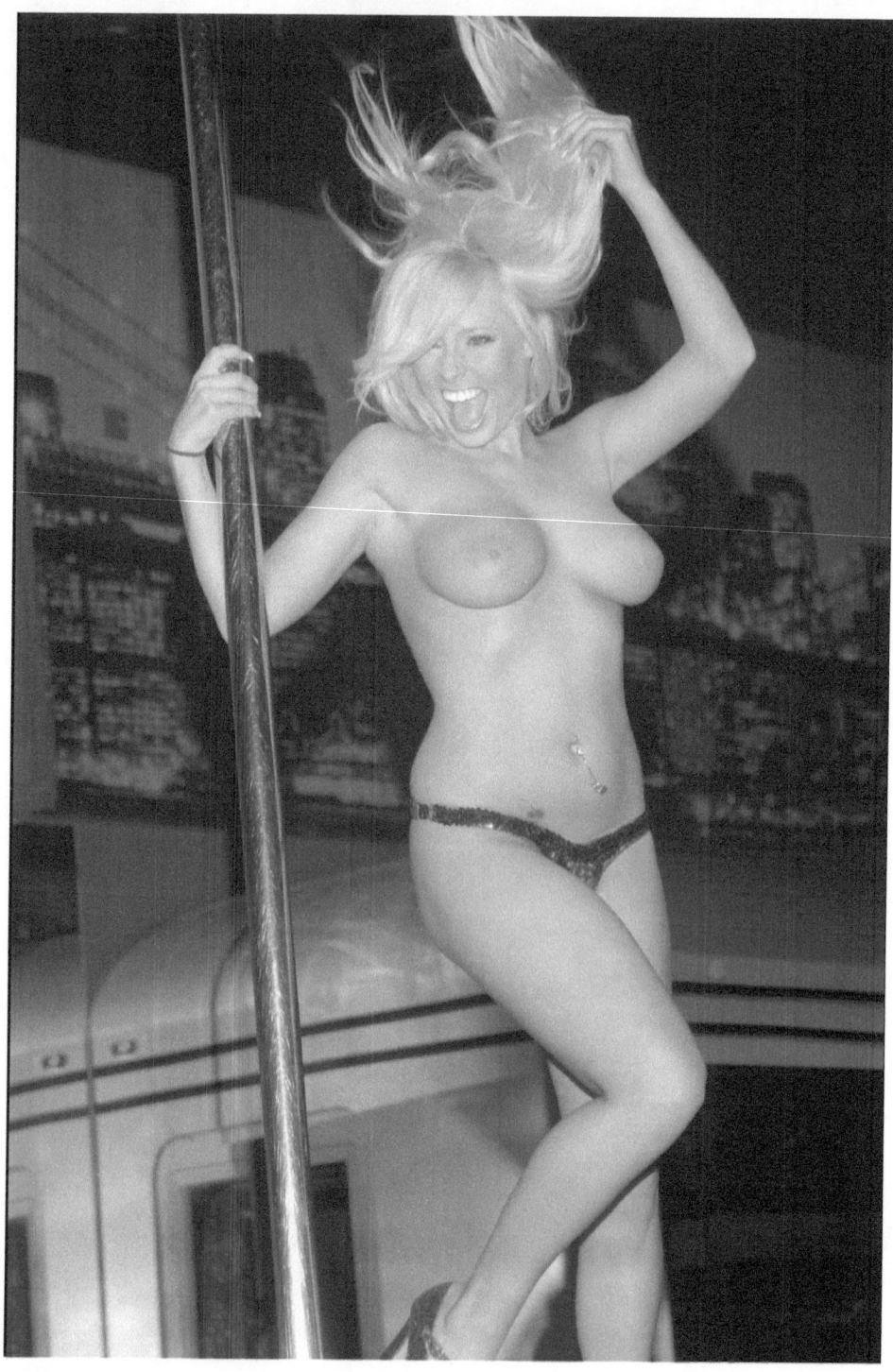

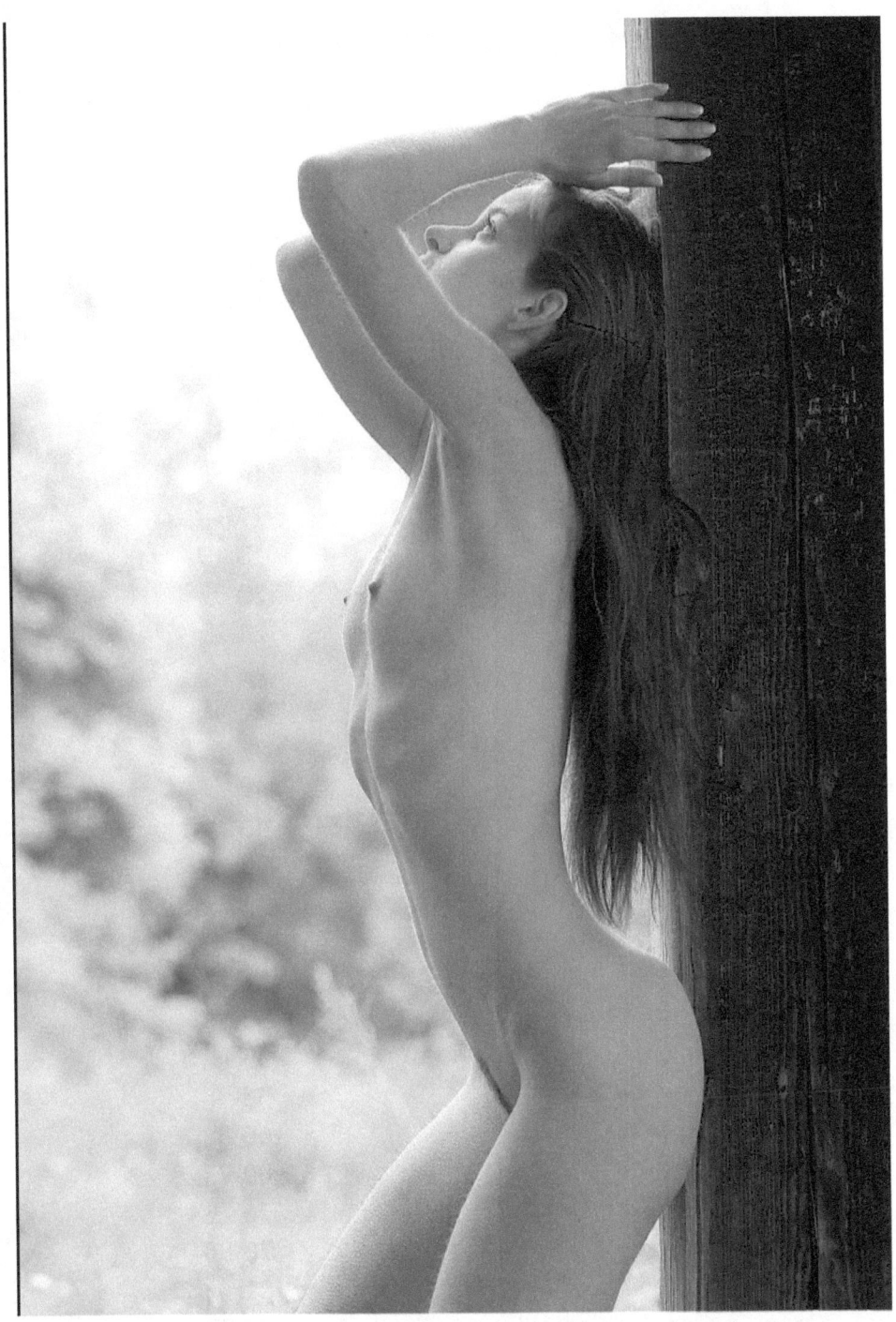

COPYRIGHT / List of Authors:

www.ingramcontent.com/pod-product-compliance
Lightning Source LLC
Chambersburg PA
CBHW021949200526
45163CB00018B/937